"*The Art Cosmic: The Magic of Traditional Astrology* is both fascinating and brilliant at the same time. The author weaves some of the ancient traditions of astrology into a wonderful approach capturing its magic embedded in the symbolism of the planets. Levi Rowland includes in the book a firsthand experience of the planets in the form of guided rituals. I have never read a traditional astrology book so thoroughly researched. The author brings the art and science of astrology from its ancient past into the modern time period of today stimulating our creative imagination. The writing is a unique user-friendly tool to empower the reader. Whether you are new to astrology or a well-informed student or even a professional astrologer I highly recommend this book!"

— **Bernie Ashman**, author of seven astrology books, including
Sun Sign Karma: Resolving Past Life Patterns with Astrology

"With so many books rehashing the same 101 material, it is so sweet to read something fresh and intriguing. Levi Rowland's The Art Cosmic: the Magic of Traditional Astrology is a delight from first to last. It encourages the reader to think beyond Sun/Moon/Venus and understand how to use the tools of astrology in the service of magic. I recommend it."

— **H. Byron Ballard**, Witch, priestess, and author of *Roots,
Branches & Spirits: The Folkways & Witchery of Appalachia*

"Not since Patricia Crowther has an Initiate of the Craft been so inspired to bring to the public his perspective and insights of the myths, innate energies and ecstatic rituals of the seven luminaries. These vast powers have inspired us from the dawn of civilization to our present-day exploration of the universe. Levi Rowland's new book, The Art Cosmic, will be a valued addition to any a occultist's shelf. Whether you're a novice or astrological adept, this work will inevitably enhance your practice and understanding of classical astrology. A must read for any magician or witch who is drawn to taking on the mantle of that magic—which comes from heaven itself."

— **Brian Cain**, Alexandrian High Priest and
author of *Initiation into Witchcraft*

exploring the infinite expanse of astrological influence. The cosmic mysteries are expressed here with wisdom, grace, intimate reverence, and awestruck humility toward the magic of 'as above, so below.'"

— **Raven Digitalis**, Author of *Esoteric Empathy*
and *Planetary Spells & Rituals*

"As a Modern Astrologer who has begun to integrate some traditional Astrology techniques into my work in my latest bestselling book, *The Complete Guide to Astrology*, and a Shamanic practitioner who loves to use ritual work to embody the energies, I found this book a marvelously comprehensive yet not overwhelming introduction to Traditional Astrology. I love the way it weaves the magical arts and ritual with Astrology, as I love to do in my own work. The very feel of the book is magical, from the fonts used to the imagery, and one of my favorite practitioners of magic wrote the forward! If you desire more than a dry Astrological text get this book and immerse yourself in the magic of the spheres."

— **Louise Edington**, Author of *The Complete
Guide to Astrology* and *Modern Astrology*

"In the past I've struggled to find books on planetary magic that have spoken to me—that are well researched yet approachable, and fun to read. That is until now. Levi Rowland's debut book The Art Cosmic is extensive yet accessible for modern audiences and now a true favorite in my book collection. Richly dripping with esotericism, Rowland passionately takes readers on a journey through the cosmos—showcasing the infinite magic in our ever-expansive universe while reminding us that we are but one ingredient in the tapestry of its magic. Including rituals, first-hand knowledge, and charming wit, this book is the perfect guide for anyone looking to deepen their connection to planetary magic."

— **Michael Herkes**, Author of *The GLAM Witch*, *The Complete
Book of Moon Spells*, and *Witchcraft for Daily Self-Care*

"From the preface, 'A Head Full of Stars', Levi Rowland invites us to dive head long into this impressively deep pool of cosmic astrological wisdom. I love the building blocks approach to traditional astrology that Levi offers whilst celebrating and encouraging the importance of intuitive interpretation for the budding astrologer to enhance their magical practice. Beautifully written passages read like poetry as you are guided down a forest path to align with ancient Moon lore, or through a tangled city maze to meet the essence of fiery Mars. The reader, Witch or non, is expertly guided in ritual practice by the author in this comprehensive offering, which, with its engaging wood cut inspired illustrations and charts, can hold pride of place in any beginner or adept's magical library."

— **Fiona Horne**, Author of *The Art of Witch, Magic of You Oracle*, and *The Naked Witch*

"Astrology is one of the most difficult topics to teach and probably the most confusing to understand, however, in The Art Cosmic, *The Magic Of Traditional Astrology*, Levi Rowland delivers a magnificent, technical, practical, informative and enjoyable work, so perfect for new adherents to the field of astrology, as a complement to those who have spent years studying the stars and its practical application.

"For those who are looking to immerse themselves in the theoretical and practical study of astrology, this book will not only be the most appropriate daily reference manual, but also a perfect complement with which to advance in all classes and workshops in the field.

"The author stands out among many others, with the appropriate use of references, and an in-depth study of the planets, also including a series of complementary rituals with perfect explanations."

— **Elhoim Leafar**, Author of *The Magical Art of Crafting Charm Bags* and *Manifestation Magic*

"A well-researched, well-reasoned guide to classical astrology made relevant for the modern practitioner."

— **Melanie Marquis**, Author *Beltane: Rituals, Recipes & Lore for May Day* and *Modern Spellcaster's Tarot*

"Rowland makes astrology approachable without dumbing anything down. *The Art Cosmic* is the perfect mix of history, magick, scholarship, and 'how to" information. An outstanding achievement."

– **Jason Mankey**, Author of *Transformative Witchcraft, The Horned God of the Witches*, and *The Witch's Book of Shadows*

"*The Art Cosmic: The Magic of Traditional Astrology* weaves together the history, practice and magical applications of astrology with clear understanding and poetic delivery. What Levi Rowland offers in this book is a way of working in relationship with the cosmos, a perspective often missing from modern astrology text. This book has everything you need to begin your journey into the deeply profound world of traditional astrology."

– **Shaheen Miro**, Author of *Lunar Alchemy: Everyday Moon Magic to Transform Your Life* and *The Uncommon Tarot*

"Levi Rowland is one of the most thought-provoking and inspiring practitioners operating today. A brilliant and challenging speaker and teacher, his first book is every bit the clear, encouraging, and pragmatic work that we would expect. *The Art Cosmic* is an approachable and thorough entry point to an intimidating discipline, and has plenty to offer more experienced readers, as well. Levi's passion is absolutely infectious."

– **Thorn Mooney**, Author of *Traditional Wicca: A Seeker's Guide* and *The Witch's Path: Advancing Your Craft at Every Level*

"*The Arts of Cosmic: The Magic of Traditional Astrology* by Levi Rowland is an inspired tome of divine celestial scholarship. Neatly organized in planetary fashion, Rowland begins with thorough explanations of our planetary system and then takes the reader on an inclusive multi denominational voyage through the cosmos.

"Rowland makes important observations on the geocentricity of astronomy and skillfully deals with the age old question by distinguishing between secular science and mysticism both ancient and modern. His conversational approach to a complex subject makes this book accessible to those new to astrology, yet there is plenty to enlighten the advanced practitioner as well.

"Steeped in lore, meticulously researched, beautifully illustrated, and lovingly rendered, The Art Cosmic is a must read for any serious astrologer.

Written with great reverence, Rowland has given us a powerful reminder to look skyward and take in the vast beauty of seen yet unknown realms and revel in their influence and power."

– **Judy Ann Nock**, Author of *The Modern Witchcraft Guide to Magickal Herbs* and *The Modern Witchcraft Book of Natural Magick*

"A rich and helpful guide for exploring the power and magick of astrology! Sincere and well-researched, Levi Rowland knowledgeably grasps the spirit and energy, art and magick of astrology. Whether you are a beginner or seasoned practitioner, there is something within these pages for all to enjoy. The work is a masterful blend of academic and mystical, practical and esoteric, serious and creative, embracing the reader with a friendly tone and easy to understand scholarly information. The author's delicious passion shines through every page, helping us embrace the unique divine cosmic soul of the heavenly bodies. Personable, easy to grasp, and brimming with valuable information the first seven chapters introduce us to the divine pattern of the planets, including their history, lore, correspondences, magick, and ritual. Succeeding chapters provide clear and concise definitions to astrological terminology and how this information relates to magick and enchantment ... and better still? How you can harness this power. I wish I had this book thirty years ago when I began studying magickal astrology! Levi Rowland provides the reader with an amazing awakening opportunity. From psychic shielding to the astral temple, from horary interpretation to clear guidance on astrological timing the author does not disappoint! You have only to open the cover to receive his wonderful gift! May we all find that holy fire-- and listen. Thank you, Levi, for this tremendous work."

– **Silver Ravenwolf**, Author of *To Ride a Silver Broomstick*, *Teen Witch*, and *Solitary Witch*

"There is that moment when we look up into the clear night sky, take a deep breath, exhale and smile. We know in that smile that there is an intimate connection between us and the vast starry sky. Levi Rowland's *The Art Cosmic: The Magic of Traditional Astrology* is an absolute must in understanding the art of Astrology. Each beautifully written chapter (complete with charts) allows us a step closer in unlocking the lost language and meaning to the sacred geometry of celestial observations. Rowland orchestrates rituals and exercises within the book to help us connect to the power and hidden secrets held within each planet. This book is invaluable for those embarking on this ancient path of divination.

– **Toni Rotonda**, Buckland Museum Of Witchcraft and Magick

"Astrology for Occultists! This is the book that I wish had been available when I was first studying planetary and astrological magics. *The Art Cosmic* is scholarly and well referenced but also clear and concise making it incredibly accessible to any that want to dip their toes into the world of the wandering stars and beyond. It is jam packed with powerful meditations, clear explanations of both traditional and modern astrological principals, and even a few fabulous mysteries hidden in plain sight. Levi Rowland is knowledgable, refreshingly honest and unafraid to speak his mind, this coupled with his fastidious attention to detail makes his book a 'must have' for any shelf regardless of the readers current level of knowledge."

– **Tara Sanchez**, Author of *Urban Faery Magick: Connecting to the Fae in the Modern World*

"*The Art Cosmic* is truly something to read. Levi goes into explanations that bring a huge understanding to this work. One of the lines in the book truly spoke to me. He said, "connection is everything." Not only is that quite a powerful statement, it is foundational for growth. If you ever wanted to learn the ins and outs of astrology I would absolutely read the wisdom in these pages."

– **Hoodoo Sen Moise**, Author of *Working Conjure: A Guide to Hoodoo Folk Magic*

"*The Art Cosmic: The Magic of Traditional Astrology* by Levi Rowland is a delicious, captivating walk through Astrological arts in a wholly extraordinary manner. Rowland's language is rich and poetic, where other Astrology books tend to be dry. Each page illustrates excellent historical research including quotes from brilliant thinkers and philosophers, and copious footnotes (thank you!). This tome explores the inspiration and guidance found in the stars-tiny bits of light inspiring language, arts, science, and society for eons. *The Art Cosmic* expresses the "as above, so below" axiom, showing how even in a modern world, the cosmic dance continues to play a role in daily life. Like the ancients, we can look to Astrology to discover anew the Angels, Guides, Ancestors, and the Gods. On a personal level Astrology offers an essential comprehension of our Higher Self, and a profound ken of the inner workings of our magical practices. It is a must read, but take it slow. Immerse yourself. Every page offers something worthy of your meditations."

– **Patricia Telesco**, Author of *A Kitchen Witch's Cookbook* and *How to Be a Wicked Witch*

"Levi Rowland has produced a wonderful text offering readers a logical, concise, and non-dogmatic approach to one of the most time-honoured Arts of the Occult world - Astrology. Offering a complete and honest account of astrological history, development, terminology and practical application; Rowland provides a solid foundation for those new to the Art and important musings for those with more experience of the Celestial. *The Art Cosmic* also offers magical and ritual application to allow the reader to immerse themselves deeper into the experience of the Heavens; truly building a meaningful relationship with the often neglected natural wonder that is available to us all – regardless of where we are. The Art Cosmic truly has something of great value for anyone drawn to the Art of astrology. Highly recommended."

– **Craig Spencer** – Author of *Aradia: A Modern Guide to Charles Godfrey Leland's Gospel of the Witches*

"*The Art Cosmic* was literally a transformative read. Levi's book is remarkable in that it not only helps to demystify some of the aspects of traditional astrology, but envelopes the reader in an experience that is timeless with wisdom shared throughout the ages, meditations, rituals and done so in the fashion of a magical grimoire from a high priest of witchcraft, truly unique. *The Art Cosmic* is a piece of art in and of itself, reading it not only helped me become illuminated in celestial mysteries in a way I did not expect but reinvigorated my enthusiasm for astrology within my magic.

"Whether the reader be a seasoned witch, sorcerer or spiritual seeker, *The Art Cosmic* will be a book of enlightenment, reference and inspiration. For me this is the consummate guide for the magic of astrology in witchcraft."

— **Witchdoctor Utu**, Author of *Conjuring Harriet 'Mama Moses' Tubman and the Spirits of the Underground Railroad*

"Serious students of astrology and magic will find a lifelong treasure in *The Art Cosmic*. In addition to being packed with useful information, this book is both an inspiration and a delight. Whether you're a beginner who wants to go far beyond the basics, a magical practitioner who wants to learn to work with planetary energy more masterfully, or an experienced astrologer who wants to gain a deeper and more dimensional understanding of the planets and their correspondences, this book is for you. It is a master key that will unlock the glittering magic and breathtaking power of the cosmos."

— **Tess Whitehurst**, Author of *You Are Magical, Holistic Energy Magic,* and *The Self-Love Superpower*

"In *The Art Cosmic*, Levi Rowland has brilliantly captured everything I was taught about why planetary magick is so vital to Witchcraft. This is the book I wish I had when I was starting my journey; I am thrilled to be able to recommend it — not only to my students, but to practitioners of all levels."

— **Sandra Mariah Wright**, Author of *Reading the Leaves* and *Lighting the Wick*

This page intentionally left blank.

The Art Cosmic
The Magic of Traditional Astrology

Levi Rowland
Forward by Sorita d'Este

Warlock Press™

The Art Cosmic: The Magic of Traditional Astrology

Published by:
Warlock Press
1219 Decatur Street
New Orleans, 70116 LA, USA

Typesetting and Cover Design: Christian Day

ISBN-10: 1-7332466-2-0

ISBN-13: 978-1-7332466-2-0

✦✶✦ACKNOWLEDGEMENTS✦✶✦

*This book is dedicated to my mother, who has always
been my North Star and showed me the way.*

*Many people were instrumental in this work coming to fruition.
Firstly, I want to thank my teachers in Craft who have always
inspired me to explore and grow. The gods have given me
some of the most incredible teachers, including Brian Cain,
Christine Stephens, Val Hughes, and countless others. These
teachers carry the wisdom and power of our Craft elders, elders
that I continue to respect and cherish. I want to specifically
thank Christian Day for his beautiful work in crafting the
images and charts that went into this work. Astrology is a
visual art and it would have been impossible to convey this
without his work. And to all of my friends, my partner, and
countless other support systems who listened to me endlessly
talk over ancient texts and complex ideas…thank you.*

TABLE OF CONTENTS

Acknowledgements XIII
Foreword XX
Preface XXII

Introduction 1

CHAPTER 1
The Moon   16
The Meeting 16
The First Sphere: Luna 19
Touchstone Texts for the Moon 21
The Moon in Astrology 22
The Moon in Magic 23
A Rite for the Moon 25
    Astrological Considerations 25
    Ritual Preparation 25
    Purification Bath 26
    The Ritual 26

CHAPTER 2
Mercury   32
The Meeting 32
The Second Sphere: Mercury 35
Touchstone Texts for Mercury 36
Mercury in Astrology 38
Mercury in Magic 39
A Rite for Mercury 40
    Astrological Considerations 41
    Ritual Preparation 41
    Purification Bath 42
    The Ritual 43

CHAPTER 3
Venus   47
The Meeting 47
The Third Sphere: Venus 50
Touchstone Texts for Venus 52

Venus in Astrology 53
Venus in Magic 54
A Rite for Venus 56
    Astrological Considerations 56
    Ritual Preparations 56
    The Ritual 57

CHAPTER 4
The Sun   60

The Meeting 60
The Fourth Sphere: Sol 63
Touchstone Texts for the Sun 65
The Sun in Astrology 66
The Sun in Magic 67
A Rite for the Sun 68
    Astrological Considerations 68
    Ritual Preparations 69
    The Ritual 69

CHAPTER 5
Mars   73

The Meeting 73
The Fifth Sphere: Mars 76
Touchstone Texts for Mars 78
Mars in Astrology 79
Mars in Magic 81
A Rite for Mars 82
    Astrological Considerations 82
    Preparations 82
    Ritual 82

CHAPTER 6
Jupiter   86

The Meeting 86
The Sixth Sphere: Jupiter 89
Touchstone Texts for Jupiter 91
Jupiter in Astrology 92
Jupiter in Magic 93
A Rite for Jupiter 94
    Astrological Considerations 94

Ritual Preparation 94

The Ritual 95

CHAPTER 7
Saturn   99

The Meeting. 99

The Seventh Sphere: Saturn 103

Touchstone Texts for Saturn 105

Saturn in Astrology 106

Saturn in Magic. 107

A Rite for Saturn 109

Astrological considerations 110

Ritual Preparation 110

The Ritual 111

CHAPTER 8
Planetary Conditions   114

Sect 115

Rulership, or Domicile 116

Exaltation 117

Detriment. 120

Fall 120

Triplicity Rulers 121

Terms and Face. 123

Peregrine 126

The Almuten 126

Reception 128

Retrograde 130

Aspects and Orb 131

Orb 131

Conjunction and Combustion 132

Opposition 134

Trine 135

Sextile 137

Square 138

Symbols. 139

Final Words: Where Are You? 140

CHAPTER 9
The Fixed Stars   141

The Old Gods 141
Within the Zodiac 145
The Behenian Stars 146
Starry Talismans 149
Fixed Stars in a Chart 150
A Ritual for the Old Stars 150
    Ritual Preparation 151
    The Ritual 151

CHAPTER 10
The Other Players   153

The Lunar Nodes 153
The Lots 156
    The Pars Fortunae 158
    The Pars Futurorum 158
    Other Lots 158
Using the Lots 160
The Outer Planets and Beyond 161

CHAPTER 11
The Architecture of Astrology   163

The Horoscope in Astrology 163
The Chart 165
Is the Zodiac Wrong? 168
The Zodiac 170
    The Triplicities 171
    Quadruplicities 173
    Terms and Face 176
    The Attributes of the Zodiac 176
The Houses 178

CHAPTER 12
Reading Nativities   185

Before the Beginning 185
What is a Nativity? 186
The Interpretation Process 186
Analyzing a Sample Chart 189

Weaving it Together 194
Literal or Figurative 197
Taking it Further 198

CHAPTER 13
Horary Astrology   200
Horary Technique 203
Keys to Beginning 205
Keeping a Holistic View 206
Example 207
Considerations 209

CHAPTER 14
Magical Astrology   212
Belief 214
Discipline and Cycles 216
Sacred and Profane 219
Mindfulness and Meditation 222
    Psychic Shielding 224
    The Astral Temple 225
Conclusion 227

CHAPTER 15
Astrological Timing   229
The Planetary Week 231
Planetary Hours 233
Magic 234

CHAPTER 16
Angels in Magic and Astrology   237
The Messengers 237
Angels and the Art 246
Embracing the Angels? 255

CHAPTER 17
Continuing   256
Make Lots of Charts 256
Research and Read Questions 257
Look at the Stars 259
Good Ritual is Learned 259

Remember to Stay Grounded. 260
Dance With Fate 261

Appendix One: A Path to Ponder 263
Appendix Two: A Rite for Diviners. 266
Appendix Three: Recommended Study. 268
Bibliography 271
Index 275

About the Author. 284

⋆⋆FOREWORD⋆⋆

> *With holy voice I call the stars on high,*
> *pure sacred lights and genii of the sky.*
> *Celestial stars, the progeny of Night,*
> *in whirling circles beaming far your light,*
> *Refulgent rays around the heavens ye throw,*
> *eternal fires, the source of all below.*
> *With flames significant of Fate ye shine,*
> *and aptly rule for men a path divine.*
> *In seven bright zones ye run with wandering flames,*
> *and heaven and earth compose your lucid frames:*
> *With course unwearied, pure and fiery*
> *bright forever shining through the veil of Night.*
> *Hail twinkling, joyful, ever wakeful fires!*
> *Propitious shine on all my just desires;*
> *These sacred rites regard with conscious rays,*
> *and end our works devoted to your praise.*"
> *– Orphic Hymns, trans. Taylor*

You don't have to be an astrologer to know that the Seven Wandering Stars have been a source of both enchantment and wonder since before the civilizations of Sumeria laid down the foundations for the modern zodiac many thousands of years ago. There is no escaping their importance in the contemporary world as their names are preserved in our current seven day week, each day, as most readers should know, named after one of the classical planets or the deities associated with them.

Astrology continues to be a serious art and science for those who study and practice it; but also frequently misunderstood and thought of as being nothing more than the short sun sign predictions familiar to readers of newspapers and magazines. There are many different systems of astrology and the differences in the approach and skill of individual astrologers ads further diversity to a system that is many thousands of years old.

Most people who consult an astrologer do so with the hope of gaining insight or wishing for a prediction of what is to come, for themselves, a loved one or a business venture. This is where Levi Rowland is different. He masterfully blends the mystical and spiritual aspects of astrology with science and practice, presenting the reader with an integrated and holistic approach that is both practical and effective. What struck me was the simplicity and ease with which the author explained the concepts and techniques and the insight with which he presents the practical aspects of the book. Best of all, Levi does not shy away from tackling challenging topics such as the simple but frequently overlooked matter of *belief*.

In the first part of the book, the reader is guided through meetings with each of the classical planets, Sun, Mercury, Venus, Moon, Mars, Jupiter and Saturn, in an exceptionally natural way, combining visuals with the essential correspondences. In the chapters that follow, the author meticulously presents the necessary steps for the reader to gain a thorough understanding of the workings of both natal and horary charts and their interpretation. He masterfully does this without getting unnecessarily complicated nor forgoing solid research, drawing inspiration from a broad spectrum of sources that includes the Chaldean Oracles, Key of Solomon and other traditional grimoires along the way.

The Art Cosmic joins the essential reading lists for magical practitioners who seek to explore both the potential for insightful predictions and the profound mysticism of astrology. I will not be alone in saying that I wish this book was available when I was first starting out. It would have made it so much easier and enjoyable! The Art Cosmic is a perfect primer, especially for those interested in both the spiritual and practical aspects of astrology, a guide that you will return to time and time again. I know I will.

> *"We are also to show forth, what Divine gifts, powers and Virtues, man receiveth from the celestial bodies (that is) the seven planets; called by the Astrologers the seven erratic or wandering stars." – Janua Magica Reserata (Sloane 3825, 17th-century magical grimoire)*

Enjoy this starry journey!

Sorita d'Este
Glastonbury, 2021

*ˣ*PREFACE*ˣ*
A Head Full of Stars

> *Non est ad astra mollis e terris via."* (*There is no easy way to the stars from the earth*)
> —*Seneca the Younger*

Out of all the things that have come to kill the mysteries of our lives, light pollution is an enemy we forget about too often. We love to blame the advent of technology for our woes, to complain about kids staring at screens or how chained we feel to the handheld devices that organize and expand our lives. We are looking down, always looking down, and we feel a twinge of guilt about this. We are rarely, if ever, looking up into the wide and glittering sky. The starry sky that proved important and inspiring for so many before us is now crowded out. The wandering stars, the constellations, the *occasional* comets, and celestial phenomena are all in competition now. City lights and airplane towers and the marvels of modern industry crowd out and shout at the old stars, letting us forget they are there. It is easy to forget to look up. It is easy to think that the only lights that matter are the ones that are trying to sell us something, or the ones that let us work late at night or stay up to watch a bad movie with our partner. We forget the infinitely expanding wonders that are above our heads. We forget what it was like when we saw them at night, perhaps away from the blinding lights of an urban area, their dazzling radiance touching from horizon to horizon. We sometimes forget that we keep our eyes too low.

But it's important to look up. The vastness that exists right above our own heads is humbling. It is also inspiring. For our ancestors, the skies held terrible beauty. They could unleash torrents of rain and yield food from the dirt. They could spit lightning and crack trees. The skies could make us write beautiful poetry, or forget heartaches, or remember to pause when the dreary toil of daily experience brought us low. We ascribed meaning to the bright specks of light we saw. We drew animals and heroes. We read fate and predicted the future. We believed that everything in the cosmos breathed meaning. It was impossible to imagine a dead world. The stars had names, so how could they be anything but alive? They ruled and created this world with us. They watched. And we watched. We lived our lives with them, a beautiful system of record-keeping that we used to mark the cycles of human lives.

Astrology and the magics it inspired have been part of our civilization in many forms and across many epochs. From Babylon to Greece, traditional Western astrology has been a bedrock for philosophy, religion, art, and magic. Vedic astrology and Chinese astrology inspired countless decisions and guided people in their daily understanding of who they were and where they fit into the universe. These systems continue to be sources of inspiration and guidance. We once ordered our lives by ordering the stars. Astrology inspired vastly different minds, but all from the same source of astral power. From the scientifically minded such as Kepler to the Hermetic philosophers like Marsilio Ficino and even unto modern psychologists in the case of Jung. This was the power of astrology. It was, and continues to be, a way for humans to understand the numinous. We were never *just* naming stars. We were naming and finding gods. We were looking for angels. We were finding reflections of our own experience, our hopes and fears. The bright lights that surrounded our home were mirrors, and we looked long and hard into them.

The magic of astrology, like any magic, has evolved. I have been working with astrology for most of my adult life and using the magics it has inspired to guide my experience, push my thinking, and transform what I can. It has been a source of inspiration, a wellspring of ideas that never seems to run dry. How could it? When the stars seem infinite above us (regardless of whether they are or are not), there is always something to marvel at and attempt to understand. And even though astrology has evolved, it is the traditional forms of it that have had a lasting impact on me and continue to ignite the fire in my work and my experience. It is this traditional form of astrology that I use and teach.

This traditional form is geocentric. It does not deny modern science—it only starts from Earth because we must all begin from Earth. We are all here, on this planet, experiencing this world together. We cannot separate ourselves from where we call home. To reach a higher destination, you must know where your starting point is. A map is useless if it does not show you where you can begin. When we look up from Earth, we can begin to experience the same awe that our ancestors did. We can think the way Claudius Ptolemy did when he wrote:

> *I know that I am mortal, the creature of one day. But when I explore the winding courses of the stars, I no longer touch with my feet the earth: I am standing near Zeus himself, drinking my fill of ambrosia, the food of the gods.*[1]

It is that connection to the stars that proves divine. By working with the systems of astrology and its magic, we can feel connected to the infinite chain of divinity in creation. We can find within our own microcosmic soul that golden light that tethers us to the macrocosmic soul of the All.

That is not to say that astrology does not have its detractors. It always has, long before the Copernican revolution or the advent of modern astronomy. To find Fate in the stars was seen as dangerous, fatalistic, or foolhardy. Modern science tends to look its nose down at astrology as a bygone superstition. I do not intend to argue with those who hold that worldview, because I genuinely believe the mistake here is that we are speaking different languages. The magic of astrology was just that: magic. It was, and is, a system of connection and power. It is an approach to the cosmos, a worldview within itself that cannot empty any part of the cosmos, from celestial to earthly, of purpose and meaning. The secular scientist and the astrologer need not be at odds, but we must realize that we are speaking of two hugely different things when we begin to talk about the stars. These stars are more than their physical beings. It is my hope that this work will introduce you to this language, this worldview that sees the divine soul reflected within the night sky and within us. These stars we see are *our* stars, woven into our history and consciousness as much as myth, legend, religion, or magic.

---

[1] Georg Luck, *Arcana Mundi Magic and the Occult in the Greek and Roman Worlds: A Collection of Ancient Texts* (Baltimore, MD: Johns Hopkins University Press, 2008), 420.

And these stars have always held sway over imagination and desire, regardless of how they were interpreted. The Egyptians chiseled prayers into stone so that souls might rejoin the starry realms. Astrological codices and star maps were carefully preserved for ages. To modern scientists all of this was just a buildup, a preamble to the advent of astronomy. The tools of science removed the god-masks of the stars to find nuclear fusion beneath. The elements revealed themselves in a cold and dread fashion. But to the magician and the seeker, nothing has been unmasked. The mysteries are still curled up in the patterns made up in the Heavenly Spheres. That magic is available to us—and it is powerful. But why would you want to study astrology? What does it offer us? Why does it still have such a hold over us that even the most fervent nonbeliever can answer the question, "What's your sign?" without a moment's hesitation? I believe it is because the power behind the system is very real.

As for what the system can teach us, I know from personal experience what it can bring to our souls. We can learn from it with the same spirit that Manilius, the Roman writer, comments upon in his *Astronomica*: "It is my delight to traverse the very air and spend my life touring the boundless skies, learning of the constellations and the contrary motions of the planets ... [for] deeper knowledge of heaven was first granted to earth by the gift of the gods." [2]

*˙*Connection *˙*

Astrology is first and foremost about connection. One of the greatest stumbling blocks to personal and spiritual development is isolation. The modern world seems hell-bent on creating situations of isolation. We are disconnected from the cycles of nature, from the food we eat, from our fellow human beings. We often experience the isolation that long work hours, commuting, and a 24-hour news cycle can create. When we step into the world of astrology and its magic, we begin to enter a world where connection is everything. Every star, every hour, every bit of our experience

---

2   Marcus Manilius, *Astronomica*, trans. G. P. Goold (Cambridge, MA: Harvard U.P., 1977), 5-7.

becomes a reflection of a higher intelligence, a greater purpose. The ensouled cosmos comes alive for us when we begin to see reflections of our own experience at the highest echelons that we can imagine or witness. To work with the stars is to elevate the soul. They begin to exist as much in our mind as they do in the firmament. And when the world feels too small, too gray, and isolated, we can drink from the rich works on the art and magic of astrology to feel connected again, to see the larger picture and wonder of life. One of the greatest Renaissance magicians and polymaths, Marsilio Ficino, believed that the regular and untroubled patterns of the stars existed to guide our own troubled souls to a deeper understanding because we, ourselves, were kin to the stars.[3] It is a therapeutic brand of magic, perhaps more so than any other in the traditions we have preserved, precisely because it breaks down the barriers of isolation and the soul-crushing singularity of mind that is the modern—and postmodern, for that matter—condition.

*∗*Destiny and Magic*∗*

Astrology walks an infinitely delicate line between fate and possibility. The anxiety of our daily experience often leads to one of two extremes: We feel trapped in patterns we cannot change, or we feel overwhelmed by choices. We are told to both "Grow up and accept things the way they are," while simultaneously being told to "Go forth! Change the world!" These conflicting messages can lead us to feel paralyzed, trapped between two seemingly impossible and contradicting realities. The wisdom behind astrology's worldview and its magic is that it understands this challenge and offers answers. The stars allow us to look above and see the larger cosmos that we inhabit, which can do wonders for our perspective. We can begin to understand that certain experiences are inevitable, predictable as an orbit or the setting Sun or the phases of the Moon. But the magic of astrology can give us tools to understand what it is we can do to change our world. Magic and astrology were intimately linked, early in

---

3   Benson Bobrick, *The Fated Sky: Astrology in History* (New York, NY: Simon & Schuster, 2007), 126.

their history, and walked a path together.[4] One of the most influential planetary grimoires, *Picatrix*, defines magic as, "... whatever is done by man, by which sense and spirit follow ... by which marvelous things are done so that the senses are led by them, contemplating and marveling."[5] Astrology's magic allows us to understand both Fate and possibility, to lay claim to both the peace of an ordered cosmos and the revolutions available to a seeker and magician. We need not be frozen by "choice anxiety." There are paths that deal with this anxiety, and they are written in starlight and math, in planetary hours, and cosmic perspective.

⁕*Discipline, Timing, and Cycles*⁕

Astrological magic requires discipline. Time matters, along with date and preparation. The Art allows us to learn discipline in our spiritual work. We must master patience if we are going to work with the planetary days, hours, the phases of the Moon, or conjunctions of the planets. We learn diligence and detail when we interpret horoscopes. We learn, in the Art, to appreciate cycles. We know the coming of seasonal changes, of tidal shifts. We know when it is the right time to act and when it may be a time to recede, to be dormant, to meditate and wait. We cannot simply rush into every idea, but must consider it from above, below, and on all sides. Astrology is a powerful focusing tool, a system that teaches us the habits necessary for any serious spiritual seeker. If a student is really craving a system that will push them to grow, and teach them both boundaries and drive, then astrology and its magics are a powerful tool. It is similar, in this way, to many other successful tools that people have used and continue to use for spiritual development. The introduction to the West of yogic principles builds on foundational ideas to even more dizzying concepts of philosophy and more strenuous forms. Astrology is no different; it lays

---

4   J. Lee Lehman, "The Conjunction of Electional Astrology and Magic," in The Celestial Art: Essays on Astrological Magic, ed. Austin Coppock and Daniel A. Schulke (Three Hands Press, 2018), 28.

5   *The Illustrated Picatrix: The Occult Classic of Astrological Magic Complete in One Volume*, trans. John Michael Greer and Christopher Warnock (Renaissance Astrology, 2015), 26.

a foundation and then builds on that foundation, bringing discipline and consistency to the practitioner.

⋆⁎⋆Foundations and Language ⋆⁎⋆

For the spiritual seeker, astrology can be a foundational Art. Throughout the currents of spiritual traditions, astrology was often at the heart of the Great Work. Hermetic works, magical texts, mystical literature, and occult organizations worked astrology into the warp and weft of their teachings. By learning the art of astrological magic, you are learning a foundational part of Western esotericism. [6] Even Christian theologians and authors wrote on and often practiced or gave credence to at least some forms of astrology. Some of the greatest writers on astrology and its magic were Jewish and Muslim. This does not even touch on the power and influence of Vedic and Chinese astrology. The Art spans across traditions, bringing a unified cosmic language that is adaptable to differing philosophies, religious practices, or spiritual aims. It gives a worldview in which to see the experience of magic and of the divine. For many seekers, the tools are easy enough to master. We can all pick up a particular system of symbols or words, but we are often left with many gaping holes in the philosophy and the approach. Astrology gives a foundation to our spiritual pathworkings and meditations. As counterintuitive as it may seem, we are truly grounding ourselves in the stars.

It is my hope that seekers will find this work a helpful guide in exploring the rich power and magic of astrology. Stretching from Babylon to Kepler and beyond, astrology has woven itself into the tapestry of our lives. Following its threads leads to a full and rewarding understanding of the world we live in and what divine magics really course through us all. I know it has done so for me, and I have seen it do so for many of my students. Every time I teach on the subject, I learn something new

---

6 For some examples and further investigation into the deep links between astrology and ritual/image magic, see: Frank Klaassen, *The Transformations of Magic: Illicit Learned Magic in the Later Middle Ages and Renaissance* (University Park, PA: The Pennsylvania State University Press, 2013) and Conjuring Spirits: Texts and Traditions of Medieval Ritual Magic, ed. Claire Fanger (University Park, PA: The Pennsylvania State University Press, 1998).

myself. I try to always be ready to let the stars teach and guide, to keep my mind sharp and open to new ideas and teachings. I often return to a fragment from the *Chaldean Oracles*, a mystical text, and a favorite of many Neoplatonist philosophers (and a favorite text of mine):

> *But when you see the formless, very holy fire shining by leaps and bounds throughout the depths of the whole world, then listen to the voice of the fire.* "[7]

May we all find that holy fire—and listen.

---

[7] *The Chaldean Oracles: Text, Translation, and Commentary*, trans. Ruth Dorothy Majercik (Dilton Marsh, Westbury, Wiltshire, UK: The Prometheus Trust, 2013), 105.

This page intentionally left blank.

INTRODUCTION

The Firmament

> " ... the God of heaven brought his servants
> to a knowledge of heaven
> and disclosed its secrets to them
> ... the first by their art to discern
> the destinies dependent on
> the wandering stars. "
> —Manilius' Astronomica.

To begin at the beginning is excellent advice, but it is not as easy as it sounds. Astrology is an ancient system with a complex vocabulary and unique tools. For the seeker, and even for someone with foundational knowledge of the system, it can be daunting. Words like *sextile* and *decans* and *imum coeli* mingle with intricate charts with alchemical-looking glyphs and precise numbers. To many, this can be a real hurdle to approaching the work and truly gaining a strong understanding of astrology and its teachings. When we add in the writings and rituals of planetary magic, with their sigils and angelic rites, then we are dealing with a subject that can seem overwhelmingly difficult.

So, we run the risk when we write about astrology of overloading the student. We run the risk of killing the mystery and magic by starting, frankly, with a math class. That is not to say that the sacred geometry and precise calculations used in astrology are not important. There is a real beauty to the precision of horoscope creation and the mandalas created by relationships between signs, planets, and houses. I am only admitting that we sometimes need to appreciate the spirit and power of a system or art before we dissect its details. That is why I am beginning with the planets.

Many astrologers prefer to teach by starting with a chart, explaining the signs of the zodiac, the house system, the elements, and other foundational tools that are indeed crucial to a working knowledge of the Art. Then, they introduce the planets: how they relate to one another (aspects), and how to interpret with them. This is an excellent way of teaching for someone who wishes to focus on reading horoscopes as a primary experience with the Art. For someone who wishes to explore both the power of astrology through horoscopes but also as a spiritual system and a magical system, it is perhaps a difficult way to begin. So, I have chosen to begin a different way.

I am beginning with the planets because they are truly the actors and intelligences behind the system. If the sky, and the horoscope as its representation here on Earth, is a stage, then the planets must dance and move across that stage. They are the spiritual sparks of creation that breathe life into the magic; they inspire and connect. We must know them first and appreciate their spirit before we can place them in a system that we can interpret and use. To put it another way, I want to taste the meal before I see exactly how it is made. It is important to truly feel the soul of each planet, to experience it across different senses and in different ways. This allows us to begin to see what each of the Heavenly Spheres can really teach us, where we find them in the cycles of our lives and in the pools of our own consciousness. Taking up the Art and magic of astrology, and truly looking into the mysteries it can teach us, requires a new worldview. It requires a worldview that we have forgotten much of after the advent of modernity.

For some astrologers, my language here might be too lofty. I may be giving too much spiritual weight to the seven wandering stars of our skies. Some would see the planets as mechanical things, acting in certain ways and producing specific effects. This was also the view of some ancient astrologers, who preferred to see the celestial bodies as emitting certain rays or properties into earthly life but not as higher spiritual beings or spheres. Christian authors often believed that the stars could predict events (particularly the weather) or influence life, but not control and truly order destiny (that role belonged only to the Triune God). Some also doubted the efficacy of astrologically guided magic. Augustine of Hippo and Isidore of Seville both refused to allot to the stars the power to truly guide fate, but they still allowed that they could be useful for mechanistic, natural explanations of phenomena. [1] There is, however, serious scholarship that sees the Art of astrology, even among classical sources, as much more akin to *divination* (coming from divinity, fortune-telling, psychism, the mystical) than what was understood as *science* (knowledge through pure observation and cause and effect). Although not the view of all classical astrological sources, this much more divinatory view of the Art shines through classical writings that work through theme and image much more than direct cause and effect. [2]

I cannot see the stars as pure mechanism, and they do not operate as such for me, either in my spiritual practice or my divination. I cannot separate astrology from its magic. Even the term "magic" has roots to the term *magi*, Persian priests who were closely linked in history with the practice of astrology. [3] I truly believe that the divinity and inner mysteries of astrology lie within an approach to the cosmos that sees it as heavy with meaning and connection, not simply a game of cause and effect. A magical approach to astrology is a worldview rooted in philosophy and religion. It draws from Neoplatonist philosophy. It draws from Hermeticism, Gnosticism, and Hellenistic religion. It breathes a magic of its own and has been the inspiration for many who want to understand what it is to be here, in the universe, and conscious of it.

Neoplatonist philosophers saw the universe as an ordered creation, a reflection of the One, and entirely divine. Thinkers in this tradition such as Iamblichus saw the cosmos as a living altar, or shrine to the gods themselves, and not simply as a fallen world. [4] The philosopher Plotinus describes the universe as " ... a life organized, effective, complex, all-com-

---

[1]   Richard Kieckhefer, *Magic in the Middle Ages, 2nd ed. (*Cambridge: Cambridge University Press, 1989), 127.

[2]   For further examination of the scholarship that interprets classical astrological sources from the divination over science perspective, see: "Interpreting Interpretations: The Aphorism in the Practice of the Renaissance Astrologers by Geoffrey Cornelius," in *From Masha'Allah to Kepler: Theory and Practice in Medieval and Renaissance Astrology* ed. Charles Burnett and Dorian Gieseler Greenbaum (Ceredigion: Sophia Centre Press, 2015).

[3]   Richard Kieckhefer, *Magic in the Middle Ages, 2nd ed.* (Cambridge: Cambridge University Press, 1989), 10.

[4]   Gregory Shaw, *Theurgy and the Soul: The Neoplatonism of Iamblichus, Second Ed.* (Kettering, OH: Angelico Press/Sophia Perennis, 2014), xxiv.

prehensive, displaying an unfathomable wisdom."[5] [6] The planets bear within themselves the spark of divinity that exists within this wise and complex creation.

The planets are almost like divine filters through which the ineffable can pass down into physical reality. They are part of the order of divine creation: steppingstones, rulers, and unique intelligences, all flowing from the eternal light of the One. They are sympathetic with plants, humans, animals, stones, and every other thing that makes up mundane existence. They are larger than their physical realities. They do not contain or restrict the divine, only existing as part of it. Iamblichus writes of the gods: "For neither is it the case that the gods are confined to certain parts of the cosmos, nor is the earthly realm devoid of them. On the contrary, it is true of the superior beings ... they are not contained by anything, so they contain everything within themselves."[7]

The planets are named for gods because they are the will of the gods made manifest. They play their role in Fate, spiritual progression, and cosmic balance. They are pathways of divine consciousness, translating an ineffable and difficult-to-understand divinity into physical reality through symbolism and relationships that we *can* understand. We can also work with them. Many Neoplatonists were *theurgists*, Iamblichus in particular. They practiced a divine form of magic that was geared toward the elevation of the soul. Iamblichus writes: "And though the soul has to a lesser degree the eternity of unchanging life and full actuality, by means of the Gods' good will and the illumination bestowed by their light, it often goes higher and is elevated to a greater rank, even to that of the angelic order."[8] The celestial spheres are a pathway for that work. Astrology

---

5   Algis Uzdavinys, *The Heart of Plotinus: The Essential Enneads Including Porphyry's On the Cave of the Nymphs* (Bloomington: World Wisdom, Inc., 2009), 82.

6   It is important to note that Plotinus criticized causal astrology in his philosophy. Later Neoplatonists would go into much deeper detail when it came to celestial hierarchies. I am referencing Plotinus here to speak to the concept of an ensouled cosmos, a differing worldview than the secular and scientific one we use today that sees the cosmos as dead space.

7   *Iamblichus: On the Mysteries*, trans. Emma C. Clarke, John M. Dillon, and Jackson P. Hershbell (Atlanta, GA: Society of Biblical Literature, 2003), 37.

8   Ibid, 85.

may have been about Fate, but it was not necessarily *fatalistic*. Magic and theurgy were part-and-parcel of the arts. Change was possible, evolution available to those willing to plunge into and accomplish the work. In the Neoplatonic sense, the cosmos was a holistic experience, a real and living thing in which the microcosm of our soul could participate, even at the highest level of the macrocosm of the Heavenly Spheres. [9]

So, when you think of the planet Venus from a magical perspective, you are not just thinking about a bright object that moves across the night sky in a regular pattern, a purely astronomical reality. You are instead thinking of an entire sphere, an entire realm of correspondences, a section of the divine cosmic soul. You may be seeing that sphere of cosmic conscious-ness as the Morning and Evening Star that is Venus, but to penetrate the magical arts you have to realize that the individual spark of light in the morning light or the evening gloom is only a mirror, a pinhole of light, a gateway to something much larger. Then, you must see that it is within yourself as much as you have seen it without. Paracelsus describes this work, instructing us to consider, "There is nothing in heaven or in earth that is not also in man. For these are the heavenly powers which work in him. For God, who is in heaven, is in man. Where else can heaven be if not in man? As we need it, it must be within us." [10] [11]

᛫᛫*What are the Planets? *᛫*᛫*

To the ancients, the planets were stars, but an incredibly special kind of star. [12] The planets were beings of light. The ancients could not see the stormy face of Jupiter, or the barren face of Mercury. They could

---

9 Richard Kieckhefer, *Magic in the Middle Ages, 2nd ed.* (Cambridge: Cambridge University Press, 1989), 130.

10 *Paracelsus: Essential Readings*, trans. Nicholas Goodrick-Clarke (Berkeley, CA: North Atlantic Books, 1999), 95.

11 Unfortunately, historical sources tend to speak only in the masculine. I have left the translations and citations in the original to respect the source, but it is important to remember that we are speaking of all human beings, not just males, and it is important to recognize the inherent misogyny in these writings.

12 This is why you will see planets referred to as "stars" in traditional texts, and throughout this book as well. For the ancients, they *were* stars.

only visualize the planets based on how they reacted with light. This is why the Greeks called Jupiter *Phaethon* (meaning "Shining One") for its brightness. It is why Mars became the "red star" with its coloration visible to stargazers on Earth. These moving stars were *planētes asteres* (πλάνητες ἀστέρες in Greek), meaning "wandering stars." The "fixed stars" in the night sky did not move across the heavens in the same way as these particular bodies did, and so they were pilgrims in the celestial realms, moving in patterns that learned peoples came to understand as regular—predictable, even. The Sun and Moon were seen as pilgrims, too, moving across the night sky in even and particular patterns. The seasons were understood in their natural cycles along with the phases of the Moon. And thus the "luminaries" of the Sun and Moon came to be understood as wandering stars as well. Even though this Greek name, with the beautiful poetic connotation that it gives, is the one that we use today, the knowledge of the planets, these "wanderers," were known long before Greek or Hellenistic culture.

In Babylon, the seven traditional planets were known, and we have textual evidence that Babylonian astrologers noted the motions of the planets. In the 7th century B.C.E., the *Enuma Anu Enlil* contained portents and prophecies based on the movements of the planets.[13] These beginnings in Mesopotamia would lay the foundations for astrology and planetary magic as it moved through the Classical Greek, Hellenistic, Roman, Muslim, Jewish, and Christian worlds. The connection to a Babylonian past becomes very evident in the proliferation of the term "Chaldean" in many texts on magic, philosophy, and astrology that came long after the height of Babylonian civilization. The mystery of the "Chaldeans" was a strong mytho-historical past for magicians and Hermetic philosophers to draw on, but it *did* have a foot in reality. Chaldeans may have been a sacred caste within the society, although the term was originally applied for people with an ethnic origin in a particular region of Babylonian territory.[14] The "Chaldeans" eventually came to be a broad term for astrologers and

---

[13]   Benson Bobrick, *The Fated Sky: Astrology in History* (New York: Simon & Schuster, 2007), 16.

[14]   Georg Luck, *Arcana Mundi Magic and the Occult in the Greek and Roman Worlds: A Collection of Ancient Texts* (Baltimore: Johns Hopkins University Press, 2008), 371.

other diviners later in Greek society.[15] Roman civilization would follow suit, labelling astrologers as "Chaldeans" and linking their art and magic to the mytho-historical past that had been built up by generations of practitioners and writers.[16] Babylonian civilization really was a cradle for the astrological arts and for planetary magic. And it was a spiritual practice from its birth, not solely an observatory one. Babylonian religion was linked closely with the stars, and the star-loving religion of Babylon would inspire the development of astrology and its deeply spiritual center.

As astrology developed in the Mediterranean, the planets were seen as governing celestial spheres. Philosophers and astrologers developed cosmologies that moved from the terrestrial experiences of humans to the divine realms of the Gods. Thinkers from Pythagoras and Parmenides to Plato and Aristotle developed complex cosmologies to explain the shape and formation of the cosmos, with Earth firmly in the center and the celestial bodies that were known moving around Earth. It was the 2nd-century polymath Claudius Ptolemy who would develop one of the most enduring understandings of planets and their celestial spheres. Although he did not invent the system entirely on his own, his enduring image of the cosmos would come to inspire many of those who came after him. This system is also known as the "Chaldean" ordering of the planets, hearkening as we mentioned above, to the Babylonian history and mythology of astrology's past. The system and number of the planets became a norm in the works of many astrologers and magicians throughout Western history. This system orders the celestial spheres in the following way:

[15] Benson Bobrick, *The Fated Sky: Astrology in History* (New York: Simon & Schuster, 2007), 18.

[16] Jörg Rüpke, *Pantheon: A New History of Roman Religion*, trans. David M. B. Richardson (Princeton, NJ: Princeton University Press, 2018), 303.

The following 16ᵗʰ century woodcut shows this sequence in context within the celestial spheres that traditional astrologers used to view the cosmos:

The celestial spheres from the *Cosmographia* of Peter Apian, 16th c.

In this system it is the Moon, that closest satellite of Earth, that is the first sphere beyond our own experience. The Sun is at the center of the list, separating out the near and distant planets, and it ends with Saturn, the slowest-moving of the planets. Beyond the planets we find the constellations of the zodiac, the fixed stars, and the Empyreum: the highest heaven, the abode of the Godhead.

The celestial spheres were frequently experienced as a journey. Pre-Christian works contain poetic references to the divine spheres, such as Cicero's *Dream of Scipio*. This image became popular later in Christian Europe in works such as Dante's *Divine Comedy* and the Portuguese epic of *The Lusiads*, both works that speak of the framework of the celestial spheres and their passage between the realms of humankind and the abode of the divine. The spheres provide a pathway for spiritual ascent and progression, a series of realms and correspondences that all link to our experience as individual souls within a wider cosmos. Their lessons and rulerships have direct relation to what we are trying to accomplish as spiritual beings, to what we wish to accomplish through magic, meditation, ritual, and art. We are carving our own place in the cosmos, and the celestial spheres are paths of creation, the unfolding of the divine will in a cosmic order. The planets are our touchstones for this, both mirrors of our own experience and gateways to a wider experience—a deeper understanding of divinity, magic, and elevation.

*⸰٭*Correspondences*⸰٭*

As this understanding of the celestial spheres and the planets grew, magical systems came to be rooted in astrological understanding. Alchemy, Kabbalah, Hermetic orders, ritual magic, Witchcraft, and more all shared a thread of truth with astrology's teachings and with planetary magic. Through the concept of sympathetic magic, the planets were associated with flora and fauna, body parts, countries and nations, minerals, and even more. The lists of magical correspondences can become quite large. It was a spiritual connection that was seen between these earthly things and the celestial bodies given rulership over them. The art of sympathetic magic was a belief in the interconnectedness of all things, the essential *oneness* within the universe that flows from the divine center outward into Creation. Drawing from Greek philosophy, magicians and astrologers saw that objects had essential *being* and that this essential being held sympathy with other beings. Thus, iron held sympathy with Mars, gold with the Sun, and so forth. This was often known as "natural magic," and it was expounded upon by writers such as Trithemius, Agrippa, Paracelsus, the Neoplatonic-inspired Marsilio Ficino, and others.

Perhaps the most enduring example of this esoteric philosophy and magical worldview is the *Emerald Tablet*. This Hermetic text appears at the earliest in Arabic in the 8th century B.C.E. [17] Its translation into Latin and proliferation in Europe made it a central text for Hermetic philosophers, magicians, alchemists, and mystics. Its author gives himself as Hermes Trismegistus (Thrice-Blessed Hermes), a figure of importance in the history of Hermetic and esoteric ideas associated both with gods and mortal philosophers, from the Egyptian Thoth to the Greek Hermes and to many human thinkers that bore their mantle. Although physical alchemy tried to interpret the text to transmute base metals into gold, the text was seen to have a spiritual significance throughout its history. Albertus Magnus, John Dee, Agrippa, and even Isaac Newton wrote on the tablet's significance and teachings. It contains references to celestial bodies and speaks to the core truth at the heart of sympathetic magic:

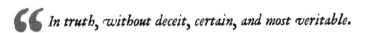 *As Above, So Below.*"

One of my favorite translations of the *Emerald Tablet* is from Dennis William Hauck's work, *The Emerald Tablet: Alchemy for Personal Trans-formation:*[18]

❝ *In truth, without deceit, certain, and most veritable.*

> *That which is Below corresponds to that which is Above, and that which is Above corresponds to that which is Below, to accomplish the miracles of the One Thing. And just as all things have come from this One Thing, through the meditation of One Mind, so do all created things originate from this One Thing, through transformation.*

---

17 Antoine Faivre and Joscelyn Godwin, *The Eternal Hermes: From Greek God to Alchemical Magus* (Grand Rapids, MI: Phanes Press, 1995), 91.

18 Dennis William Hauck, *The Emerald Tablet: Alchemy for Personal Transformation* (New York: Penguin, 1999), 45.

Its father is the Sun; its mother the Moon. The Wind carries it in its belly; its nurse is the Earth. It is the origin of All, the consecration of the Universe; its inherent Strength is perfected, if it is turned into Earth.

Separate the Earth from Fire, the Subtle from the Gross, gently and with great Ingenuity. It rises from Earth to Heaven and descends again to Earth, thereby combining within Itself the power of both the Above and the Below.

Thus will you obtain the Glory of the Whole Universe. All Obscurity will be clear to you. This is the greatest Force of all powers, because it overcomes every Subtle thing and penetrates every Solid thing.

In this way was the Universe created. From this comes many wondrous Applications, because this is the Pattern.

Therefore am I called Thrice Greatest Hermes, having all three parts of the wisdom of the Whole Universe. Herein have I completely explained the Operation of the Sun."

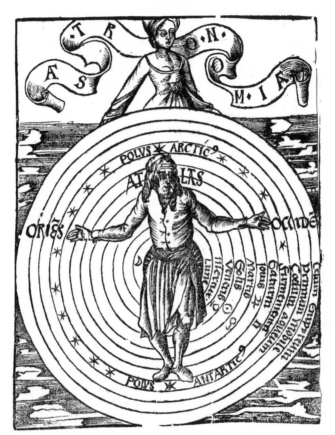

16th c. depiction of a human being at the center of the celestial spheres.

This understanding of the world as full of sympathetic processes and divine reflections fueled alchemy's desire to transformation, both physical and spiritual. It influenced astrology and planetary magic just as profoundly as it did alchemy. Planetary magic sees the spheres as pathways between the "Above" and the "Below," and it is the Great Work to unite the two, to realize the connectedness. That is the spiritual power behind astrology and the magic of the stars. It is the power of uniting the cosmic to the terrestrial, the divine One to the myriad and varied experiences of our souls here in Creation.

Therefore, the planets exist in herbs, stones, and the human body. They exist in the Below. And they lead to the Above. This is the magic at the heart of correspondences.

Finally, it is important to remember that correspondences may differ between authors, traditions, or systems, but it is the core truth that is crucial for the seeker: it is all connected. Sympathetic magic, Hermetic philosophy, Neoplatonist theurgy, and more are all philosophies and practices that ground themselves in the understanding of the cosmos as interconnected, meaningful, and divine. Astrology and its magic are tools for the Great Work, the eternal goal of the mystic, the seeker, the sage, the magician, the witch, the hero. We use correspondences to connect ourselves to higher planes, higher experiences of consciousness. We work them into our magic and our divination to connect to the various expressions of Creation that share a profound common unity. Do not get bogged down too far in lists. They are especially useful, but it is the heart of the work that matters, the eternal return to that sacred unity, the crucible of imagination, life, and magic.

With this view of As Above, So Below, and the understanding of the divine connection within Creation, we can become conduits for celestial magic. Paracelsus says, "The magus is not born of the natural stars but of the supernatural stars."[19] It is the theurgy of astrological magic that allows us to tap into the divinity of the cosmos and channel it into action, meditation, and change. The stars go from their purely physical image to their supernatural image, their higher meaning. Correspondences are the microcosmic, earth-bound tools that we use to connect our souls to higher power.

✷✶✷Meeting the Planets ✷✶✷

The first seven chapters will introduce you to the seven planets. We will go in the traditional order, starting from the Moon. Each chapter will have a pathworking, which is a guided meditation meant to introduce you to the correspondences, spirit, and magic of each planet that you will encounter. I recommend coming back to these chapters as you progress through the book, remembering the images and experiences of each planet. You can

[19] *Paracelsus: Essential Readings,* trans. Nicholas Goodrick-Clarke (Berkeley, CA: North Atlantic Books, 1999), 143.

record the meditations to use later, or use them as touchstones for your own meditations and writing. Journaling after experiencing a meditation or pathworking is always a good idea, and even better to do so after a ritual. The important thing is to experience the totality of each and begin to form your own connection to the stars. These pathworkings are not a litany of rigid rules and expectations, but a guide to place your mind in the right place to experience the spheres, and to make and continue to make connections with the celestial world.

We will begin to introduce the planetary magic of each of the Heavenly Spheres, referring to the corpus of historical works. You will know the relationship each planet has to the world we inhabit and how we can channel and work with those relationships. At the end, there is a traditional table of correspondences for your own magical practices. These correspondences are drawn from historical sources and my personal experiences and workings with each planet. I have drawn from multiple traditional sources, from Hellenistic sources such as Ptolemy and Valens, Arabic language sources such as al-Qabisi and al-Biruni, and to later Christian sources such as William Lilly. I have also pulled from the rich grimoire tradition, with *Picatrix* and *The Key of Solomon* serving as central resources. I have tried to avoid correspondences that are too difficult to procure, possibly dangerous, or where translations were difficult, and we are unsure of the original author's intent.

Finally, there is ritual. Ritual is crucial to magic. Magic was never something one only thought about; it is something one does. It is a living and breathing Art in which we place our entire selves and all our senses. Incenses awaken our senses of smell and taste. Ritual clothing and tools shake our mind free of the mundane world to a different world rich with possibility, beauty, and daring. We touch and see the objects, sigils, and creations of the Art. Each planet will be given a ritual. I recommend following the planetary days and hours[20] for these rituals and taking time to prepare for each one. There is no need to rush through them. Let them be guides for your own personal ritual development and magic. We

---

[20] Each planet will have this information in its correspondences. Also, see the chapter on planetary hours and timing.

will go further into ritual later in the book, but, for now, these rites are beginning gateways into the power of ceremony, sensation, and magic. For centuries, ritual magic and astrological magic went hand in hand. They were inseparable Arts, all part of a theurgic process of uniting our souls to the divine and effecting change in the universe and within our own bodies.

When approaching the rituals, do not get bogged down in details early. Precision and mindfulness are crucial for good ritual, but good ritual is a learned skill and not an immediate ability. Ritual space doesn't need to be elaborate, but care should go into it. The same can be said for ritual tools, clothing, and incenses. Go over all rituals before engaging with them, and make sure you are ready. Nothing can destroy the power of good ritual more than stopping and starting in the middle of the work. Effort is what truly matters. When we engage in ritual, we are triggering certain responses in our psyche and building up a sort of astral muscle memory. Approaching ritual with consciousness and an eye for beauty will do wonders in developing good habits and getting the results you desire. The words, actions, and implements of ritual all serve a purpose. Sometimes it is to shake us out of our mundane experience. Sometimes it is to unite our thought with the built egregores of the past. Whatever the purpose, our intention must be present, and our mind engaged fully, to truly benefit from ritual work.

With that, we meet our wandering stars—our seven pilgrims that will guide us through the Heavenly Spheres. We look up with the same wonder and awe that every generation before us did, our feet firmly planted on Earth and our minds with the stars. We must forever keep that spark of curiosity and awesome wonder that exists when we see the night sky full of lights.

THE MOON

Mother. Water. Memory.

⋆⋆⋆ The Meeting ⋆⋆⋆

The air is humid. The cool, light dew seems to cling to your clothes, soaking through to the skin. The forest is eerie at night, cast in a pale glow from the Full Moon visible above the treetops. Frogs croak in the night and crickets chirp, a noisy reminder that this place is alive, even at night. Stumbling slightly in the tree roots and underbrush, you move large fern fronds out of your way. They seem prehistoric in size, milky-green in the moonlight and dripping wet. Snails cling to your clothes, left there by the vegetation you press and move against. You pick them off and set them back onto the forest floor. The path is not clear, not yet at least, but you keep moving forward. In the distance is the light sound of water in motion, and that becomes your goal. You need to find the water. Every part of you wants to find it, every part of you eager and curious to find the source of the sound. The night time is confusing. It makes monsters out of the trees and seems to turn you in circles, making the way harder and harder to find.

Just as the need to find the water grows to a fevered pitch, the tree line breaks, and the forest is behind you. The break in the woods is a soft stretch of ground, muddy soil mingling and then giving way to a sandy beach. The body of water is a lake, its soft rippling waves lapping against the shoreline in a gentle, rhythmic pattern. It stretches far, but in the distant haze of the moonlight, you can make out islands, inlets, and a far shore on the other side. The slow push and pull of the water against the sand is soporific, lulling you almost into a hazy sleep where you stand until you notice the woman.

She is standing by a small fire that is barely lit and fizzling in the dewy night air. She sits down on a small stool, tending the flames, wearing a plain white gown and nothing upon her feet. Her hair is dark and long, thick and unruly. You cautiously come nearer to her presence, and as you do, you see a boat bobbing gently in the water, tied to a small sapling that grows near the banks of the lake. The small vessel is pale and silvery-white, paint chipping away from the old wood.

The woman looks up at you, unstartled, her face calm and placid. She reaches behind her and takes a basket from the ground along with a small grate. She places the grate over the fire, which grows hotter as she adds what seems to be small clods of earthen material. You sit down, close enough to the fire to feel its warmth but not close enough to disturb what she is doing. From the woven basket, she takes out small freshwater crayfish and long, silvery skewers of wood with pointed ends. Her nimble fingers work quickly, unadorned save for a silver ring with something lustrous catching the moonlight, maybe mother of pearl. You watch as she pierces the crustaceans and places them on the heated grate. The crackle of food on hot metal breaks the quiet evening, and the scent of cooked fish fills the space around you.

You sit and watch as she cooks. She finally removes her meal carefully and shells the crayfish as they cool. She eats. You are offered to take part, and you may or may not—she does not insist. She places the shells in her basket and stands up. You notice she is pregnant, her abdomen filling out the simple white dress. You cannot remember if you noticed this before. You are sure you could not have missed it. Her form is different, fuller, holding itself upright and proud. Feeling out of place and not trusting your own perception, you stand up with her.

She motions to the boat, and you feel a sense of unease. It is small and unsteady on the surface of the lake. Motioning again, she turns from you and places a bare foot on the edge of the craft. Wanting to help, you take her hand and walk with her into the boat. It pitches and moves beneath you, but she does not seem to notice, taking her place on one of two benches. She looks at you, impatient. It is time to go. We must cross the water. We have no choice but to cross the water. You reach back and unhook the rope that tethers you both to the safety of the shore. She looks at you again, that same sense of impatience and readiness to move written on her face. You look around for oars, something, anything, to propel you forward.

The boat slips away from the shore independently, moving across the clear water. The moonlight bathes everything in its glow, and the woman nods slowly as you begin your journey. Your gaze drifts from the Full Moon above to the water and back to the woman. She seems different. Each time your eyes fall back to her, she is somehow the same and yet not the same. Her expressions are mutable, her form shifting in the night's shadows. At times, you would swear she is young, too young even to bear a child, and yet still other times as you glide across the lake water you would swear she is older, ancient even. The feeling is unnerving, and you doubt, not for the first time this night, your own senses. The dreamlike moment is unsteadying yet curious. You need to know who she is, where you are going, why you are moving across the water with her.

Her eyes grow larger, a sense of urgency in her face. She clutches at the side of the boat and looks behind her. Your eyes follow where her gaze falls and you see a small, green island in the middle of the lake, far from the shore where you began. Pale flowers bloom around the island, and the floral scent fills your nose, heady and sweet. The boat moves toward the shore of this isle, the woman standing and moving to leave the vessel. You help her from the boat. You have questions to ask, but you cannot find your voice to ask them, and you know she will not answer, not yet. You stumble behind her as she moves away from the boat that has brought you both to this place, this blooming, lush and wet place in the center of the dark waters of the lake.

There is a clearing in the vegetation on the island, a place for her to lie down. She holds her belly, gazing up into the night sky. Her hair is silvery-white, her entire frame different, but it is still her. She is breathing heavily, her form still mutable, shifting hazily in your vision, causing you to pitch and reel while you kneel to help her. She looks into your eyes and in the reflection, you see flashes of memory, bits and pieces of something from a different place, someplace familiar to you, comfortable. Your eyes are dazzled by the flickering in her eyes as a thunderbolt crashes near the lake, the roar of it in your ears. The bright flash illuminates the sky, and for a moment you are dazzled. You hear the woman cry out in birth pangs, and everything goes white, your ears ringing.

The woman is gone. Your eyes readjust, but it is dark; there is nothing. The lush smell of vegetation is gone, the heady scent of the flowers, the dewy wetness on your skin—all has evaporated. You squint and struggle in the darkness until you make out three shining lights, small and flickering. They are close, awfully close. The haze of your vision begins to clear, and you see three small candles, pierced into the thick white frosting of a round cake. Family is around you, and friends. Everyone is here for you. There are wrapped presents and music in the background. Everything seems larger. You adjust, but only briefly, before you lean closer and blow out the candles.

*.*The First Sphere: Luna *.*

The Moon is the first of the Heavenly Spheres, the closest celestial light to our terrestrial home. Because of this intimate relationship we have with her, she has come to figure centrally in the mythology and social consciousness of most peoples. We keep time by her, evident in the naming of "month" for the Moon. We know that she influences the tides of the sea. She has entered our metaphors and daily speech in terms like "Moonstruck," "shoot for the Moon" and "lunatic." Her influence is everywhere in magical texts and astrological workings. Her associations with fertility, motherhood, planting cycles, the agricultural year, and more have made her the closest relative and maternal figure for our own planet. She is honored in the pre-Christian pantheons as a deity, worked into angelic magic in Renaissance grimoires, and is a central focus in the modern rebirth of religious Witchcraft. The occult and magical worlds seem to have been "Moonstruck" since the beginning, always placing her in the highest honor and seeing the light reflected within the night as a beacon, a focal point for the elevation of the soul.

She is, in many ways, the first gate to the heavens. She is the astral path, the shifting, nocturnal secret door that opens to the higher planes and the inner mysteries. She is keeper of those mysteries and must be propitiated first before we can reach the higher spheres. All things begin with a mother, and the heavens are no different. Many of the goddesses who bore lunar crowns also bore heavy associations with Witchcraft, with midwifery, and with magical operations and divination. From Hekate and Thoth to the Triple-Goddess of contemporary pagan and Witchcraft movements, she is a mistress of magic, psychism, and the occult (which is, by its definition, hidden).

With the advent of modern psychology, this mythical history became transferred to conversations about the subconscious. Esoteric thought mixed with psychoanalysis in the works of astrology-obsessed Jung and his followers to firmly place the Moon in the archetypal role of subconscious magic, memory, and motherhood.[1] She never lost her connection to those mystical and difficult-to-comprehend areas within the map of our minds and souls. She will not be understood by pure logic. She requires emotional intelligence, magic, and a willingness to understand the poetry of life as much as the mechanics of it.

It is no surprise that she is the first Heavenly Sphere to which we ascend: the subconscious mind, imagination, and magic. These are requirements for any seeker, any would-be initiate, magician, witch, or hero. We must first confront that Great Mother, that place within ourselves that believes in possibility, which feels and reacts, before we can order the stars or understand our own souls. She creates no light of her own, only reflects that of the Sun, and receives and transmits its force, as well as the celestial powers of the other wandering stars. She is a reflection, and we must always begin in the mirror before we move to any higher worlds.

---

[1] For more information, see: C.G. Jung, *Jung on Astrology*, ed. Safron Rossi and Keiron Le Grice (New York, NY: Routledge, 2018).

TOUCHSTONE TEXTS

"...the lady of great beauty, the mistress of rain and waters, the giver of riches, the nurse of mankind, the governor of all states, kind, merciful, protecting men by sea and land, mitigating all tempests of fortune, dispensing with fate, nourishing all things growing on the Earth, wandering into divers woods, restraining the rage of goblins, shutting the openings of the Earth, dispensing the light of the heaven, the wholesome rivers of the sea, and the deplored silence of the infernals ... treading hell under her feet ..."[2]

—Cornelius Agrippa

* * * * * *

"May God bless you, O Moon, you who are the blessed lady, fortunate, cold and moist, equitable and lovely. You are the chief and the key of all the other planets, swift in your motion, having light that shines, lady of happiness and joy, of good words, good reputation, and fortunate realms...you are apt to good and evil, you join the planets together, you carry their light, and

---

[2] Henricus Cornelius Agrippa, *Three Books of Occult Philosophy*, ed. Donald Tyson (St. Paul, MN: Llewellyn, 1993), 427.

by your goodness you rectify all things whatsoever...you are the beginning of all things and you are the end thereof." [3]

—Lunar prayer from *Picatrix*

* ✳ ⁎ ✱ ⁎ ✳ •

"Most of the moon's power consists of humidifying, clearly because it is close to the earth and because of the moist exhalations therefrom. Its action therefore is precisely this, to soften and cause putrefaction in bodies for the most part, but it shares moderately also in heating power because of the light which it receives from the sun." [4]

—From the *Tetrabiblos* of Claudius Ptolemy

✳˙⁎˙The Moon in Astrology ✳˙⁎˙

In astrology, the Moon is linked closely with all things motherly and female. She is often referred to as the Great Mother or given the epithets of great female deities in the pre-Christian pantheons. She rules the sign of Cancer, a summer sign, due to her great light. The other luminary, her brother the Sun, rules another summer sign: Leo. The two luminaries stand in the center, near the brightest and hottest part of the year. Vettius Valens gives her associations in the following list: "The moon, lit by the reflection of the sun's light and possessing a borrowed light, in a nativity indicates man's life, body, the mother, conception...housekeeping, the queen, the mistress of the house, possessions, fortune, the city, the assembly of the people, gains, expenses, the household, voyages, travel and wanderings."[5]

---

[3] *The Illustrated Picatrix: The Occult Classic of Astrological Magic Complete in One Volume*, trans. John Michael Greer and Christopher Warnock (Renaissance Astrology, 2015),183-4.

[4] Claudius Ptolemy, *Tetrabiblos*, trans. F.E. Robbins (Cambridge, MA: Harvard University Press, 1956), 35.

[5] Vettius Valens, *Anthologies*, trans. Mark Riley, accessed June 2020, https://www.csus.edu/indiv/r/rileymt/Vettius%20Valens%20entire.pdf, 1.

The Moon is cold and humid in traditional astrology, a nocturnal planet. She is exalted in the sign of Taurus, the earthy bull. The Moon's joy is the 3rd house, which governs siblings, short-term journeys, and more. The 3rd house is the House of the Goddess and thus a fit house of joy for the divine mother of the celestial spheres.[6] The 3rd house's relationship to short journeys is also important to consider, given that the Moon governs such trips, her ever-changing form a perfect guide for the traveler. Her detriment is in the wintry and earthen Capricorn, and her fall is in the fixed water sign of Scorpio.[7]

In horoscopes she is often consulted about a client's mother, a client's emotional well-being and sanity, journeys (particularly across the water), secrets, and mysteries. She is consulted with Venus in questions of marriage. Being one of the great luminaries—and the closest Heavenly Sphere—her aspects with other planets are taken seriously when interpreting a chart, and she is a quintessential tool for interpreting many areas of one's life path, strengths, tribulations, predilections, and abilities. The Moon is also crucial in determining certain astrological points such as the nodes and the lots, which we will examine later. All of this makes her one of the most central players in the sky, a Titaness in the Art (which her Greek namesake, Selene, was).

⸱⸱The Moon in Magic*⸱*⸱

Given her astrological associations, it is no surprise where the strengths of the Moon lie within magical operations. *The Key of Solomon* gives immense precedence to the Sun and the Moon as the great luminaries, noting that the Moon is the "first and main receptacle of the Sun's influences."[8] Works are to be timed in accordance with the Moon's phases and when she is in beneficial conjunctions with other planets.

---

6   Ibid, 29.

7   We will explore these terms and their role in horoscope reading further in chapter 8.

8   Stephen Skinner and David Rankine, *The Veritable Key of Solomon: Three Different Texts from Those Translated by S.L. MacGregor Mathers* (Singapore: Golden Hoard Press, 2017), 87.

Since the Moon is used as a measure of time for humans, she is frequently used as the marker for when we desire to complete a magical work. Full Moons, New Moons, waxing and waning, all take on significance in the timing of our work. In occult workings, the Moon was seen as receiving the power of all the higher spheres, and thus as the main gate through which power might pass down.[9] She has the most direct influence upon Earth, given her proximity and her visible effects on Earth's bodies of water. Bonatti says of the Moon: "She of all the Planets has the greatest similitude and correspondence with inferior things ... to pass by her daily effects which she causes in all things here, and the frequent revolutions about the Elements and Elementary Bodies by reason of the nearness of her Orb to the Earth, and smaller circle than any other Planet; so she seems a Mediatrix between Superior and Inferior Bodies."[10]

She is the protectress of journeys and is used in protection magic for wanderers and voyagers. She is particularly associated with journeys across the water and with all bodies of water on Earth, from rivers and lakes to the seas. This means that she is also useful for all goods, monies, or processions that can be procured because of the waters. Shipping, fishing, dock work, and boating all belong to her. Her watery associations extend to rain magic and the ending of droughts.

Being the emotional and watery mother, she is also worked into con-jurations and spells for divination, scrying, sacred dreams, and astral travel. The Moon is mother of visions, given over to emotional intelligence and central to the forms of magic employed by Witchcraft, both folkloric and in the modern contemporary Witchcraft revival. Her association with the human psyche makes her a powerful celestial pathway for engaging with the more occluded and secretive aspects of our own souls. She holds what we believe to be possible, what we wish to hide, what we want to bring to fruition but perhaps only in the dark of the night.

Because she changes, in her predictable phases, the Moon was used for magical timing along with other systems such as the planetary hours we

---

9   Henricus Cornelius Agrippa, *Three Books of Occult Philosophy*, ed. Donald Tyson (St. Paul, MN: Llewellyn, 1993), 366.

10   Guido Bonatti, *Liber Astronomiae*, trans. William Lilly & Henry Coley, accessed September 2020, https://www.renaissanceastrology.com/bonatti146considerations.html.

will discuss later. The Moon's phases were interpreted in different ways, across systems, but most magical systems did take into consideration the phase of the Moon when planning magic. In *The Greek Magical Papyri*, a simple system was used wherein the Waning Moon was more suited to works of negativity and destruction, whereas the Waxing Moon was for works that build up or increase.[11] In Vettius Valens' *Anthologies*, the Full Moon was given dominion over both terrible events and great ones, highlighting the power of that celestial orb that could bear and reflect the light of all the others.[12]

˙˙*A Rite for the Moon *˙*˙*

To receive prophetic dreams, nocturnal visions, and lucid dreaming.

To be performed on the day and hour of the Moon, at night.

ASTROLOGICAL CONSIDERATIONS

Better it be that Mercury and the Moon are well aspected. The Moon in the 3rd or 9th house is beneficial. Avoid negative aspects between the Moon and Mercury, Saturn, or Mars. A New Moon is best. A Moon in an Earth sign is strongest.

RITUAL PREPARATION

Have a space for your ritual. A simple altar is best, with white or silvery cloth. Place a silver or white candle at the center of the altar or a silver oil lamp, filled and ready with a clean wick. Have a receptacle for incense ready, a censer or small cauldron with sand placed to the East of your candle or lamp. To the West of your lamp or candle, place a small bowl of saltwater. Heat your charcoal before the rite so that you are ready to begin when you enter the ritual space. Have a lit candle ready to the side of your altar that you may work from so that you do not need an external source

---

[11] Stephen Skinner, *Techniques of Graeco-Egyptian Magic* (Singapore: Golden Hoard Press, 2017), 58.

[12] Vettius Valens, *Anthologies*, trans. Mark Riley, accessed October 2020, https://www.csus.edu/indiv/r/rileymt/Vettius%20Valens%20entire.pdf, 46.

of fire for your working candle or lamp once the ritual begins. You may perform this rite nude or in clean, white, pale-yellow, or silver clothing. A simple robe can be used, or loose-fitting, clean garments.

PURIFICATION BATH

Before the ritual, you will take a purification bath. Fill your bathtub with water, with no distractions around you. As the water fills the tub, center your breathing and focus on the sound of the water. When the bath is ready and you feel centered and calm, add salt, rosemary, hyssop and dried flowers (jasmine, or any other dried pale-yellow or white flower) to the water. Submerse yourself three times in the water and then relax, focusing again on your breathing. Visualize the water as a silvery, lunar light entering and exiting your body in a calm, rhythmic fashion. It enters through your pores and exits, continually cleansing and purifying you. Relax each area of your body by clenching and releasing your muscles in groups in the warm water. Begin at your feet and ankles and move up your legs, torso, arms, neck, and, finally, your head. Take as long as you need with this process, repeating the muscle relaxations if necessary.

Completely relaxed in this manner, and with your hands in the water, vibrate the sacred vowels, resonating each one forcefully, three times.

IIIII, AAAA, OOOO!

IIIII, AAAA, OOOO!

IIIII, AAAA, OOOO!

Let the sound fill your entire body, just as the water did, echoing in your space until you are centered completely. Exit your bath and dry your body carefully, preparing to move to your ritual space.

THE RITUAL

Enter your ritual space and approach your altar. Upon the charcoal place a small amount of the following incense mixture:

Incense of the Moon
1 part myrrh resin
1 part frankincense resin
Pinch of dried mugwort
Pinch of powdered white sandalwood

As the incense smoke begins to rise, focus on it, watching the smoke billow and move across the air. Your mind should be focused on the incense smoke. Do not grasp onto any thoughts as they arise but instead let them come and pass easily. Take three deep breaths, inhaling through the nose and exhaling through the mouth. When you are ready, raise your hands with palms out before the altar and invoke:

> "Spirit of Revelation, throned and thrice-formed: a burnt offering before the face of the New Moon! To She who travels the boundless chasms of Time and Night, receive my prayer in this creature of smoke. Rise, rise, offering of air and fire before the one who bears the arrows, dread Lady, wheel of light and mother of the jackal and the hound. Part the veil of the temple and let my devotion mingle with this smoke. Eater of ashes and giver of sight to those that work the mysteries, silver-crowned queen, draw near to your altar and hear your supplicant."

Visualize a strong, bright silver ray of light descending upon your altar. See it filling your entire sacred space, bathing everything in its soft, ethereal light. It works across your body, crowning you in silver, focusing on the center of your forehead, right above the space between your brows.

Take up the saltwater and move to the East of your ritual space. Sprinkle the water three times, saying:

> "Eastern Powers, come at my call and stand guard over the temple."

Repeat at the South:

> "Southern Powers, come at my call and stand guard over
> the temple."

Pause in the West. In the West, you will kneel and sprinkle the water
three times with a different invocation:

> "Western Powers, open the doors of dreams. Hypnos,
> Morpheus, Hekate! Split the bitter sea and part the infernal
> rivers that I may see your face and hear your voice. Guard
> this temple and the gates of mystery that you open for your
> servant."

Rise and move to the North. Invoke:

> "Northern Powers, come at my call and stand guard over
> the temple."

Return to your altar and center yourself again, seeing the silver light
descending upon the candle or lamp. Add another small piece of your
incense mixture and focus on the center light to be used. Light your candle
or lamp and place your palms flat on the altar, to each side.

Invoke:

> "Come and make yourself known, spirits who have the power
> for this work. I call you! You who are appointed by the
> gods to show all revelations; I call you by the eternal father
> and mother of you all, ISIS, OSIRIS. Show me your forms
> and that which is concealed beneath the starry robe of Nyx.
> Mother of dreams, I call you. White Moon, New Moon,
> Triple-Faced!

Great Goddess, many named, many formed, dread Lady, dark and terrible maiden, night-crier, from whom all things were formed, bearer of the celestial lights, reflection of the titan-born, answer me!

Eternal One, bull-faced, serpent-twined, SELENE, ARTEMIS, HEKATE!

From the Silver Mansion part wide the river of night and make clear my divination. High-minded Queen, fatal thread-spinner of mortal life, blessed One, shining radiance, send the revelation!

Resonating forcefully, invoke:

MOU AMOU! MOU AMOU! IIIIAAAAOOOO! IIIIAAAAOOOO! IIIIAAAAOOOO!"

Strike the altar three times with your palms.

Seat yourself before the altar and watch the fire of the candle or lamp burn. Add incense as needed, focusing on the flame. As you breathe evenly and deeply, see the silver light of the altar suffusing into your body, in through your breath and then out from the pores of your skin. Focus on the lamp as long as needed until you feel a loosening of your conscious self, a soft relaxation and peace. You may extinguish the flame for safety but before leaving the ritual space make a small nod to each of the quarters with the following invocations.

"Powers of the East, you have guarded this temple in Her glories. I thank you and bid you peace."

"Powers of the South, you have guarded this temple in Her glories. I thank you and bid you peace."

"Powers of the North, you have guarded this temple in Her glories. I thank you and bid you peace."

And at the West:

"Powers of the primordial waters, leave wide the gates of dream through which I will know the revelations of Her, even unto sleep. Guard my soul in the realms of shade. I thank you and bid you peace."

Leave your ritual space and prepare for sleep. Keep a journal beside your bed for recording dreams. You can place a bit of the unburned incense mixture, along with a lunar stone, lunar herbs, or a piece of silver in a silver-colored or white sachet under your pillow as well. This ritual can be repeated until a desired revelation occurs.

MOON CORRESPONDENCES
Cold, Moist, Nocturnal, Feminine

IN THE HOROSCOPE

Domicile	Cancer
Exaltation	Taurus
Detriment	Capricorn
Fall	Scorpio
House of Joy	3rd

THE MAGICAL WORLD

Day	Monday
Colors	Silver, white, pale yellows, pale greens
Archangel	Gabriel
Sephirah	Yesod (Foundation)
Tarot	The High Priestess
Divinities	Selene, Luna, Artemis, Diana, Hekate, Isis, Khonsu, Arianrhod, Sin, Thoth
Magical Intent	Journeys, safe passage, childbirth, fertility, emotional disturbance, peace of mind, journeys across or to the water, psychism, visions, dreams, nocturnal work, illusion, motherhood, works for mothers or female family, secrecy, occultation, invisibility

THE NATURAL WORLD

Mineral	Silver, pearls, chalcedony, selenite, moonstone, crystal (quartz), glass
Flora	Palms, hyssop, rosemary, cabbages, melons, mandrake, poppy, lettuce, cucumber, aloe
Fauna	Toads, frogs, dogs, hares, rabbits, baboons, crabs, waterfowl, cats, snails, owls, otters, weasels, crayfish, crustaceans and mollusks, eels, tortoises
Fumigations	Myrrh, camphor, white sandalwood, mugwort, aloes, jasmine

2

MERCURY

Intellect. Mutable. Swift.

⋆⋆⋆The Meeting⋆⋆⋆

The two figures in the distance seem hazy as you raise yourself up from the ground. It's raining lightly, but the sun is still shining, visible past a small group of thundering clouds that are currently spilling out over you. Your eyes go back to the hazy figures as they approach. You raise yourself up further from the ground and realize you are in a large parking lot outside of a drab building with locked, gray doors. The two figures become clearer. They are children, looking about 12 years old, walking hand in hand. The boy has straight dark hair, the girl long, thin brown hair done up into braids around her head. They are dressed in matching uniforms of a sky-blue color with polished gray shoes and dull white knee socks.

You hear a noise as you stand up entirely from the blacktop of the place and realize there is a large, colorful parrot perched on the boy's shoulder. The boy pats the emerald-and-blue creature affectionately and hands up a seed from his pocket. The bird expertly opens it and drops the shells behind the twins as they approach you. You dust yourself off as the twins stand in front of you now, both of them looking up, hand in hand.

"Time to go," the girl says. She points toward the doors of the large, drab building and heads toward it.

You start to follow the twins but realize that they are far from you, somehow. You begin to speed up, finally breaking into a run to catch up with them. You squint and rub at your eyes because the twins seem to walk calmly, easily strolling toward the gate, but they stay so far ahead that you are almost out of breath with running just to keep up. You close your eyes and bear down, running faster, feet hitting the pavement. You open your eyes and finally see the doors much closer. You stop to take a breath, hand on the doorpost, waiting.

The twins are gone. The woman standing by the door is thin and short, with a colorful, almost-rainbow-printed dress and large glasses that make her gray eyes appear larger than they should. She motions toward the door with an impatient sigh, her foot tapping on the cement. You go to open the door and realize there is no knob, no handle, no pull. There is a wooden box bolted into the center of the doors. You look up to the woman and she motions again, impatiently, smirking.

You kneel down and see a series of sliding wooden panels on the box, each marked with an image and a number. Blue circles. Green triangles. Red squares. Purple diamonds. There are more, and you count each symbol, looking for matching pairs or opposing panels. The numbers are 0-9 and do not correspond to the shapes at all. You slide the panels around. There is a satisfying little click as one panel slides into a new position, changing the shape of the box. You begin to play with it, pushing and pulling and trying your best to match symbols, colors, numbers, finding the pattern that will unlock the box. When you look up, the woman only smiles at you and winks.

The shape of the box has changed dramatically. You are able to work it into the shape of a heart, a jagged circle, and even something akin to a face, but nothing seems to unlock the puzzle. You begin to feel frustrated, so you focus harder, sweat beading on your forehead, your hands even and steady. You begin to realize the patterns. They align beautifully in front of you. You do not remember the twins, the girl, or whatever shape is standing next to you. You work. You focus everything toward this pattern. It is working. It is working well. The last strip of wood clicks into place and you hear a whirring, mechanical sound from inside. The shape is of a six-pointed star, each piece perfectly aligned and coordinated. The star begins to click and spin, and it flowers in front of you, opening up with that ticking, mechanical noise. A silvery key drops out of the center of the open star, and you snatch it up.

The man beside you claps, and you look over. He is tall and dignified with a trimmed, gray beard, and bright eyes that seem to shift in color. He is wearing a toga, and nothing upon his feet. In the crook of his arm he carries a large green stone. He congratulates you and motions for you to use your key. You slip it into the now-exposed keyhole and easily unlock the large doors. He follows you into the space as you hear the doors shut behind you.

You are mildly disappointed to find yourself in a school. It even resembles one from your past. The walls look so familiar, the open rooms showing lines of desks and tables that are so easily recognizable. Even the smell of the place is nostalgic, save for a different odor mingling with it, something chemical and tangy. You walk down the halls with the man and look into each classroom as you pass. There are no students, but there are books open, pencils, pens and notebooks full of writing. The blackboards contain equations, sentences parsed out carefully in cursive writing, images of planets and stars, diagrams of cells and the usual imagery of education. There are labs with bubbling beakers, thick white clouds boiling over from flasks and droplets of water sliding down the curlicue glassware of a chemistry set.

The man takes the lead, his toga out of place in the modern schoolhouse as he turns the corner and takes you into a large classroom. You instinctively take a seat as he begins to write on the blackboard with a large piece of chalk. The marks he is making are foreign to you. They are a chicken scratch of arcane tracings that you cannot even place. Yet, the words begin to coalesce in your mind. You can read. You can read everything he is writing. You follow his frenetic hand, the chalk scratching and squeaking against the blackboard, filling up the space at an unnatural speed. You read, you hear yourself speaking the words out loud, words of power, words of memory, answers to things you've asked and asked over and over again since before you can remember. Your mind is so clear, you feel alive and quick. The blackboard begins to shake slightly, humming with energy.

He stops, the chalk crumbling to dust. The writing glows a brilliant hue, opalescent shifting colors, a rainbow on white and silver, blinding and dazzling. You are transfixed on the glowing words as he turns to face you. He is not the old man. Or the twins. Or the girl. He is young, and perfect, and winged. His eyes are many, his hands uncountable, his height beyond the scope of the room, as it explodes away from his radiance. From his many mouths he sings, he sings in a new language, and it rings in your ears. You cannot see the writing anymore, but you can hear it in the song that he sings and you join in, echoing the words of creation. You feel the stars begin to come into form, you feel life springing from somewhere, some muddy, raining, thundering place of prehistory and primeval memory. The words teach you the names of great people, forgotten people, and show you where there are treasures buried in this world, and in many other worlds that you cannot place in your mind's memory. But you know them. You feel the opening of new ideas like flowers, feel the pangs of silencing and tyranny. The speed of the song is unbearable, but you cannot stop. *You cannot stop.* You see it all. Everything unfolds in a bright, new knowledge. Everything is accounted for. It is always coming into being. The song never stops.

⋆ ⋆ ⋆ The Second Sphere: Mercury ⋆ ⋆ ⋆

We began with the Moon, our first Heavenly Sphere. She is heavily tied to emotional intelligence, the psychism and magic of our experience, and even to lunacy. When we enter the second sphere, we begin to see logic and order. Mercury is the planet of intelligence, wit, logic, and change. It has no gender, being both feminine and masculine, and taking on the attributes of the planets and phenomena around it. It is mutable, fast and nimble. Even its correspondences do not follow a purely solid path, instead being fluid just like the metal that takes its name from this planet. To the Greeks, it was Hermes, the messenger of the gods, fleet-footed and filling many roles, both playful trickster and solemn psychopomp. Perhaps the greatest symbol of this planet is Hermes Trismegistus, the "Thrice-Great Hermes." Born from Hermetic writings and carried throughout European occult circles, this figure had many faces (perfect as a representation for such a mutable planet). He was the sage, the philosopher, the alchemist, the great teacher. He was god and mortal, both a deity in his own right, and a living, human sage linked to real figures throughout history. His image drew from Egyptian and Hellenistic sources. His teachings, aimed at drawing the human soul to a higher state, were linked to the sciences, to art, and to magic. Spiritual alchemy, more concerned with transmuting the soul than lead, became a framework for esoteric teachings and practices.

If the Moon is a witch and a midwife, then Mercury is a magician and scientist. Mercury brings all of our tools of language, our ability to make connections and inferences from the natural world. Mercury is our power to link our understanding with both the teachings of the past and the revolutionary promises of the future. It is the ever-moving mind, our racing thoughts and ideas. It is hard to pin down because *we* are hard to pin down. We defy labels and shift perspective regularly. Mercury embraces this, ready and willing to teach and adapt to new information. As ancient as the images for this planet are, it is just as comfortable in the information age, where we have unlimited access to knowledge and can transmit it at lightning speeds through the ether. Computer science, portable communication, artificial intelligence, robotics, nanotechnology, high-speed rails, and space flight. All of this is Mercurial. All of this is tied to the great sage, the sphere of thought and cunning.

TOUCHSTONE TEXTS

"Mercury indicates education, letters, disputation, reasoning, brotherhood, interpretation, embassies, number, accounts, geometry, markets, youth, games, theft, association, communication, service, gain, discoveries, obedience, sport, wrestling, declamation, certification, supervision, weighing and measuring, the testing of coinage, hearing, versatility. It is the bestower of forethought and intelligence...the creator of all marketing and banking... It also rules those skilled interpreters of the heavens, those who by using pleasure or winning charm, earn fame for their amazing feats."[1]

—Vettius Valens, *Anthologies*

* ✳ ✳ ✳ ✳ ✳ ·

"... he is more of a 'journeyer' than a 'traveler.' Just as the geographical goal of a honeymoon is of little importance, so Mercury wanders about and communicates for the sheer pleasure of it. His route is not the shortest distance between two points: it is a world in itself, made of serpentine paths where chance and the unforeseen may happen."[2]

—Antoine Faivre, *The Eternal Hermes*

* ✳ ✳ ✳ ✳ ✳ ·

"I am the light you saw, mind, your god ... who existed before the watery nature that appeared out of darkness. The lightgiving word who comes from mind is the son of god."[3]

—Hermes Trismesgistus speaking in *Corpus Hermeticum*

[1] Vettius Valens, *Anthologies*, trans. Mark Riley, accessed June 2020, https://www.csus.edu/indiv/r/rileymt/Vettius%20Valens%20entire.pdf, 2.

[2] Antoine Faivre and Joscelyn Godwin, *The Eternal Hermes: From Greek God to Alchemical Magus* (Grand Rapids, MI: Phanes Press, 1995), 13-14.

[3] *Hermetica: The Greek Corpus Hermeticum and the Latin Asclepius in a New English Translation with Notes and Introduction*, trans. Brian P. Copenhaver (Cambridge, UK: Cambridge University Press, 1992), 2.

⋆⁎⋆Mercury in Astrology ⋆⁎⋆

Mercury is the ruler of Virgo and Gemini. This planet is neither masculine nor feminine, but both. It is neither diurnal nor nocturnal, but again: both. It is shifting and mutable, able to take on the characteristics of other planets around it. The planet finds its joy in the 1st house, the Ascendant, the ego. This makes sense given Mercury's association with mind. It is the voice, the tongue that first says: I AM. It is the beginning of the desire to know, the eagerness of the scholar and the magician. Mercury is in detriment in Pisces and Sagittarius. It falls in Pisces but is exalted in Virgo.

In chart reading, he[4] is looked to as a symbol of communication, ruling over language. He is the guiding star for education, teachers, studies, and science. He is the patron of magicians and occultists, looked to for skills in arcane arts and even for the finding of hidden treasures, both literal and spiritual. He can be tricky when ill-aspected, a spy or a thief, a liar or a silver-tongued weasel. He has much to say for commerce, banking, and money exchanges. In charts for questions of money, a well-aspected Mercury can portend quickness of action and cunning in business dealings. Ill-aspected he can be a cheat. In all aspects of how we build our life through relationships and communication: Mercury is present.

This planet can be a strong indicator of particular skills and abilities, particularly when interpreted with the Midheaven, the 10th house, and other areas where knowledge of a career path or a public life is needed. Our public and business life can be found in his interpretations. Our styles of communication with friends, family, or significant others will take into account his disposition in the chart. Beyond just communication, the state of our mental faculties in general are tied to his Heavenly Sphere. From our mental acuity, to anxiety and adaptability, the realm of the mind will always take Mercury into consideration.

Being the patron of alchemists, Mercury is always transforming, and this is one of the areas where both traditional and modern forms of as-

---

4   I have kept gender-neutral language earlier, while introducing Mercury, but I do reference the planet as "he" at times, due to the male deity that the planet takes its name from: Mercury, or Hermes. It is important to remember, however, that the planet can be either masculine or feminine.

trology tend to find agreement. They both see in Mercury the supreme mutability of life. Adaptation and evolution are the keywords here, and a distaste for stasis and dullness. We prize our ability to change with the times, to adapt to new circumstances. We can also, however, be swept up in change and rapid transformation, losing ourselves in the process and giving in to whims and fancies. Mercury, the swift-footed messenger, is both of these possibilities, thrilling at its best and nerve-wracked at its worst.

*⋅*Mercury in Magic *⋅*

Being a patron of magicians, this planet is a powerful tool in magical workings. Mercury speeds our magic, carries information for us, and ensures clear and meaningful communication with both higher intelligences and within our own minds. Mercury helps to order our world, imposes logic, but with a playfulness and quickness that avoids the stultifying boredom of a tedious life or a colorless magic. Being the great Magus, Mercury can be called upon to guide studies, ensure success in a magical process, or a course of education. He brings success in the occult and the sciences. He is a natural resource for students, both autodidacts and those in institutions of higher learning. He sharpens the mind for examinations, for defenses, and for writing.

Being the trickster, the mutable one, he is also invoked and worked with for success at games of chance, in business dealings where we need cunning and craft, and to avoid situations of constraint. He is a despiser of slavery and shackles. *The Key of Solomon* contains a pentacle for Mercury specifically designed to ward against prison and slavery.[5] The quick-footed, free-minded Mercury is a liberator, both of our mental traps and of physical oppression.

Whenever negotiations are at hand, Mercury is our ally. We can call and invoke this planetary intelligence, this Celestial Sphere, when we need our wits to win, we need a good argument or for the odds to tip in our favor. Risky ventures, gambling, and shooting for the Moon are enhanced

---

5 Stephen Skinner and David Rankine, *The Veritable Key of Solomon: Three Different Texts from Those Translated by S.L. MacGregor Mathers* (Singapore: Golden Hoard Press, 2017), 162.

by the quicksilver planet. Entrepreneurial spirit thrives with Mercury, and suggestive writing and speech-giving. He is a showman, a natural winner, lucky and intelligent. When we invoke the spirit of Mercury, his familiar spirits, his intelligences, or his power we are invoking our natural drive to know, to win, to adapt and thrive.

Mercury was so powerfully linked to intelligence and learning that he was made patron of the "notory art." This system of magic included mnemonics and spells to increase the magician's knowledge of certain subjects, to retain information, and to learn more quickly and efficiently.[6] It is the magic of learning how to learn, a mystical form of pedagogy and memory retention. Any subject could be guided and strengthened by the magic of Mercury, from grammar and language to astronomy and medicine. The mind, always elastic, is reflected in the fastest of the planets, that twinkling brightness so near to the Sun.

His alchemical associations are central to his magics as well. Mercury is the great alchemist, the patron of all those that will tread the inner paths and try to forge their baser instincts into the divine gold of spiritual fulfillment. In a Hellenistic framework, we can remember Hermes as the psychopomp that guided souls to the afterlife, as comfortable in that solemn role as he was being a trickster or messenger. The two are not separable and this planet will never be pinned down to a singular role in our spiritual workings.

*˙.˙*A Rite for Mercury *˙.˙*

To receive an answer or solution quickly to a problem, to remove an obstacle to communication or shorten a period of waiting for results.

To be completed on the day and hour of Mercury.

---

6   *The Illustrated Picatrix: The Occult Classic of Astrological Magic Complete in One Volume*, trans. John Michael Greer and Christopher Warnock (Renaissance Astrology, 2015), 138.

Astrological Considerations

A well-aspected Mercury, free of any hindrances. Avoid ill aspects with Saturn or Mars. Positive aspects with Venus and Jupiter when possible. Better if Mercury be rising, or exalted (in Virgo).

Ritual Preparation

Have your ritual space ready. A simple altar should be placed in the East, with an altar cloth of multi-colored fabric or a print. Upon the altar have a bowl of water in the West, a censer or cauldron for incense in the East, a pentacle (any metal disc) with salt in the North and a small lit candle in the South. In the center of your altar you will have a piece of clean fresh parchment and pen and ink prepared to create a sigil. It should be a square piece of parchment, not creased or marred in any way.

If you are able, you can create your own magical ink. *The Key of Solomon*, as well as other traditional grimoires, contain specific recipes and benedictions for the "ink of the Art." Creating your materials in this way can be a meditative exercise, and I do recommend that students try to craft at least some of their materials in the traditional way as a matter of experience and discipline.

PURIFICATION BATH

Before the ritual, take a bath in water purified with a bit of salt. Prepare the bath by filling your tub and making the banishing pentagram of Water over the water.

As you draw the banishing pentagram over the water, say:

> "Creature of primordial Water, I banish all hindrances you bear within you. I make of you a new creature that you may serve to cleanse and purify all that you touch."

Sprinkle salt.

> "Creature of Earth, may you bless and consecrate this exorcised water. As the salt touches the water, so the body and mind are one."

Immerse yourself fully in the water.

While bathing, focus on the intent of your working. Keep a measured and even breath and if distracting thoughts come, try not to grasp onto them but let them pass and go. When you are ready, leave your ritual bath, dry your body and dress for your ritual.

The Ritual

Enter your ritual space and approach your altar. Salute your altar and invoke:

"Thrice-Greatest and fleet of foot, come now, THOTH, ape and ibis, winged son. I invoke and call on you, by the virtues of your celestial lights. By Mercury, by the East, by the spirits of the Air and by my sacred breath."

Place an incense of Mercury on the burning coals, watching as the smoke rises from your Eastern altar, using the following mixture:

Incense of Mercury
1 part frankincense
¼ part storax
Pinch of powdered clove
Pinch of dried marjoram

Speak aloud:

"An offering, a fumigation, for the Spirits of the Air."

Lift incense and offer at the four directions, starting at the East, above your altar. Return it when finished.

Mix the salt and water on your altar, reciting the same water and salt blessings from above, the ritual bath blessings, before lifting it to each direction and sprinkling in the four directions. At each quarter, invoke:

"Spirits of the gates of Air (Fire, Water, Earth), I bless and consecrate this space by the name above all names, by the One, the endless and undying one from which springs Mind."

Lift the candle from your altar and offer at each direction.

"I kindle again the sacred fires of the East (South, West, North). The temple is constructed. The light is eternal."

Return to your altar space and prepare your ink and parchment. Focus your entire intent on the desired outcome of this work, taking up your pen to begin. Carefully and slowly draw out the following sigil of Mercury.

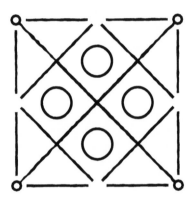

When you are finished, take up the parchment and show it, image facing away from you, to the four quarters, saying:

"Spirits of the East (S, W, N), a sign is brought. Be quick in the Great Work and send your aid to me, quick as the wind. I salute you and thank you for your guardianship of my rite."

Return to the altar and leave your parchment near the burning candle. You can use this time to meditate, but direct all thoughts to the desired outcome, imagining it as a reality in the present, currently occurring, easily accomplished.

Leave your sigil on your altar until the work is accomplished. Afterward it can be burned under a well-aspected Mercury or on the hour or day of Mercury with this:

"Spirit of Air, Heavenly Mind, I thank you for your aid."

MERCURY CORRESPONDENCES

As Above — So Below

Mutable—neither purely male nor female

IN THE HOROSCOPE

Domicile	Virgo and Gemini
Exaltation	Virgo
Detriment	Sagittarius and Pisces
Fall	Pisces
House of Joy	1st

THE MAGICAL WORLD

Day	Wednesday
Colors	Mixed colors, rainbow, opalescent
Archangel	Raphael
Sephirah	Hod (Splendor)
Tarot	The Magician
Divinities	Mercury, Hermes, Thoth, Iris, Hermes Trismegistus, Woden (Odin)
Magical Intent	Education, speed, removing obstacles, wit, freedom, games of chance and gambling, notory arts, teachers, mindfulness, public speaking and persuasion, communication, letters and writing, technology, excelling in the magical arts, divination

THE NATURAL WORLD

Mineral	Quicksilver (Mercury), topaz (of variegated colors), red marble, opal, emerald, all stones that shimmer or show multiple colors
Flora	Hazel, marjoram, parsley, nutmeg, vervain, ash, arnica, walnut, elder, anise, lungwort, cinquefoil
Fauna	Apes, monkeys, dogs, foxes, weasels, cranes ibis, parrots, hyena, spiders, locusts, mullet
Fumigations	Frankincense, amber, cinnamon, cloves, golden copal

VENUS

Mirth. Pleasure. Generation.

✦₊The Meeting₊✦

The Sun is setting as you approach the windowless brick building with the green door. A man stands outside, in sunglasses, dark clothing, an imposing stature and stern face. He guards the green door on the side of this building that your feet carry you toward. A bright twinkle in the evening sky draws your eye as you stumble over the curb, walking quicker, closer and closer to the man and the green metal door. There is sound coming from the building, musical and loud, muffled only by the door, the door, the door, *you must get past the door.*

The man raises his hand, and you stumble again. Your heart begins to pound inside your chest. You feel sweat trickle down your back and under your arms, pooling in the warm recesses of your body. Your clothes are sticky. A cool breeze hits you, and you shiver slightly. The man lowers his hand and asks you for the password. Your mind goes blank. No word comes to you. He asks again, and you stammer. Something, anything, should come out. It doesn't. He waits, patiently, unmoving, refusing you entry to the green door, to the life and music within.

A flock of birds startles you, flying across the street behind you. You turn around to see before returning your gaze to the guard and absentmindedly lean in and kiss the man on the cheek, grasping his hand in yours. Then there is no man. Your lips press against the cool green metal door, and it swings open easily, almost causing you to fall inward. You catch yourself and regain your footing, letting the door close behind you as the sound of music surrounds you. It is lively and loud, played well, the band on a raised stage above a floor of dancers. Couples twirl and press against one another to the beat, bodies mingling. Laughter and shouts of encouragement from bystanders to the dance floor ring out in the crowded place.

The scents and sounds are overwhelming. The smell of bodies, of sweat, mixes with food and the sharp tang of wine and spirits. Something sweet and light tickles your nose before a headier, muskier odor invades. The lights are low and rosy, glinting off the copper and brass of the bar that you are now walking toward. You take a drink from the bar, and when you go to find something in your pocket with which to pay, your offer is waved away by the smiling man behind the counter. You thank him and turn to watch the dancers. They move and twirl across the floor, the music filling the entire space, guiding their movements. You move toward them, wanting to join. A woman grasps your hand the moment you set down your drink, pulling you into the swarm of bodies.

She is graceful and quick, her laughter rising up above the music as she spins with you and moves in graceful arcs. You can dance freely here, easily, your body light and entirely your own, unencumbered by self-doubt, missteps, or shame. You realize she is moving you both across the dance floor, easily avoiding the other couples, pressing further and further into the space until you see a new set of doors, copper, aged with verdigris and etched in intricate designs. Your dance partner presses you on, moving you toward the doors. Your line of vision twirls with your body, from the crowd, to the bar, to the lights, to her face, and back to the doors. It is nauseating to spin this much, but you are laughing, almost giddy with it, your ears hot, your heart beating. Finally, she releases you, propelling you toward those doors.

The aged carvings are botanical, vines and roses climbing up the copper. Swans arch from the metal, next to little doves and ripe pomegranates, their seeds greened by time and air. You run your fingers across the carvings. They are so cool to the touch, so perfectly etched as to seem real. Even the lines on the birds' feathers and on the leaves stand out, the veins within each leaf so real you are sure they could move at any moment, stirred by a breeze or brushed by one of the animals that make up the scene. You take hold of the carved doorknobs and they give entry to you, the music disappearing to complete silence as you shut the door behind you.

The room is large, and your eyes struggle to take in the space. There is nothing left bare. The walls hang with thick damask and embroidered tapestry. Rich greens, chartreuse, white, silver, blue, and gold all mingle in thread and fabric. Lamps with feathered shades and an enormous chandelier illuminate a rich table laden with food on copper platters interspersed with glasses of red wine and green bottles of sweet-smelling liquor. Cushioned chairs with down pillows surround the table. Figurines in lapis lazuli, coral, and emerald stand on lacquered tables. They show dancers, musicians, couples in embrace, and wild beasts.

She invites you to take a seat. Your body whips around to find the source of the voice and you see the woman coming from behind a curtain. She is exceptionally beautiful, a kind of beauty that few would try to deny. She walks with ease, her dress shimmering as she walks, beaded in green and blue. Around her neck two sparrows meet, carved in the same etched copper as the doors to this place. Her thick auburn hair is loose around her shoulders, with round curls. Her voice is soft and low, and something inside your chest pinches and aches. It feels like longing but also like jealousy. For some reason, you laugh. She laughs with you, and she motions again for you to take a seat. She raises an eyebrow at your hesitation before you finally fall into the comfortable chair and take in the spread of food in front of you.

She makes herself a small plate, on the brass charger in front of her. She mixes together berries and walnuts, drizzling them with honey. The entire spread before you is open. You can eat and drink whatever you choose. Your hands feel the food, the cool glasses of wine and other drinks, everything available to you. Take. Eat. Drink. Experience whatever you are led to taste. She watches as you explore and sample everything, her own fingers going back and forth to her plate, eating slowly, eyes never leaving you.

When your meal together is done, she stands and takes your hand. She raises you from the comfortable chair and begins to dance with you, moving toward a large, expanding room of rich color. The sunlight is dying through the large window in the back, a sunset casting everything in low, warm hues. Your mind is hazy now, your body full and satiated completely from her table, from the experience of the evening. She dances slowly, body close. You laugh with her as she tells you things, little things, about yourself. She knows about your desires, your thoughts, your memories both petty and great. She teases, but kindly. What does she say to you? What memory does she bring you to think about and see again, entirely? You listen to her clear, sweet voice and move across the floor, the milky-white and pale-green tiles beneath your feet so beautifully connected in intricate mosaic designs. She spins you a final time and you release, falling. The floor does not catch you. The wall does not catch you. There is nothing but the coolness and gentle push of the air around you as you fall. You twist and turn, free as a falling bird. Nothing constrains you, and you feel your heart race. Your toes and fingers curl against themselves, your eyes pinch closed. Warmth and release wash over you. Every part of you can feel this, experience this electric jolt, this pure joy. You are almost like water. And all you see are stars.

. The Third Sphere: Venus *.*

Venus is the Morning and Evening Star, so named for her visibility on the horizon during the dawn and the dusk. She is named for the goddess of love, associated with the deities that govern sensuality, mirth, sex, and generation. She is Ishtar, who is Inanna and Astarte. She is Aphrodite, mother of Eros. As the Moon is the emotions of the psyche, she is the emotions made manifest as desire. She is lust and the drive to procreate. She is mirth and revelry, delighting in the social sphere. She is not a planet of loneliness but of connection and human touch. She is the party to which everyone is invited, the consummate hostess, the loving partner, the muse almost too beautiful to contemplate. To the theurgic philosopher, the Heavenly Sphere of Venus is where our souls first gain their ability to desire. [1]

---

1   Matilde Battistini, *Astrology, Magic, and Alchemy in Art*, trans. Rosanna M Giammanco Frongia (Los Angeles, CA: Getty Publications, 2007), 76.

She is lush as well, warm and sometimes cool, given to the almost-prof-ligate diversity of life and the biosphere. She is vegetation and birthing and placenta and arousal. She is not just sex, but friendship and camaraderie as well. She delights when we delight, gives honors, favors, tokens of ap-preciation, gifts and rewards. According to Valens, the careers she rules are those that work with gold and precious metals, as well as hairdressers, entertainers, and all those tied to luxury and artistic creation. [2]

She is beauty, and the magic that lies behind all glamour. She is the care and effort we put into our bodies, the luxuries of life. Fine dining, beautiful clothing, jewels, and adornments are hers. She delights in a beautiful home, a domestic sphere that impresses and comforts. She can turn with these gifts, however, reminding us of the difficult and painful side of love and desire. She can deal with caprice, and malice. She can engender spite, gossip, jealousy, revenge, and the craven use of others. But that is what love must be, a totality, an experience both divine and infernal. It is no surprise that the "Morning Star" became associated with Lucifer, the Devil himself. It is no surprise that "venereal" in reference to sexual illness comes from Venus.

Venus, as the ecstasy of love, is both divine and mortal. She is the *eros* of erotic love and the *agape* of divine love. In Greece, Aphrodite had two incarnations. She was Aphrodite Pandemos, the Aphrodite of the people, who governed love affairs, sex, and partnering. She was also Aphrodite Ourania, the heavenly Aphrodite, who was the higher, divine love that enraptures the soul. But we must not make the dichotomy too black and white. We experience divine love when we experience human love. The famous statue of Saint Teresa of Avila in the Vatican, by Bernini, shows the saint in visitation by an angel, in the throes of ecstasy. It is a statement of the power of the divine, but to the casual onlooker it appears, to be frank, like an orgasm and not so much a divine revelation. The more prudish aspects of our minds would do well to ask if they are not very much one and the same experience.

---

2   Vettius Valens, *Anthologies*, trans. Mark Riley, accessed June 2020, https://www.csus.edu/indiv/r/rileymt/Vettius%20Valens%20entire.pdf, 1-2.

TOUCHSTONE TEXTS

"Goddess of marriage, charming to the sight,
mother of Loves, whom banquetings delight;
Source of persuasion, secret, fav'ring queen,
illustrious born, apparent and unseen:
Spousal, lupercal, and to men inclin'd,
prolific, most-desir'd, life-giving, kind:
Great sceptre-bearer of the Gods, 'tis thine,
mortals in necessary bands to join;
And ev'ry tribe of savage monsters dire in magic chains to bind
thro' mad desire.
Come, Cyprus-born, and to my pray'r incline ...
exalted in the heav'ns you shine..."[3]
—*Orphic Hymn to Aphrodite*, Thomas Taylor Translation

✦ ✶ ✦ ✱ ✦ ✶ ✦

"May God bless you, O Venus, you who are queen and fortune,
and are cold and moist, equitable in your effects and complexion,
pure and lovely and sweetly scented, beautiful and ornate. You
are the lady of ornament, of gold and silver; you delight in
love, joy, ornaments and jests, elegance, songs and music that

---

³ *Hymns of Orpheus*, trans. Thomas Taylor, 2015 E-book ed., Loc: 1463-1478, Kindle.

are sung or played on strings, written music and songs played on organs, games and comforts, rest and love." [4]

—*Picatrix*

* ✱ ✱ ✱ *

"On earth there's nothing better
Than fair and noble love,
Through which we will turn godlike,
And none do other harm.
Therefore sing unto the King,
Make the whole sea to resound,
We ask you—answer us." [5]

—"Song of the Nymphs" from *The Chemical Wedding of Christian Rosenkreuz*

*.*Venus in Astrology *.*

Venus is the ruler of Libra and Taurus. She is exalted in Pisces, finds her detriment in Aries and Scorpio, and she falls in Virgo. Her planetary joy is the 5th house, the house of good fortune, where our friendships, joys, and pleasures find their fulfilment and exposition. She, along with Jupiter, is a "benefic" planet, largely seen as positive and exerting a good influence over the world. When positively aspected, she brings desire, love, partnership, and mirth. When ill aspected, she destroys relationships, turns the mind to spite and vindictive bickering, and robs us of our little joys.

In chart interpretation she is consulted frequently for questions of love, marriage, and progeny. She rules over luxury goods, the acquisition of property and fine things. She governs favors and public recognition. She can make one well-liked, popular, and desired. She is sought for in

---

[4] *The Illustrated Picatrix: The Occult Classic of Astrological Magic Complete in One Volume*, trans. John Michael Greer and Christopher Warnock (Renaissance Astrology, 2015), 179.

[5] *Rosicrucian Trilogy*, trans. Joscelyn Godwin, Christopher McIntosh, & Donate Pahnke McIntosh (Newsburyport, MA: Weiser Books, 2016), 147.

questions of the fine arts, of music and creativity, especially of its public reception and appreciation. In conjunction with the other planets and house positions, she is where we go to determine our fate with lovers, the partners that will come into our lives and what they will bring. She can determine our own approach to love and relationships, and to the greater social sphere of connections and friendships.

She can be women in our lives, being the other female planet apart from the Moon. She can be our pleasures and sources of joy. When we have questions about our successes in love and money, she will be part of the conversation. She will come into questions of fertility and childbirth. The generative aspects of life are all under her domain, exalted in her Heavenly Sphere and properly understood in conjunction with the other planets.

Venus is often that part of life that is most joyous, the parts that make us laugh or intrigue us. She is a playful and vital planet, very much *full of life*. Although the "lesser benefic" planet, she is often the benefic influence we most care about in our daily experience. The influences of the greater benefic, Jupiter, often come with much higher concepts of responsibility, power, religion, and duty. Venus comes with that daily joy of a life well-lived, the tickles of desire and interest that make our life here meaningful. All of the magic and power in the celestial realms are useless without love, and it truly is her domain.

⋆͙⋆ Venus in Magic ⋆͙⋆

It will be no surprise that Venus rules over the libraries of love spells that have been written in the grimoires and traditional magical texts we have access to. In the Greek Magical Papyri, we find the name of Aphrodite, the Greek Venus, invoked for love spells along with her son Eros, her mother Dione, and other deities and *daimons*.[6] It is not surprising that the inverse of a love spell is invoked in these charms as well, spells to slander others and to break up relationships. The pentacles for Venus in *The Key*

---

6   Stephen Skinner, *Techniques of Graeco-Egyptian Magic* (Singapore: Golden Hoard Press, 2017), 218-219.

of Solomon include magic to acquire lovers, to be found more attractive by desired partners, and for keeping love affairs secret. [7]

Beyond just sexual attraction and love partnerships, Venus can influence magic for friendships, and concord between parties. In *Picatrix*, invocations to Venus include, "… from you flow good friendship and mutual delight among people." [8] Her sweetening power is invoked in these operations to bend others to our side, to influence those in positions of authority to notice and respect us. Her Heavenly Sphere will govern that magic which works toward harmony, mutual benefit, and even a bit of ladder-climbing in the social world. In *The Book of Angels*, her planetary square can be used to remove disagreements with others, improve our businesses, crops, and naturally our sex lives. [9] Agrippa gives the power of her square to include changing one's mood as well, causing joy and removing melancholy. [10] This power can be worked into magic that desires to improve outlook and perspective, to invite joy and wonder back into life if one is struggling to see positive aspects to a situation, a person, or a decision. Venus is the "little benefic" or the "lesser of the good fortunes" [11] that is a positive influence, even in the smallest or seemingly small tasks of our lives. For Marsilio Ficino, the famed magician, she could even make learning sweeter, and turn our minds to see the beauty in knowledge and thought. [12]

Her darker aspects, as mentioned above, can be invoked as well. She is the terrible goddess of love, fickle and capricious when she wants to be. She can be worked in magic for discord and jealousy, to sow spite and

---

7   Stephen Skinner and David Rankine, *The Veritable Key of Solomon: Three Different Texts from Those Translated by S.L. MacGregor Mathers* (Singapore: Golden Hoard Press, 2017), 194-197.

8   *The Illustrated Picatrix: The Occult Classic of Astrological Magic Complete in One Volume*, trans. John Michael Greer and Christopher Warnock (Renaissance Astrology, 2015), 180.

9   *Conjuring Spirits: Texts and Traditions of Medieval Ritual Magic*, ed. Claire Fanger (University Park, PA: The Pennsylvania State University Press, 1998), 69-71.

10   Henricus Cornelius Agrippa, *Three Books of Occult Philosophy*, ed. Donald Tyson (St. Paul, MN: Llewellyn, 1993), 319.

11   In traditional texts, Jupiter and Venus are given as the benefic planets. The former is seen as the greater of the two.

12   Matilde Battistini, *Astrology, Magic, and Alchemy in Art*, trans. Rosanna M Giammanco Frongia (Los Angeles, CA: Getty Publications, 2007), 76.

to kill romance, attraction, or sexual performance. I have found, however, that most works focus on the benefic nature of Venus and prefer to use her magic in situations of increase and love magic. Baneful magic that seeks to tear relationships apart, ruin others, or bring enemies low is often allotted to Saturn or Mars, both of which were seen as malefic planets in traditional sources.

∗∗∗A Rite for Venus∗∗∗

To begin an artistic endeavor, for inspiration when preparing to create, to make an object of your creation attractive and beautiful.

To be completed on the day and hour of Venus.

ASTROLOGICAL CONSIDERATIONS

Venus exalted or in domicile is best, well-aspected to the Moon, the Sun, or Jupiter. Avoid all ill aspects with Mars or Saturn. Helpful if Venus is not in a cadent house. A Waxing Moon is useful.

RITUAL PREPARATIONS

Your ritual space should be freshly cleaned with an altar in the center. Upon the altar have a soft green cloth and two large taper candles made of beeswax. On your altar, place a vase of fresh roses between the candles, which you can mingle with other flowers of Venus. Usually, a simple altar is best, but with this working, add to your altar symbols and attributes of Venus. You can add small mirrors, bits of colored glass, stones of Venus (see table), almonds, fruits, boughs or leaves of fruit-bearing trees, small figurines, a statue of the Goddess, copper or brass jewelry, and any other accoutrements of Venus. Abundance and beauty are key. The altar should be visually arresting, and you should find it pleasing. Have a censer or cauldron with sand ready for your incense blend. Also, a feather is used in the oil you will be making, but it is useful to have a white feather or the feather of a creature sacred to Venus ready for the fumigation.

Incense of Venus
1 part frankincense
½ part benzoin
Pinch of powdered sandalwood
Pinch of crushed, dried rose petals
1 crushed, dried bay leaf

You will also need to have the following ready for the creation of an oil blend, as well as a bottle to contain it:

Oil of Venus
Fractionated coconut oil, grapeseed oil, or apricot kernel oil
Rose petals, dried and crushed to a powder
1 small piece of amber
1 small seashell, crushed
1 white bird feather, cleaned, dried, and pulverized to small pieces

THE RITUAL

You can take a ritual bath before your working. Working nude or in loose clothing is best for Venus. Approach the altar, light two candles upon the altar, and center your breathing. Focus on the images on the altar, the collection of symbols and items that you have created here for this working. Have your materials ready. Invoke when ready.

> "From the sea is born the Morning Star; light of love and light of life, come again and breathe upon the sacred altar. Astarte, Ourania, Genetrix, do I call now, beneath the light of the Heavenly Sphere of Venus. Unlock the gates of inspiration and pour forth the waters of creation. Make smooth the path of the muses. Gate of Beauty, helpmate of mortal beings, under your gaze and within my heart is accomplished the Great Work."

Place your incense blend on the charcoal and direct the smoke over your altar, tools, and ingredients with a feather.

When you are ready, begin to create your oil. Focus on the images and items on your altar, and on the desired outcome of the work. When finished, bottle your oil and hold it near your chest.

> **"I consecrate and anoint this creation in Her many names. Flesh of my flesh, and spirit on high: both breathe life into the Earth. Within me is the sacred marriage complete. It is done."**

VENUS
CORRESPONDENCES
Cold, Moist, Nocturnal, Feminine

As Above — **So Below**

IN THE HOROSCOPE

Domicile	Libra and Taurus
Exaltation	Pisces
Detriment	Aries and Scorpio
Fall	Virgo
House of Joy	5th

THE MAGICAL WORLD

Day	Friday
Colors	Greens, milky whites, turquoise, aquas
Archangel	Anael
Sephirah	Netzach (Victory)
Tarot	The Empress
Divinities	Venus, Aphrodite, Ishtar, Inanna, Astarte, Freya, Blodeuwedd, Aengus, Eros, Lucifer
Magical Intent	Love, attraction, artistic inspiration, spite, sweetening deals, childbirth, popularity, event planning, engagement, gardening social influence, crowds, likeability, mending heartbreak, sowing jealousy, sexual prowess, fertility, musical ability

THE NATURAL WORLD

Mineral	Copper, brass, emeralds, beryl, sapphire, green jasper, lapis lazuli, coral, alabaster, turquoise, mother of pearl
Flora	Myrtle, roses, saffron, peach, fig, apple, lily of the valley orange, almond, apricot, plum, lemon, water lilies, maidenhair
Fauna	Dove, sparrows, goats, cows, swans, wrens, pheasant, dolphin, nightingale, panthers
Fumigations	Sandalwood, myrtle, musk, rose, ambergris, benzoin

4
THE SUN

Monarch. Illumination. Golden.

✦⁎✦ The Meeting ✦⁎✦

The weather is warm, a bright light suffusing the entire scene. The lush forest expands around you, verdant summer green mingling with sprays of color as flowering plants reach up from between the foliage and seek toward the sky. You are on a clean, paved road and you hear the click of wheels beside you. You look over. Beside you, keeping time with your pace, is a large chariot with a raised dais in the center. The body of the chariot is gold, intricately mixed with shining red stones. The vehicle is blindingly bright in the sunlight. The carvings in the soft gold are of agricultural scenes, laborers growing corn and harvesting wheat. Bodies are shown raising obelisks and stone monuments. Great litanies in a script that you can barely decipher, all seem to praise a raised figure, carved in the metal. In front of the conveyance are two pure white rams, their horns massive, curling backward, shimmering as if they, too, were made of the same gold of the chariot. The lightest of chains link the great beasts to the weight they pull.

Riding on the chariot and seated upon the dais is a young boy. He holds no reins, does not instruct the animals, only looks forward, unmoving. He is draped in yellow and saffron fabrics; gold chains and stone beads crowd his neck. Clanging bracelets line his arms, and every finger is adorned in a carbuncle, a ruby, a chrysolite. His dais is strewn in marigolds, sewn into garlands with heliotropes and palm fronds. A strong scent wafts from his form, frankincense and ginger, with warm amber and cedar.

You keep pace, eyeing the glittering beauty of the chariot, unsure of where you are headed. You watch the rams' hooves evenly click against the stone pavement as the road moves forward, unbending. The boy looks at you, smiles, even his teeth capped in gold. His eyes seem to shine even in the daylight, and you notice the crown on his head. It is seven-pointed, plain, but perfectly worked. He reaches his hand across the side of his vehicle and you hesitate. His ringed fingers beckon gently. You take a deep breath and reach out. You feel his fingers touch your hand. A gentle warmth suffuses your entire body, a vigor and liveliness. You are filled with energy and feel as though you could run the course of the Earth and never tire. He smiles, grasping tighter. Your heart races. You feel taller, stronger, your aches and petty grievances melting away. When he finally releases, you feel a pang of sadness, missing the light of his presence.

The road breaks into a clearing, and the rams pick up their pace. You walk faster, in time with the boy beside you in his chariot. Wheat fields blossom to either side of you, large corn stalks in even rows are ripe and perfectly spaced. You hear the bustle of workers before you see them. When they do come into vision they kneel as the chariot passes, hands flat upon the Earth. You nod as their eyes meet yours. They stay kneeling until you have passed, and you hear them returning to their work as you continue. The scent of upturned Earth and vegetation fills your nose, mingling with the heady incenses coming from the chariot and the animal scent of the rams, now slick with sweat.

The fields of crops begin to dissipate and then evaporate completely. Something new breaks on the horizon. It is a wide and empty expanse of cracked mud. There is no color, only the endless brown of a dried lake, or a river basin. Along the banks are workers from the fields you passed, no longer kneeling. They stand in silence, holding scythes and sickles, farming instruments, spades and pointed seeding spikes. You feel a tightness in your chest. The line of workers keeps their eyes firmly placed on the young boy arriving in the chariot. His expression does not change, and the rams do not slow their pace, approaching the line of workers, the endless basin of dried earth, with its violent cracks and terrible emptiness.

The bright Sun is no longer pleasant. It feels brutal. Rivulets of sweat trickle down your body as the rams stop abruptly. Two workers approach, a man and a woman. They offer their hands and the young boy lightly steps from the chariot, his feet in curled golden slippers embroidered with ruby flowers. He follows the workers to the edge of the basin, and you trail behind, nervous to follow but unable not to finish this journey.

The boy and the two workers on each side kneel into the edge of the mud, digging their hands into the dead soil. You begin to hear their prayers. They sing. They sing to the Earth, and to the Sun, and to the stars. The other workers begin to take up the song, and before you can stop yourself, your own mouth opens. You know these words. You have been in this chorus before. This chorus is eternal.

The boy stands and the song ends. Your heart beats faster as he turns to face the crowd, to face you. His eyes meet yours and inside them you see two bright suns, burning, eternal, so bright you fight to keep his gaze. His hands go to the simple golden crown. He raises it from his head slowly. You start to move forward but cannot. You want to stop this, but something scratches inside of you, nips at you, stops you from stopping anything. The boy lets out a cry, loud and deep, stronger than a full-grown man. He hurls the golden crown behind him, and it flies into the light of a setting Sun, toward the wide, broken Earth. The workers raise their sickles, blades catching the dying light, glinting and bright. You finally manage to close your eyes. There are two loud, wet thuds. One is metal falling into mud. One is a young body falling into eternity.

You calm yourself. Take a deep breath. You open your eyes, hesitating and shaking. The boy is gone. The workers have evaporated into the ether. The Sun is low and red, setting in the far West. The basin is no longer dry. At first you believe that you see a lake that has caught the red light of the setting Sun. It takes you a moment to realize that it is not water *but living fire.* The entire basin is filled with licking, swirling flame, a symphony of yellow and gold, scarlet, deep oxblood, orange, and gaseous blue. Fingers of fire spit up from the great expanse, the heat pressing against you, beckoning you.

Your feet move you forward, closer and closer to the inferno of color and heat. There is nothing but this fire, this endless power at the center of your sight. It expands in all directions before you. You will walk. You will feel it. Your hands come together, in prayer, in supplication, in a gesture of warding. You are not sure. You feel yourself kneel. You are coming closer to the swirling flame. It is a sacrament. You realize this. You must partake. Your cupped hands lower closer to the brutal heat until, finally, you plunge them inside of the light.

There is no pain. There is only the shock of the sight of it. You feel your hands fill with fire, a real substance, a weighty reality against your soft skin. You remain unburned. You bring your hands up, holding the fire and watching it dance against your palms. You raise your hands further, and before the fear can stop you, you drink. You drink in thirsty, greedy gulps. The fire pours down your throat, seeming to fill your entire body. Light surrounds you, an aura of golden hues expanding from your flesh. You dip your hands again and drink. Over and over you go to the fire, taking in the heat and cleansing power of the flame. Soon, the light is all you can see. The light overtakes your vision. All is gold.

*.*The Fourth Sphere: Sol *.*

The Sun lies at the center of our Solar System, but for traditional astrology it rules its own Heavenly Sphere. We see the Sun as it moves across our sky, even if we know that it is the Earth that is orbiting around the great furnace that allows life to exist on our planet. For the magician, the astrologer, and the seeker we see the movement of the Sun and can work with that knowledge, spiritually, with no dissonance with our astronomical understanding of how the Solar System functions.

When I teach astrology or have discussions about it, the Sun is often a place where my students and conversation partners get confused. Because the acceptance of the Copernican model of the Universe has influenced how we think, many people believe the Sun to be the most important planet in traditional astrology. In modern astrology, I often see it equated with the ego, the sense of self, the very heart of the entire system. For the ancients, this was not so. All planets were important, all stars crucial to the interpretation of charts and the working of planetary magic. The Sun was not given sole precedence over any other celestial figure. And as for the ego, or the sense of self, many ancient sources prefer to give that place to the sign that is rising in the East, the Ascendant, and its planetary ruler and not to the Sun.

Nor were Sun signs the center of astrology, which we will discuss further on. The preeminence of the Sun in modern conceptual frameworks of astrology has much to do, in my opinion, with the preeminence we place on our own egos and how we have drifted from our sense of community and divine purpose. And although the ancients did understand the Sun's placement as important, it was not until the advent of tabloid newspapers and quick-read horoscopes that Sun signs were given their absolute central importance. An astrology obsessed with Sun signs is really a 20th-century game and does not take into account the entire chart of a person, which is much more how astrology was traditionally done. [1]

That is not to devalue the Sun. For the ancients, it was the life-giving Father of the Heavens. He made agriculture possible, lit the way for hunting and building. He was the king, the monarch, the divine ruler. Sun gods were central deities in their pantheons, and powerful. In Egypt, the solar cult was crucial to the religious order of the people, and solar cults were found in all of Egyptian society. Apollo, in Greece, took on the role of Sun god from the titan Helios, and became the light-bearing deity of culture, art, prophecy, and more.

And even if the ancients did not see the Sun as the center of the universe, they did see his sphere as the center of the other spheres, lying between the inner and outer orbits, and thus in a prominent position. This is not a weak place, or a demotion. He is powerful. He is power itself. Lilly writes that the Sun bears, "an almost itching desire to rule and sway." [2] He is associated with kingship, rulers, and authority. He is patron of nobility and those who take the mantle of leadership. It is no wonder the absolutist monarchs invoked him, such as Louis XIV becoming *Le Roi Soleil*, the "Sun King," or Ramses lining the temple at Abu Simbel with howling baboons and solar discs, greeting the rising sun, cementing the royal house with the cult of the Sun.

---

[1] Alexander Boxer, *A Scheme of Heaven: The History of Astrology and the Search for our Destiny in Data* (New York, NY: W.W. Norton & Company, Inc., 2020), 84.

[2] William Lilly, *Christian Astrology: Books 1 & 2*, ed. David R. Roell (Bel Air, MD: Astrology Classics, 2004), 70.

TOUCHSTONE TEXTS

"The Sun also aids, when it is familiar with the planet that governs the temperament of the soul, in an honourable position modifying it in the direction of justice, success, honour, dignity, and reverence for the gods..."[3]
—Ptolemy, *Tetrabiblos*

✷ ✷ ✷ ✷

"This divine and wholly beautiful universe, from the highest vault of heaven to the lowest limit of the earth, is held together by the continuous providence of the god, has existed from eternity ungenerated, is imperishable for all time to come, and is guarded immediately by nothing else than the Fifth Substance whose culmination is the beams of the sun."[4]
—*Hymn to King Helios*, Emperor Julian "the Apostate"

✷ ✷ ✷ ✷

"Come Heavenly Spirits, who are bright and resplendent with the rays of the Sun. Luminous Spirits, who are most prompt to obey the powerful voices of the great and wondrous Tetragrammaton, come to assist me in my Operation, which I undertake

[3] Claudius Ptolemy, *Tetrabiblos*, trans. F.E. Robbins (Cambridge, MA: Harvard University Press, 1956), 361-363.

[4] Julian, *Hymn to King Helios*, trans. Emily Wilmer Crave Wright, accessed October 2020, https://en.wikisource.org/wiki/Hymn_to_King_Helios.

under the auspices of the torch of the day, which our creator has created for the use of all Nature." [5]
—Invocation for Sunday, from *The Key of Solomon*

∗˙∗ The Sun in Astrology *∗˙∗*

The Sun and the Moon are the two brightest luminaries in the sky and, therefore, are given to rulership of the summer, when the light of day lasts longest. The Sun rules Leo, a hot summer month. He finds his exaltation in the fiery sign of the ram, Aries. He is in detriment in wintry Aquarius and finds his fall in Libra. He is a masculine, diurnal planet, hot and dry. The Sun's joy is in the 9th house, the house of religion, gods, travel, philosophy, and priests. In astrology, he is representative of the father, of kings, the masculine, the powerful, and those in positions of authority over us, including high priesthood. [6] He is associated with the public sphere, including reputation and perceived dignity.

The Sun is largely seen as positive, associated with robust health, good reputation, and a noble character. The Sun is also, however, extremely bright and fiery. This leads us to the concept of *combustion* in astrology. When the Sun is near to another planet in our field of vision, or *conjunct*, then that star is no longer visible. This is seen as affecting the star in question, which is combusted by the Sun, eaten up by its bright fire, which can cause disharmony, weakening, or negativity. This is taken even further in Vedic astrology, where combustion is seen as seriously debilitating in certain circumstances. Different astrologers will use different methods for determining how near to the Sun the planet in question must be to be combusted, but as a general rule, 10 degrees to either side is a useful

5   Stephen Skinner and David Rankine, *The Veritable Key of Solomon: Three Different Texts* from Those Translated by S.L. MacGregor Mathers (Singapore: Golden Hoard Press, 2017), 105.

6   Vettius Valens, *Anthologies*, trans. Mark Riley, accessed October 2020, https://www.csus.edu/indiv/r/rileymt/vettius%20valens%20entire.pdf, 1.

measure. It is also important to note that whether or not the star is rising above or below the Sun will determine the nature of the combustion.

As for the Sun representing our ego, this seems to be a bit more of a modern interpretation. Throughout my teaching and experience using astrology, I have found the Ascendant, its house, and its ruling planet to be a much better tool for interpreting one's sense of self than the Sun sign. When looking at the Sun, I find it a much better representation of how one relates to authority, to public perception, and in some questions of health. In a horary chart, I look to the Sun in questions of a person's boss, their political leaders, their father, and their sense of accomplishment in public settings.

*٭*The Sun in Magic*٭*

The Sun, in magic, is a powerful tool. Solar magic has been woven into multiple cultures, a sensible and almost self-evident truth when we consider that life itself is impossible without the Sun. We rely on it for our heat, our food, our ability to exist at the basest biological foundation. The plant kingdom turns sunlight into energy itself. This power runs as a golden chain throughout magical systems, from Egyptian and Hellenistic Sun worship, to the celebration of Sabbats in contemporary Witchcraft. The Sun was once *Sol Invictus*, the invincible Sun, worshipped by emperors and commoners alike. He was the titan Helios. He was Apollo, the god of prophecy, light, music, art, and perhaps the best incarnation of Hellenistic ideas in one deity. His cult in Egypt was omnipresent, found in the deities of Ra and his incarnations of Kephri, Aten, and of Sekhmet the ferocious lioness, and many more. In Neoplatonism, the Sun was often seen as the best example of the supreme One, the Monad, the underlying divinity within all existence that was manifested throughout creation as light.

In astrological magic throughout the Renaissance, he was associated with Michael the Archangel, the vanquishing commander of the divine host, often shown piercing the Dragon, destroying Satan himself in a blaze of glory. He was the ruler of the element of gold, the goal of all alchemy. As alchemy became spiritualized, this gold was the *aurum solis*, the "gold of the Sun" that existed within the human soul. We transmute our own lead selves into this gold of the Sun.

Pentacles to the Sun in *The Key of Solomon* were used to gain public honor, for protection against dangerous animals, to annihilate fear, win at lawsuits, and to bring others under our sway and obey our authority.[7] Planetary squares for the Sun were made to influence kings and princes of the Earth, and to bring luck.[8] Agrippa gives the table of the Sun as able to, "… render him that wears it to be renowned, amiable, acceptable, potent in all his works, and equals a man to kings, and princes, elevating him to high fortunes, enabling to do whatsoever he pleaseth."[9] This use of the Sun to gain favor with those in power, or to put ourselves in positions of power is echoed in *Picatrix*.[10] Traditional grimoires and occult works frequently see the Sun as our pathway to the feet of the King … or the pathway to taking his throne for ourselves.

⋆⁎⋆A Rite for the Sun ⋆⁎⋆

To gain the confidence or respect of someone in a position of authority, to gain promotion or respect in an endeavor at work, to succeed in the public eye.

To be completed on the day and hour of the Sun.

ASTROLOGICAL CONSIDERATIONS

To be done with a well-aspected Sun, particularly with no negative aspects to the malefics (Mars or Saturn). During the daylight, with a bright and

---

[7] Stephen Skinner and David Rankine, *The Veritable Key of Solomon: Three Different Texts* from Those Translated by S.L. MacGregor Mathers (Singapore: Golden Hoard Press, 2017), 111-118.

[8] *Conjuring Spirits: Texts and Traditions of Medieval Ritual Magic*, ed. Claire Fanger (University Park, PA: The Pennsylvania State University Press, 1998), 69.

[9] Henricus Cornelius Agrippa, *Three Books of Occult Philosophy*, ed. Donald Tyson (St. Paul, MN: Llewellyn, 1993), 319.

[10] *The Illustrated Picatrix: The Occult Classic of Astrological Magic Complete in One Volume*, trans. John Michael Greer and Christopher Warnock (Renaissance Astrology, 2015), 175-76.

clear Sun above. Avoid stormy, overcast weather. Better out of doors, with bright light. Sun not in detriment or fall.

RITUAL PREPARATIONS

Have an altar with golden cloth and a beeswax candle in a brass or copper holder. Have a censer or cauldron of sand for your incense, ready with lit and smoldering charcoals. Centrally display an image of the Sun, preferably in a solar metal or made of items corresponding to the Sun. A purifying bath before ritual is always a good idea, even better if sprinkled with herbs of the Sun. Have a talisman, piece of jewelry, or small stone (solar) in the center of your image upon the altar.

Incense of the Sun
1 part frankincense
1 part copal
Pinch of cinnamon
1–3 drops amber oil
Pinch of dried, crushed sunflower petals, calendula blossoms, or marigold

THE RITUAL

Place a portion of your incense on the hot coals. Center yourself before the altar, breathing in slowly, and exhaling with intent, focusing on the work at hand and the desired outcome. Light your candle and invoke:

"Splendorous Light, Crown of Gold, King of the Heavenly Hosts, an offering to you."

Carry the incense carefully to the four corners, offering it up to the Sun with the following words:

At the East:

"**Bright** and glorious Dawn. The **Light** breaks upon my work and births my Will in the starry ether."

At the South:

"**Height** of Noon, eye of God. The **Light** illuminates and gives strength to my Will."

At the West:

"**Setting** Sun, luminous upon the water. The **Light** carries forth my will."

At the North:

"**Hidden** Father of Midnight, warrior beneath the Earth. My Will destroys the serpent and makes manifest the Great Work. The enemy is defeated, as it was, and is, and always shall be."

Return your censer to the altar. Place your right hand firmly on the image of the Sun, pressing down.

"**Beneath** my right hand is the crown of glory.

Beneath my feet is the kingdom.

Upon my forehead is the Invincible **Light**.

My belly eats the dawn.

My maw is filled with stars.

My neck is bared to the golden torc.

My right eye is the Eye of Heaven.

My left eye is the hidden door.

My mouth is the jaw of the Dragon.

My reign is in days uncountable.

My hosts are numbered like grains of sand.

My cry is the rattling of a great wheel.

My decree is heard and answered."

Focus your intent. You can voice your specific desire here. Leave the talisman in the Sun throughout the day. You can wear or carry it with you after the rite as long as needed.

Finish by taking the incense to the four directions, saying:

"Light of Heaven, ever-present, ever-returning."

SUN CORRESPONDENCES

As Above — So Below

Hot, Dry, Diurnal, Masculine

IN THE HOROSCOPE

Domicile	Leo
Exaltation	Aries
Detriment	Aquarius
Fall	Libra
House of Joy	9th

THE MAGICAL WORLD

Day	Sunday
Colors	Gold, yellows, fiery oranges and reds, scarlet
Archangel	Michael
Sephirah	Tiphareth (Beauty)
Tarot	The Sun
Divinities	Apollo, Helios, Ra, Kephri (the scarab), Aten, Mithras, Sol Invictus, Surya
Magical Intent	Gaining authority, good relationships with power structures, mental health, clarity, sense of purpose, attainment of prestige or promotion in the public sphere, to bring someone more powerful than you to heel, to conquer something nobly

THE NATURAL WORLD

Mineral	Gold, chrysolite, diamonds, carbuncle, aventurine, ruby
Flora	Laurel, marigold, rosemary, saffron, Corn, St. John's wort, eyebright, sunflowers, heliotropes, barley, angelica
Fauna	Lions, seals, eagles, falcons, hawks, horses, rams, crocodiles, alligators, bulls, rooster, wolves, oxen, glowworms, starfish
Fumigations	Frankincense, amber, cinnamon, cloves, golden copal

MARS

Calamitous. Militant. Iron.

*⋆⋆⋆The Meeting⋆⋆⋆

The city around you is dark. Lights do not shine from the broken windows or busted streetlights that litter the area. Glass crunches under your feet, mingled with nails and shrapnel. There is a dull reddish glow to the evening as the half-charred, skeletal buildings look down from all sides. The streets are uneven and pockmarked. You keep walking. There are so many noises. Your heart beats a little faster, hoping the sources of these noises are far away. There are shots ringing out in the dim light, voices raised, shouts in languages you cannot make out. Bodies run past you, sometimes their faces glancing back into yours. Their eyes are twisted up in anger, their mouths set in determination. They carry makeshift weapons, pieces of metal and wood, some fashioned into impressive instruments of carnage. You slip against the wall of one of the large brick buildings on the street, trying to avoid the crowds of armed runners that seem so eager to move toward the chaos and not away, as part of you wishes to.

You start to walk faster, the maze of the city difficult to make out. Signs that may have once proven helpful to a wandering stranger are twisted up, illegible, scrawled in dripping graffiti. Posters plaster the walls, simple and stark images that inspire horror: images of strength, of armed bodies, all carrying threatening lines to dissidents. Most of these posters have been defaced in some way, but their underlying warning still shines through. The shouts and blasts sound louder. You cannot make out from what side they are coming from. Each turn seems to lead closer to the sound. You turn down alleys, squeeze past the growing crowds of runners, trying to avoid them, your legs pumping now, your body caked in sweat and the filth of the city. You wipe your face as the sting of something chemical and metallic pokes at your eyes. Your fingers feel grit.

There must be fires. Smoke snakes around the corners, sulfurous and choking. The blasts and roving sound of machinery are louder and louder, almost deafening, as whistling rockets and crumbling stones echo in the red city. Some of the runners try to pull you, egg you on, wave at you to join. You press against the stone and weigh the situation. They do not wait. They shake their heads and keep running, running ever toward the growing sounds of destruction. You hear more explosions and begin to run faster, crossing over ruined streets, past emptied vehicles and piles of trash.

You come upon a plaza, thronged with loud and screaming people. They call for righteousness, for justice, for the end. You feel the stomping feet of enforcers, bodies blacked out in armored masks and carrying firepower that makes your stomach knot. The gathered crowd is unafraid. Your eyes follow the crowd to the center, a massive statue, a male body with arm raised, face grim and empty. The statue is wobbling as bodies crawl across its base.

You see the ropes fly up, like spider web shot through the air. They cross and mingle until they find purchase on the great monolith. It shifts again. Shots ring out. Fire explodes from windows. You stifle a scream. The great monstrosity begins to tumble as the roar of the crowd becomes deafening, and the rushing enforcers begin to bear down on the crowd. Bodies press against you from every side. The air is barely breathable, filled with the smell of destruction, with heat and an acrid taste. The statue collapses, crumbling into pieces that fall to the Earth as huge plumes of dust rise and billow out from the scene.

The dust-clogged air, the bodies, all of it becomes unbearable. Your clothing is ripped and hanging in threads around your scarred and bruised skin. You escape the throng you are caught up in and turn down an abandoned alley, empty of people, empty of trash or rubble. You run, eyes so blurry from grit that you can barely see. You only make out the hazy outline of the walls to either side of you. They seem to want to close in on you, trap you here, your blood running hot, your head pounding. You are angry. No, you are furious. You do not know exactly why. There is something wrong. You pump your legs harder, hearing your teeth grind inside your skull, feeling your fingernails digging into the soft flesh of your palms. You keep running.

Just as you feel you will collapse, the alley is filled with light. You feel at first that it must be a weapon, an explosion, something that has come to end you. So, you hunker down, covering your head instinctively with your hands. Your eyes see red, even behind your closed eyelids. You wait for the pain, for the end, but it does not come. You just hear your breathing, ragged and heavy.

You slowly open your eyes and stand. You blink in pain as the light from the sand hits your face. It's all sand. For miles and miles, you see sand, an endless desert. In the distance there is a break in the brown-and-red nothingness: a skyline. You see billows of smoke rising from the distant city, hear vague and hard-to-decipher noises of destruction. It is the city you have left, burning and changing. As you gaze at the far-off city in the desert, a noise behind you causes you to spin around and face what is waiting for you.

The man is enormously tall, inhuman and imposing. He is shirtless, body both sculpted by discipline and marred by frequent scars and divots in the flesh. You cannot see his face, as it is covered by a dull, iron mask. It is a grotesque covering, a mask in the form of the head of a warhorse, nostrils flared, eyes cast in anger, teeth bared. Every detail stands out in the mask, bits of rust and patina coloring the entire thing in a mix of metallic hues. The man holds a spear, taller than he is, pointed in a star-shape. There are strips hanging from its points. You hope they are bits of rag, but something in you knows it to be flesh. His breathing echoes loudly, mingling with your own, the only sounds outside of the distant explosions from the city.

You stare at him, both of you as unflinching as stone. Your eyes look into the hollows of the iron, trying to see his eyes. There are only black hollows. He clenches the spear, the wood splintering slightly at his strength. The sound wakes you from your stillness and your mind fills with images. There are chains. And bars. Screams echo in your head as you see bodies separated, children taken from their mothers, doors smashed to dust by heavy clubs, fists connecting to soft flesh. You see fire. There is much fire.

The man does not move. The great mask stares at you as the visions fade. You feel an intense heat burning at your breastbone, moving through your veins like molten metal. You clench your fists once more, grit your teeth and set your heels. The man widens his stance. The point of the spear lowers. You feel the sand blow against you from behind, egging you on, challenging you. The man will not be moved. He will match you, meet you, beat you ... or at least try. You begin to run, not from but toward him this time. You will not stop. You will not turn. He waits for you. He stares and waits for you. Your feet carry you faster. Your eyes look into the great mask once more before all is red. You taste metal, coppery and bright. You feel connection, bone to bone, body to body, fire to fire. And everything is still red. All of it is red.

*˙.*The Fifth Sphere: Mars *˙.*

The Red Star is a malefic influence in most traditional works on astrology, whether it be for chart interpretation or astrologically guided magic. He is a beacon of war, change, and revolution. As positively as modern astrology tries to spin every negative statement made in traditional texts, it is difficult to remove the ominous omens and dark predictions tied to this planet. Even though he can be positively aspected and give himself over to discussions of bravery, courage, military honors, strength, and physical robustness, he is often lurking as the malefic influence that can bring quick ruin when least expected. When we read in traditional sources of a "bad star" or a malefic influence from the heavens influencing our earthly experience, we often find Mars in the discussion. In *Picatrix*, the image of Mars is a man holding a decapitated head.[1] The grimoire goes on to say that Mars is the "spiller of blood, and giver of illness."[2]

---

1 *The Illustrated Picatrix: The Occult Classic of Astrological Magic Complete in One Volume*, trans. John Michael Greer and Christopher Warnock (Renaissance Astrology, 2015), 103.

2 Ibid,171.

There is a lot to be said of rehabilitating the darker aspects within magic and divination, of trying to find the positive within the negative. It is a good habit. It can also be dishonest and, frankly, saccharine. There is an attempt in some New Age teachings to completely render all negative statements as positive, to try desperately and constantly to spin something harrowing into a good thing. Mars has been recast in the eyes of many as "misunderstood," a good omen, a bringer of change. We are told to understand Mars as the sharp changes in life that bring us lessons. If you are familiar with tarot reading, it is similar to how some readers try to re-read the Tower card as a positive. I often read modern astrological horoscopes thanking Mars for a tough lesson, or interpreting his influence as solely about action or drive, and never about something negative. *No, no ... all must be good.* It is the hallmark of modernism to smile, even when things are going poorly, to rewrite it all as geared toward love, and convince ourselves that everything and everyone really, truly wants us to succeed.

I cannot support this rewrite. I believe that if astrology is going to speak to all of human experience, it must include the ugly, the dangerous, the violent, and the terrifying. War, destruction, enslavement, injustice, and violence are part of the human experience. History is a bloody textbook. We cannot have a spiritual system that will truly teach us to understand our experience as ensouled creatures if we are going to try and gloss over the parts of it that are negative. If we are searching for the One, for the numinous, the divine, then we will never see it as well-defined as when it is contrasted to the darkness. I am reminded of many Christians who grow up hearing the Bible read and interpreted from the pulpit, but never read it for themselves. They are often quite shocked and horrified by the violence and terrifying imagery that sometimes comes up in scripture. They shouldn't be. Any system of spirituality is going to include the terror of life. If it doesn't, how will we ever find the good? How are we going to learn and grow from this system?

I will admit that Mars has its positive influences. He can push us, give us a fiery drive to accomplish goals and destroy our enemies, even if those enemies are our own moral and mental shortcomings. Mars can be the torch, the ignition, the powerful engine of change that is necessary for evolution. What I cannot do is say that this is easy, or that it is always beautiful. It is sometimes an ugly and heartbreaking experience. If the Red Star is anything, he is that realization: pain is here, and it isn't going anywhere. Change is here, and it is unavoidable. Sometimes, the lightning strikes when we least expect it. Mars was often seen as the harbinger of quick, violent ends. He is the unexpected and seemingly pointless horrors that could arrive when we are not ready, leaving us questioning and regrouping.

And there is a revolutionary spark within the Red Star, perhaps why a red star became a revolutionary symbol in itself. Agrippa gives Mars the power to remove kings from their thrones, to upend the powerful, and to give boldness to those who need it.[3] If there is a benefic force within the Martial Sphere, it is this revolutionary seed, this possibility of destroying tyranny and deposing the wicked. But again, it isn't guaranteed to be beautiful, or easy.

TOUCHSTONE TEXTS

"Shed down a kindly ray from above upon my life, and strength of war, that I may be able to drive away bitter cowardice from my head and crush down the deceitful impulses of my soul. Restrain also the keen fury of my heart which provokes me to tread the ways of blood-curdling strife."[4]

---

[3] Henricus Cornelius Agrippa, *Three Books of Occult Philosophy*, ed. Donald Tyson (St. Paul, MN: Llewellyn, 1993), 426.

[4] *Homeric Hymns*, trans. H.G. Evelyn-White, accessed August 2020, https://www. theoi.com/Text/HomericHymns3.html#8.

—From the *Homeric Hymn to Ares*

· ✳ · ✳ · ✳ ·

"And their nature is to cause and stir up war, murder, destruction, and mortality of people and of all earthly things, and their bodies are of a mean stature, dry and lean. Their color is red like to burning coals burning red, and their region or abiding is the South." [5]

—Description of the Spirits under Mars in *The Sworn Book of Honorius*

· ✳ · ✳ · ✳ ·

"My head is split. The crashing axe
Of the agony of things shears through
The stupid skull: out spurt the brains.
The universe revolves, then cracks,
Then roars in dissolution due;
And I am counting up the gains
And losses of a life afire
With dust of thought and dulled desire." [6]
—From Aleister Crowley's *The Rite of Mars*

✳ Mars in Astrology ✳

Mars rules fiery Aries and the fixed water sign of Scorpio. He finds his exaltation in Capricorn, his detriment in Taurus and Libra, and his fall in Cancer. His house of joy is the 6th house, known as the house of ill fortune, a place of illness and calamity. He is a hot and dry planet, malefic, masculine and nocturnal. His red coloring is significant of bloodshed, fiery temperaments, and war. Vettius Valens gives him rulership over such dark

---

5 "Liber Jurata Honorii," Esoteric Archives, accessed October 2020, http://www.esotericarchives.com/juratus/juratus.htm.

6 Aleister Crowley, *The Rite of Mars*, accessed August 2020, https://hermetic.com/crowley/the-rites-of-eleusis/mars.

themes as banishment, abuse, the deaths of spouses, murder, torture, and in the bodily realm: fevers, boils, and strokes. [7]

In more positive aspects he speaks to courage, bravery, the desire to unseat tyrants, and the impetus to action and resolve. He is a striker, quick to action, aggressive and powerful. This is why, in his most malefic aspects, he is "calamitous." Mars is often the unexpected tragedy, the lesson that comes from the Heavens like a lightning strike. Sometimes there is no lesson, and it is more the simple "acts of God" that we must all deal with in this mortal coil.

In electional astrology, we look to him for question of quarrels, wars, enemies, sudden acute illnesses, and strife. He is frequently consulted for military careers. Lilly, however, gives him rulership over not only military careers, but also to those that use knives such as butchers and surgeons as well as to those who work with iron tools such as blacksmiths. [8]

He is ravenous and sharp, eating up health when ill-aspected and causing anxiety and fear. Mars' moons are named for Ares' sons, Phobos and Demos, "fear" and "terror." And he can represent anxieties, mental distress, and phobias.

In politics, Mars is sought in readings about revolutions. The deposing of kings, political change, election surprises, and assassinations can fall under his purview. This is tied to his rulership of sharp change and fear itself. Sahl bin Bishr, the Persian astrologer, in his *On Questions*, writes that when we want to interpret answers to what someone fears, the malefic planets (Mars being one) bring death, imprisonment, capture and punishment when they are "Lord." [9] Masha'allah, also a Persian astrologer of the same strain as Salh bin Bishr, ties Mars and his aspects to revolutions, bloodshed, and the killing of kings. [10]

---

7   Vettius Valens, *Anthologies*, trans. Mark Riley, https://www.csus.edu/indiv/r/rileymt/vettius%20valens%20entire.pdf, 1.

8   William Lilly, *Christian Astrology: Books 1 & 2*, ed. David R. Roell (Bel Air, MD: Astrology Classics, 2004), 67.

9   *Works of Sahl & Masha'allah*, trans. Benjamin N. Dykes (Minneapolis, MN: Cazimi Press, 2010), 174.

10   Ibid, 358.

. Mars in Magic *.*

From what we have written about Mars, it is no surprise that in astrological magic, the Red Star was the planet par excellence for cursing and baneful magic. It is also no surprise that he was invoked in matters as lofty as war and revolution. In *The Key of Solomon*, his pentacles' usages range from simply "military matters" to the inciting of civil wars, protection from traitors, and for invulnerability and magical weapons. [11]

I find that Mars is often the influence needed when we are wronged in some way. We have had a calamity, or we experience injustice, and we feel that we need to right this. Meditations and occult workings for Mars can be powerful tools to channel righteous indignation. He can be a balm to feelings of shame, helplessness, or rage. Mars can aid us to reclaim our power and to topple the mighty, even if we understand that this is often an internal, painful work.

In angelic correspondences, Mars is tied to Samael, who in some interpretations is akin in certain aspects to Satan. Although they are not the same figure, there is a strong link between these two angelic intelligences. It is important to note that Samael—and even Satan, for that matter—were not seen in every system as fallen angels who worked for the destruction of humankind. In some theological interpretations, Satan and angels associated with him, such as Samael, were more like God's prosecuting attorneys, forces of judgment, discipline, and punishment. In Hermetic, Christian interpretations of Kabbalah, Samael was associated with the sephirah of *geburah*, along with Mars. This sephirah was about God's judgment, his severity, and even his wrath.

So, Mars can be baneful, or he can be the force of drive and change. He is lusty and violent, quick to anger and does not work slowly. I find Mars workings to be rapid, sometimes with unforeseen consequences if we are not meticulous in our approach and our wording. When we want to work with Mars, we must be ready to bear the consequences of playing with fire, of invoking the most primal and bloody parts of our nature to

---

11 Stephen Skinner and David Rankine, *The Veritable Key of Solomon: Three Different Texts from Those Translated by S.L. MacGregor Mathers* (Singapore: Golden Hoard Press, 2017), 146-154.

be made manifest in our spiritual path. Whether by a headbutting ram or the sting of a scorpion, we will get what we want. Come hell or highwater … or red stars.

✦˙✦ A Rite for Mars ✦˙✦

To discover a traitor, to unearth a negative secret in someone, to make clear an enemy's intentions or ill will, to discover gossip.

To be completed on the day and hour of Mars.

ASTROLOGICAL CONSIDERATIONS

Mars nocturnal, and well-aspected to other planets. A Waxing or Full Moon. Avoid a poorly aspected Sun or Saturn.

PREPARATIONS

Have your altar plain and mostly bare, with a simple red cloth across the center. Have one candle, in red or saffron-yellow, in an iron candlestick. Prepare a small poppet or doll in red cloth with black stitching. Have a length of black cord, 3 feet, cut and ready. You can further connect with Martial correspondences by stuffing the poppet with corresponding stones or herbs of the planet. Place it on your altar, face-down. Braid together three pieces of leather and have it ready, knotted on both ends.

RITUAL

Approach your altar with candles lit and invoke:

"Red.
Black.
Malefic Star.
Red Star.
Black Star.
Father-Brother.
Warmonger.
Lust.

Bright, Flickering-Flame.
Heathen Star.
Spy and General.
Come! Come!"

Take up the leather braid and strike it forcefully three times on the altar.

"Iron son.
Morning-Star-Lover.
Red-eyed and wild-handed.
COME."

Strike again, three times, forcefully.

"Mad as an Amazon, wild as a hare. Shield-bearer. Guard
and charger."

Strike again, once.

"Come!"

Take up the poppet and the black cord. Begin to wind the cord around,
clockwise, near the flame of the lit candle.

"Bound in Heaven. Bound in Earth. Red above me, and
red within. Vein to vein, iron of blood. Sword of clarity,
cut, unsheathed. Reveal and contain. Reveal and master.
Tie and knot. Bear within and without. Star to soil, and
soul to Heaven. Under the eye. Under the hand. Extended
and gnarled. Branch of fire. Branch of metal. Wound
tight and bright. Omen and soothsayer. Prince and maker.
Come. Come!"

Finish by knotting the end of the cord in an uneven number of knots. You can repeat the above incantation as many times as needed before you feel the rise of power and finish with the knotting.

Seal the poppet and the wound-up cord with candle wax, invoking:

"Fallen tyrant.
Silent spy.
Quiet mouth.
Eager for freedom.
Truth and justice.
Served and worshiped."

Leave the working until the desired outcome is complete. Get rid of the working items under a New Moon.

MARS CORRESPONDENCES

As Above — So Below

Hot, Dry, Nocturnal, Masculine

IN THE HOROSCOPE

Domicile	Aries and Scorpio
Exaltation	Capricorn
Detriment	Taurus and Libra
Fall	Cancer
House of Joy	6th

THE MAGICAL WORLD

Day	Tuesday
Colors	Red, fiery colors, saffron
Archangel	Samael
Sephirah	Geburah (Severity)
Tarot	The Tower (La Maison de Dieu)
Divinities	Mars, Ares, Tyr, Enyo, Eris, Sobek, Kartikeya
Magical Intent	Violence, cursing, strengthening weapons, finding enemies, hiding secrets, uncovering sabotage, protecting or unearthing a spy, conquest, bloodlust, courage, fearlessness in the face of adversity, purpose, revolution, ending tyranny, domination, liberation

THE NATURAL WORLD

Mineral	Iron, antimony, bloodstone, red jasper, red and jagged stones, brimstone, lodestones,
Flora	Nettles, thistles, onion, garlic, ginger, galangal, hemlock, radish, all things with a sharp and spicy taste
Fauna	Horse, mule, goats, serpents, baboon, flies, gnats, tigers, vulture, leopard, shark, crows, kites, worms, scorpions, bears
Fumigations	Red sandalwood, cypress, all things with a sharp, unpleasant, or bitter odor

JUPITER

Beneficence. Expanse. Philosopher.

⋆⋅⋆ The Meeting ⋆⋅⋆

The man who takes your coat smiles, handing you a small purple ticket with a number. You place it in your pocket, checking yourself in a long mirror in the hall. You are in very formal clothing. You shift in it, getting comfortable, straightening out the fabric and tidying your appearance. The long hall you find yourself in has deep, darkly colored wood floors, interlocking in complex starburst patterns. The walls are papered in rich prints of foliage and natural landscapes, every detail painted with care. It seems so realistic that you could walk into the painting and find yourself in a familiar location. As you are examining the walls, two doormen open the gilded doors at the end of the room and smile, motioning for you to enter. You take one last look and move into the space, leaving the entrance hall and walking into an impressive ballroom filled with bodies. The event is black tie. Dancers move gracefully across the parquet floor, smiling under the glowing chandeliers that hang with blue sapphires and strung crystal.

Waiters move with large silver platters, offering food and precariously balanced glasses of champagne and cordials. Plates of food move past you, glinting under the light. You take your fill, tasting the warm spice on ripe figs, the tang of briny olives, rich cheese, and other delicacies. Every person you pass grasps your arm, smiles at you, greets you by name. They are happy you are here. You are welcome in this space. You know these faces. The music is lively and bright, the band playing on a raised dais behind large open windows that show a stormy night outside. The rain and lightning stand in stark contrast to the brightly lit, happy place where you mingle and move in ease and comfort.

The groups of people shift and move around you, inviting you into conversations. You find yourself catching only bits of their conversation, pieces of stories, tales of long journeys, of conquered difficulties, and new ideas. Heated debates pop up around you, and women and men argue passionately, hands moving rapidly to drive their points home as they place their palms over their glasses so as not to spill wine on the dancefloor. Take your time among the people. Explore and see what they say. Find what you agree with, what inspires you to contradict their little speeches and arguments. There is no shortage of people to speak with, no difficulty in finding a welcoming place to listen and speak.

Large tables are placed around the ballroom, draped in blue and white. Candles burn in glass votives, sitting on wide oak leaves. Violets and other flowers are strewn around, mingling between the candlelight and foliage. The scent is sweet and pleasant. The bar and buffet are filled with diners, chatting and laughing together as they fill their plates to overflowing, moving to their tables and sipping their drinks. You search for your name, moving through the crowd. You hear so many languages, the lilt and fall of a thousand tongues from every corner of the Earth fills your ears. Every stripe of person seems represented here, every group mingling together and finding space. You cannot help but smile and greet the partygoers. The sheer diversity of humanity is on display here, with no two persons looking alike in any way. Everything is effulgent with newness and a unique quality of sharpness.

You notice your name in elegant calligraphy on a white placard. Your seat is waiting. At your table are others, all speaking their own language, but you converse with ease. You know these faces; you are welcome here. A server brings you rich wine and offers to bring you a plate of food from the smorgasbord. You can take what you want, taste whatever is brought to you. The music is still playing as you dine, your foot tapping to the beat, your belly full and your mind slightly buzzing from the atmosphere.

You notice, for the first time, a very tall man on a dais at the front of the ballroom. He is dignified, with graying hair and a trimmed beard. His eyes sparkle in the room, catching the light of the chandeliers and the glow of the candles. There are others at the long table he presides over, all with small blue and purple sashes denoting rank or position. His own sash carries a metallic pin, beaten out of tin: an eagle in flight. A woman is standing beside him, arm interlaced with his, her eyes sparkling as brightly as his own. They look out over the crowd, and the music fades peacefully to silence, the conversation of the partygoers quieting as if willed by the couple at the dais. Standing in front of the crowd, the couple is calm and collected, but their presence is commanding. They do not need to raise their hands for attention or signal to the room that they are ready to speak. You know when they are ready. And you listen.

His voice comes in a language you do not understand, just like at the table, but you still manage to grasp. It is a booming voice that matches the thunder crashing just outside the warm, safe ballroom. He speaks louder, his arms raising. You feel a rumble in the floor. As you look around to see if anyone else noticed, you realize that the crowd is gone. You sit alone, watching the man speak from the raised dais at the front of the room. Gone are the dancers, the musicians, the servers, and concierges that packed the room just moments ago. Now it is only his voice echoing in the empty space, filling it completely, filling your mind and ears. It is so loud, so powerfully loud, that you almost cover your ears. But you cannot. You feel that you must hear him, hear this voice speaking into the empty room.

He looks into your eyes, his own irises so piercing that you try to look away, flinching slightly at the gaze. In that moment you see yourself bare and free, seen through as if you were transparent. You remember so many things in that moment. You remember why you began so many projects, what inspired you to be where you are, what you were given and what was expected from you. There is drive here, a push to understand that all of this is pushing you to something more, to something you were destined to finish. The images pour so rapidly that you cannot differentiate time or space anymore. There is only the possibility of becoming what you were supposed to be, here, in this moment. You were brought here because of who you are, because of what you will become.

And you are on the dais, before an empty room, a room that expands seemingly forever. Bright light pours in from all directions, bathing the space and your body in an effervescent glow. Light the color of lightning flashes across your body, crowning above your head, crackling, and arcing out from your skin. You are moving, moving forever upward at a speed you do not comprehend. The light loosens your hold on any sense of space, time, or location. Everything moves, growing, expanding, and creating from the central point that is you.

And you feel them, the stars, as friends and lovers, as children you did not know were yours, as partners and coworkers. They are everywhere in this light, exploding in proportions that you struggle to comprehend. Threads of explosive blue light and ethereal, milky purple link every point of light before your field of vision until the web around you is infinite, and infinitely connected. The music of this dance rings out everywhere, announcing the ever-expanding field you now know to be real, more real than any vision of earthly experience your eyes have seen. The eternal voice echoes with your own, a shout of ecstasy, a prayer, a full sound of beginnings and of authority. All of it is here. All of it is right.

*.*The Sixth Sphere: Jupiter *.*

The planet Jupiter is the great benefic in traditional astrology, the other lesser benefic being Venus. It is a bright, shining light in the night sky, large and imposing. This presence led the wandering star to be named after the King of the Gods—Jupiter, or Zeus. Jupiter was the star of kings, philosophers, priests, and philanthropists. Nobility was written into this bright light, so glaringly powerful as to inspire connection with all those that use mindfulness and chivalry to rule and control. This star is the part of us that desires more than what we are born into, whether it be ambition in career, or desires to explore new places and far-off lands. This Heavenly Sphere is our inspiration in philosophy and thought, eager to expand our horizons beyond the tight and constricting space we can inhabit in our lives.

Traditional astrologers and magicians saw in Jupiter the epitome of a just and wise ruler, a benefic leader who inspires rather than rules by fear or absolute fiat. In a world of warring nobles, difficult princes, and frequent war, the image of a ruler who was guided by higher principles would have been a beautiful hope to aim for, something to inspire better societies and more involved citizens. As much as we may malign rulers (and rightfully so) in the modern world, this wandering star can hold for us the image of what it feels like when leadership is done right. It can hold for us what a real teacher can inspire and what a real cleric can communicate.

Given Jupiter's great light, it is no surprise that the planet was linked to religion. Our search for meaning, our experience of the numinous, and our drive toward the divine is reflected in this benefic planet. Even Vedic astrology, developing separately from the Western tradition, links this planet to a sage who instructs even the gods. The clergy of the world, and their massive institutions and movements, find correspondence with this star.

It is also no shock that this bright star was given to the King of the Gods, the thunderer, in Hellenistic systems. Jupiter's astrological symbol is a stylized version of Zeus' lightning-bolt, a symbol of his divine power. Although Zeus' image is often read in modern times as a philandering husband, traditional believers still saw in him the image of controlled power and lofty rulership. He was more than his dalliances with nymphs. He was the ruler of the Air, the King of Olympus, whose name was used as a synonym in more philosophical pagan systems for the supreme and unified Godhead itself, the Monad and sacred One.

TOUCHSTONE TEXTS

"When Jupiter and the sun are together, they produce noble and distinguished men, rulers, governors, dictators, vigorous men, honored and blessed by the crowd. These men are wealthy, rich, living with much spectacle."[1]
—Vettius Valens, *Anthologies*

* ✳ ✳ ✳ *

"Jupiter is moderately warm and moist. The greater benefic. Male. Diurnal. Sweet, bitter-sweet, delicious. Dust-colour and white mixed with yellow and brown, shining, glittering."[2]
—Al-Biruni

* ✳ ✳ ✳ *

"From Jupiter an unshaken prudence, temperance, benignity, piety, modesty, justice, faith, grace, religion, equity & regality..."[3]
—*Janua Magica Reserata*

[1] Vettius Valens, *Anthologies*, trans. Mark Riley, https://www.csus.edu/indiv/r/rileymt/vettius%20valens%20entire.pdf, 17.

[2] Al-Biruni, *The Book of Instructions in the Elements of the Art of Astrology*, trans. R. Ramsay Wright (Bel Air, MD: Astrology Classics, 2006), 32.

[3] Stephen Skinner and David Rankine, *The Keys to the Gateway of Magic: Summoning the Solomonic Archangels and Demon Princes* (Singapore: Golden Hoard Press, 2005), 91.

*₊*Jupiter in Astrology *₊*

Jupiter is benefic, powerful, and a strong, positive influence when well-positioned in the chart. He is the ruler of Sagittarius and Pisces and exalted in Cancer. The planet's fall is in Capricorn, and he is in detriment in the signs of Gemini and Virgo. He is a diurnal, masculine planet, happy in the bright day. When the Sun's light is not overpowering, Jupiter can even be seen with the naked eye during the daylight hours.

Jupiter will be associated with long-distance travels, philosophy, religion, rulership, and public power. Any question a client might have, either in their natal charts or in other techniques, can look to Jupiter's situation in the chart when questions about these corresponding areas of life need an answer.

A well-aspected Jupiter, with much dignity, is going to influence things strongly, being such a powerful benefic planet. Anything involving power, or public perception and relationships, is strengthened with a well-positioned Jupiter. Kings, and potentates of all stripes, were deeply concerned with Jupiter in charts, and we can expand this in the modern world to include Jupiter's influence on all things relating to public connection and societal expectation. Lilly takes it down to even mundane aspects, noting that a good Jupiter in a chart makes one strong in conversation, affable, and known for charity.[4]

When Jupiter is negatively aspected or positioned within a chart, it reeks of the dangers always associated with rulers and religious leaders: hypocrisy, lack of wisdom, schisms, and tyranny. Because of Jupiter's association with religion, a debilitated Jupiter could portend a heretic, or a misguided thinker. I have seen Jupiter exact a negative influence on thought patterns, creating obsessions, religious fanaticism, or even ego-driven cruelty. It is a powerful planet, just like the ego is a powerful thing in us, and it can be a positive or a negative influence.

---

4   William Lilly, *Christian Astrology: Books 1 & 2*, ed. David R. Roell (Bel Air, MD: Astrology Classics, 2004), 62.

He is also the law, and judges, magistrates, councilors, and those who work in universities and colleges. He is the planet of lawyers, to Lilly.[5] Higher learning belongs to him, just like it did with the Church at one point. The two were inextricably linked historically, and for many in Catholic education, continue to be so. Scholarship and faith find their home in the sixth Heavenly Sphere. It is no surprise that foreign travel and emissaries, ambassadors, and their like are tied in with this. Nothing is more powerful and instructive for a student than travel.

Jupiterian (or *jovian*), physical appearances were considered striking, strong, and noble. He was given to those that were tall of stature, with good complexion and a fleshy, filled-out body.[6] Everything that we may associate with a strong, well-liked, and just king or knight could be associated with the characteristics of a Jupiterian figure.

*᛭*Jupiter in Magic *᛭*

Jupiterian magic is benefic and largely focused on growth, long-distance travel, religious faith, or those in positions of power. The powerful influence of Jupiter can be petitioned in any working that is geared toward abundance, overflow, growth of mind. In short—this is *the* planet for benevolent workings and increase.

In Agrippa we see a table for Jupiter able to bring "… gain and riches, favour and love, peace and concord, and to appease enemies, to confirm honours, dignities, and counsels; and dissolve enchantments, if it be engraven on a coral."[7] This confirming of honor or dignity links Jupiter to its power over those in positions of authority such as rulers, judges, clerics, or teachers. Any working to gain entrée into a circle of power will benefit from this planet's spirit.

Picatrix gives a talisman for Jupiter with the following information: "Make it in the hour of Jupiter when Jupiter is rising in his exaltation, and

---

5   Ibid., 63.

6   Ibid.

7   Henricus Cornelius Agrippa, *Three Books of Occult Philosophy*, ed. Donald Tyson (St. Paul, MN: Llewellyn, 1993), 318.

make it in a clear and white stone. Those who carry this image will have an increase in riches and honor and lead a good life and have many sons and be able to perform good things and not be injured by enemies."[8] The key here is increase. The magic of Jupiter is expansive. It grows and rules evenly. The goal here is not unfettered growth or wild attainment. The goal is always a measured and controlled rulership over what we need to achieve our means.

The Key of Solomon contains pentacles for the planet Jupiter, almost uniformly positive. Many lead to finding riches, protection against evil, obtaining glory and honor, and the invocation of good spirits. The grimoire tradition is as enamored with Jupiter as traditional astrological texts, using the spirits of Jupiter such as the angel Sachiel to increase honor and dignity, and to grow riches and esteem. This planet and its spiritual force embody the meaning of the term *benefic*, so often encountered in traditional astrological sources.

⋆⁎⋆A Rite for Jupiter⋆⁎⋆

To have protection on a journey, to begin a new journey or plan great travel, to be successful in a trip for business or personal gain.

To be completed on the day and hour of Jupiter.

ASTROLOGICAL CONSIDERATIONS

Diurnal working with a well-aspected Jupiter. A Jupiter with positive dignity is best. Avoid the New Moon. Avoid a poorly aspected Mars, Saturn, or Sun.

RITUAL PREPARATION

Have the altar covered with purple or deep-blue cloth. Two silver or gold-colored candlesticks should be placed to either side of the working space, with lit candles in blue, purple, or gold. White may be substituted

---

8 *The Illustrated Picatrix: The Occult Classic of Astrological Magic Complete in One Volume*, trans. John Michael Greer and Christopher Warnock (Renaissance Astrology, 2015), 106.

if nothing else is available. Have a censer or cauldron with sand ready for your incense, with hot coals smoldering and ready. On the altar, place the image of an eagle. This can be a sculpture, a drawing, a handmade image, or a collection of feathers (ethically sourced) bound in twine. Also have ready a wand of oak, or if you do not have one, a small branch of oak or a bound collection of dried oak leaves. Beneath your items have either a piece of information about your journey (tickets, itinerary, maps, images, etc.) or a detailed description in your own hand. Have a bowl of water mixed with salt available on the altar.

Prepare with a ritual bath, or calming meditation, well in advance of the hour of Jupiter so that you have time to mentally prepare. When you are ready, enter your space and approach the altar in comfortable ritual clothing.

THE RITUAL

Invoke:

> "Jove, Amun-Zeus, Sachiel. By the oak and beech. Under the sphere of kings. Potentate. Judge. Fly! Eagle-strong. A prayer of strength. A call to the wheel. Turn! Turn! Move and make. Father of Heaven, olive-bearing chieftain, come! Lord! Lord!...

> ...of suppliants,
> ...of hospitality,
> ...of the rains,
> ...of the lots,
> ...of refuge,

> Come! Come! Quick as a bird, fast as the hunter, now and now and ever now. Flash of light, and thundercrack, upon the brow a crown and upon the breast a rod. King of Kings. Mighty breaker, release! Release! Free and righteous is the path to the ascent."

Place your incense blend upon the coal, allowing the smoke to build up around the altar space.

Incense of Jupiter
Frankincense
Pinch of ground nutmeg
Small pinch of ground clove
1 crushed olive leaf, finely ground

Take up the eagle and pass it through the smoke. Invoke:

> "Purifier. Sanctifier. Chief of priests. Teacher of gods and mortals. Make bright the way. Turn the wheel. Make clear the path. Cast the lots. Unburden. Unleash."

Pass the image over and around the two candle flames.

> "Altar of the highest, shining Light of Heaven. Crucible of the Stars. Make bright the way. Turn the wheel. Make clear the path. Cast the lots. Unburden. Unleash."

Sprinkle the image with salt and water.

> "First of all that come, and last to concede. Mystery of the vaults of Heaven. Make bright the way. Turn the wheel. Make clear the path. Cast the lots. Unburden. Unleash."

Place the eagle back on the items of your journey and take up the oak. Draw the invoking pentagram of Air over the eagle, while invoking.

"Clear skies break over the Earth. Fly! Fly! Creature of my hand, and breath of my soul—carry forth and go! By the crown and sandal. No pauper, but king! APEMIOS! LAOITES! ELEUTHEREUS! ARIEUS! CLARIUS! HYPATUS!"

Leave the image of the eagle upon the journey materials, letting the candles burn down completely under your watch. The incense can be burned throughout the process.

JUPITER CORRESPONDENCES

Hot, Moist, Diurnal, Masculine

IN THE HOROSCOPE

Domicile	Sagittarius and Pisces
Exaltation	Cancer
Detriment	Gemini and Virgo
Fall	Capricorn
House of Joy	11th

THE MAGICAL WORLD

Day	Thursday
Colors	Purple, azure blue
Archangel	Sachiel
Sephirah	Chesed (Mercy)
Tarot	The Wheel of Fortune
Divinities	Jupiter, Zeus, Thor, Amun, Marduk, Ba'al, Perun, Indra
Magical Intent	Public honors, dignities, religious clarity, long-distance travel, success in university or higher learning, good relations with leaders, guidance from a teacher or guru, riches and treasures, benevolent spirits and their protection, avoidance of harm

THE NATURAL WORLD

Mineral	Tin, amethyst, sapphire, topaz, marble, hyacinth, beryl, emerald, jasper
Flora	Cloves, mulberry, oak, olives, figs, ash, hazel, beech, ivy, nutmeg, betony, fumitory, peony, rhubarb, balsam, flax, basil, poplar, corn, wheat, barley, licorice, almond
Fauna	Eagle, dolphin, whale, sheep, stag, cuckoo, elephant, tiger, unicorn, stork, peacock, hen, partridge, pheasant
Fumigations	Nutmeg, storax, mastic, cloves, frankincense

SATURN

Discipline. Time. Reaping.

⋆⁺⋆The Meeting⋆⁺⋆⁺

The long corridor in front of you stretches out under a dim, fluorescent light. The floor is slick, freshly cleaned, as spotless as anything you have seen. It is gray tile, and as you walk forward the click of your footsteps echoes against the walls of the hall. There are heavy doors with dark handles evenly spaced on either side of the corridor that you are exploring. The dull lights above cast everything in shadow. You cannot see into the rooms, but there are plates with names beside each one. The thin black windows in the center of each of the doors reveal nothing. You continue walking down the hall of heavy doors, across the uniform, clean tiles.

Your measured breathing and rhythmic, clacking footsteps now mingle with another, even set of sounds. You hear evenly spaced beeps. You hear evenly spaced hissing. You hear evenly spaced clicks. They are like metronomes, these sounds, so even and continual. You realize they are machines. There are ventilators here, and monitors. As you realize what place you are in, the scent fills your nose. It is antiseptic, clean, but it hides beneath it something else, a scent of decay, of age. It is the scent of a hospital, that unmistakable odor that is somehow both alien and sterile while being all-too human at the same time.

You realize the corridor is coming to an end. Two large gray doors of metal stand at the end. The word above the doors is etched out of stone, out of place in the modernity of the hospital. They carry a word that can only mean that the dead are here. They come here. They pass through. They know this place. And now you are heading to see, to feel, to know. Your stomach grows heavy, your feet fighting against walking toward the doors. But you must. You know that you must push them open and enter this space. The lights begin to fade behind you, the corridor sinking into darkness behind you, utter and complete, until only the doors are lit, waiting for you. You take a deep inhale, the scent overpowering, and you push against them.

They give way, and you are in a better-lit space, rectangular and clean. Chrome and steel glint from everywhere, instruments on sanitized paper, tables ready for what must lie on them, and washbasins with exposed pipes. You adjust to the new light, the sterile-yet-decayed odor, only stronger here. The wall of drawers, large and metallic, on the far wall sends a shiver to the roots of your body, churning in the pit of your stomach.

The man comes out from the shadows of the back of the room. He is lean, with an aquiline nose and dark eyes. He walks with an odd gait, giving slightly to one of his legs, a mildly pronounced limp. His uniform is black but dull, the mask covering his mouth tattered from use but clean. You are startled at first, but he does not ask anything, nor does he seem to be surprised that you are here. He motions for you to come closer to the wall of large, metal drawers. Your footsteps again echo as you move closer to him, closer to what must be seen, what must be done.

He effortlessly slides the drawer out between you and him. The thing that lies upon it, covered in linen, is unmistakably a human form. You catch your breath a little as he pulls the linen slowly up from the feet of the body, leaving the head covered, for modesty. It is so pale, so blue in places. The man begins laying out the instruments, setting up for the work that is to be done. He asks you, wordlessly, to help him to move the body and you comply, unable to stop the trajectory of this task. You help move the gurney and then gently slide the person into place. The instrument tray is prepped, the body moved, the lights brighten above in blinding clinical brightness. It is time.

The first incisions and cuttings are difficult. He performs them alone at first, hands gloved, working meticulously. His precision is absolute, his movements timed, even, and patient. But he will not let you be an idle watcher. He pulls your hands, his fingers cold as ice and dry as sandpaper, toward the body, slips your fingers around the tools and guides your movements. The sounds and sensations fill your field of vision, your ears. You cannot focus on anything besides the precise cutting. The blurring of saw and metal and blood all move as you cut and cut and cut. You are guided to open up the form, to lay bare what most were never meant to see, the slick butterfly of human life bared to the sickles of science and necessity.

The work is mostly done, the body displayed for both of you, lying between your forms. He slips his hands slowly into the open cavity and pulls out a black and shining fruit. It is a fig, a dark-skinned and plump fig. He washes it carefully in the basin beside the table and places it down. Again his hands go in and he slides out an earthy, stony lump. It is like coal, or unpolished onyx, black and crystalline and hard. Again, he rinses it carefully and places it beside the body. Each time, your eyes try to understand. Before you is the body, its viscera plainly visible, human, wet, organic. And yet his hands slip inside again and he removes nothing that was meant to be inside of this frame. Again the hands go in, and he pulls out flowers, untouched by blood or any stain, large and ghostly purple. He carefully places them down. He looks at you and his hands rest by his side. He nods at you.

You brace yourself and look into the cavern left inside this creature of flesh, this person. You see things you can identify, but you do not trust your senses here. Taking a breath, you slip your hand inside and feel. It is wet, and cold. There is nothing unnatural here. It is human and was once alive. It is where all must go. Here. This place. This experience of the empty house of a body that has lost its soul.

Something slides across your fingers, and you recoil in terror. The man grasps your arm, stopping you from removing your hand. His grip is so strong. You fight against him, but it is to no avail. It is like a vice on your upper arm, and you struggle as the slick, moving thing inside the body continues to brush against your hand and fingers. You feel it quivering and squirming, pressing against, sliding past. You try to scream, but silence erupts from your mouth.

You brace yourself and extend your fingers in the moist hollow. The thing slips between, and you close your fist, grasping tightly. It thrashes violently, whatever it is. The man releases your arm and you pull backward. The black serpent coils around your arm, hissing violently, its black scales shimmering in the fluorescent lights of the morgue. You cannot drop it. It tightens and constricts around your upper arm. You stare back at the man as he watches calmly while you fight with the creature. Tables are knocked over and needles, scalpels, pincers, all go scattering across the floor. The snake will not let go. You try again to scream as you realize the man is approaching the body again. He quickly snaps the linen away from the cadaver's face, and you are looking in a mirror. The body is your body. The face is your face. It has changed and transmuted. You are on the metal slab, your chest now sewn into a perfect Y, the sutures black and glossy. The serpent releases and falls to the ground, slithering toward the man.

When you look up, the room is dark. The table with that body, that body that bore your face, is gone. The serpent is what you see, moving toward the man in the dark room, only enough light to barely illuminate him. He is tall now and shrouded in black, his face hooded, his surgical mask gone. The serpent twines up his body, slowly, as the glint of the scalpel in his hand reveals it to no longer be a scalpel but an ancient, rusting scythe. He raises it high above his head and you curl down, bracing for the impact. You press yourself into yourself, your breath shallow, your hands clammy. The moment lasts too long to seem real. You hear it swing through air, the metal singing almost as it slices through air. There is a sound like glass shattering, of a familiar voice crying, of rumbling deep in the Earth, and a cold sensation surrounds your body. There is no pain, only coolness. And the singing metal of the scythe swings again. And again. And again. It sings you to sleep.

*⋆*The Seventh Sphere: Saturn *⋆*

Saturn is the second of the malefic planets, the ruler of the final Heavenly Sphere before the realm of the fixed stars and the Empyrean Heaven of the Godhead. From Earth, Saturn is a grayish, dull star that moves quite slowly. Named after the titan father of the Olympians, Chronos in Greece and Saturn in Rome, this star was truly the last gateway before the great void of space. Carrying a sickle, he is "Falcifer," or The Scythe-Bearer, the cutter of things, the lord of time, delineation, discipline, death, and finality. He is an arbiter and some-times bitter teacher. He is the Fates, holding the thread of life and deciding when to cut. He is the black-clad figure in the Night, the Devil of the Witches' Sabbat, and the incarnation of Father Time.

In traditional texts, Saturn was dour and dark, a Heavenly Sphere associated with death, decay, and the end of things. Saturn is the spiritual teacher that we can struggle with the most, the *momento mori* planet that is slow and steady because he knows the beginning and end of things. Saturn was lead, heavy objects, and flowers that were soporific and dangerous. He ruled over the elements of life that made us realize our own mortality, but also our inner power.

In the world of creation, Saturn is the boundary-maker, the solidification of spirit into matter, ensoulment of the divine spark into physical, mundane reality. His nature is both brooding and alarming, at times awakening that tremulous inner spark in us that sometimes we feel at funerals, in graveyards, in grand, abandoned cathedrals or empty city streets. He is the great wall of time that we cannot seem to surmount. In Hermetic interpretations of Kabbalah, he is *Binah*, the dark cosmic mother of "understanding." Saturn is the limit-maker, the only thing that makes creation a possibility. Without Saturn's outlining, creation is untenable. It cannot be. Without the possibility of non-being, being is meaningless, an endless and amorphous nothing that can go nowhere. With Saturn, the boundaries are set, and we can begin to understand our place in the cosmos.

This concept of Saturn as the materialization of spirit, the boundary-maker, can be seen in Bonatti, who writes that Saturn is, "the first circle of the planets, and is the first planet in their order, and whom all others follow, and is even the first one who exercises his operation in a conceived child after the falling of the seed into the womb, by binding and uniting together the matter from which the conceived child is formed."[1] This explains why Saturn is seen as the father, the ultimate progenitor. We see mortality in our own fathers, and Saturn reflects this back to us.

It is interesting to note that, depending on the scheme we are using, Saturn is either the first planet we are going to encounter, or the last. If we are beginning from God and descending from the fixed stars into the planets, then he is first. If we are starting from Earth and moving outward, he is the last. Either way, his significance is unchanged, and that is significant. When we fall from the heights of the Godhead, our first planet is boundary. Our first stop is the realization that death is an inevitability. If we start from Earth and climb up, we can only go so far before, again, we confront death and limitation. We must break through the discipline and dark reminder of Saturn, either way we decide to travel. Whether we are climbing high to meet God, or falling from the heights to taste creation, he is waiting patiently to swing the sickle and teach a lesson.

---

[1] Guido Bonatti, *Bonatti on Basic Astrology: Treatises 1-3 of Guido Bonatti's Book of Astronomy: Theory, Signs, Houses, Planets, Configurations*, trans. Benjamin N. Dykes (Minneapolis, MN: The Cazimi Press, 2010), 150.

TOUCHSTONE TEXTS

"Grave persons, with a certain austerity, advised, excogitating profound matters, taciturn, solitary, laborious, patient, preservers of riches, sparing and thrifty, studious for their own profit, zealous, mistrustful."[2]
—William Lilly's descriptions of the manners of those with a strong and well-affected Saturn

* * * * * *

"Saturn makes serfs and farmers because of its rule over the land, and it causes men to be renters of property, tax farmers, and violent in action. It puts into one's hands great ranks and distinguished positions, supervisions, management of others' property, and the fathership of others' children. Of materials, it rules lead, wood, and stone."[3]
—Vettius Valens

* * * * * *

"If Saturn were in his own domicile, his works will be strong, and the native will be mixed with those who know sciences;

[2] William Lilly, *Christian Astrology: Book Three* (Abingdon, MD: Astrology Classics, 2004), 539.

[3] Vettius Valens, *Anthologies*, trans. Mark Riley, accessed June 2020, https://www.csus.edu/indiv/r/rileymt/Vettius%20Valens%20entire.pdf, 1.

> and if the nativity were in the day, it will be stronger; if in the night, it will be with anguish." [4]
> —Masha'Allah, on the significance of Saturn in his own sign

✦⭐✦ Saturn in Astrology ✦⭐✦

Saturn is the ruler of wintry Capricorn and Aquarius. He is exalted in Libra, in detriment in Cancer and Leo, and in complete fall in Aries. His house of joy is the 12th house, a house of bad fortune and imprisonment in many cases, but perhaps also a connection to his love for order, discipline, delineation, and time. Saturn, along with Mars, is often listed as a malefic planet. Malefic with Saturn, a diurnal planet, can mean a different thing than with Mars. In traditional writings, the malefic nature of Saturn seemed to be tied much more strongly to concepts of discipline, limits, and rules, than the inherent violence or catastrophic spirit of Mars. When positively aspected and in a good position, Saturn can come off more as the great teacher than the great malevolent spirit of death. He can bring a sense of duty and purpose, an ability to wait for the things that matter, and even bring us to an understanding about mortality. He is also tied to the things of the Earth, hearkening to his agricultural namesake. He is lead and dirt and growing and cutting and the scythe and much more.

It is interesting to note that he is a diurnal planet, even though he is associated with death, darkness, reaping, or time. The fact, however, is that Saturn to the Romans was an agricultural god as well. The reaping of the crops is not necessarily a *nocturnal* activity, is it? The fact is that sometimes the most difficult things we face are not bumps in the night or challenges fought in the moments of darkness we encounter. No, sometimes the most difficult challenges of life are in the everyday, right here in the full light of the Sun. There are other reasons that Saturn was a diurnal planet in historical astrology, but I like this philosophical approach to Saturn

---

4 *Works of Sahl & Masha'Allah*, trans. Benjamin N. Dykes (Minneapolis, MN: Cazimi Press, 2010), 463.

because I think it teaches us how to approach this planet and what he can do for us and teach us in our magic and our divination.

In chart interpretation, Saturn is looked to for the father, for timing, for death, and ending. He is sought in areas where hard lessons will be delivered, or where the reaping must happen. What must be cut away? What must be reformed, restrained, and taught? In good aspects of his teaching role, he is associated with the sciences, with good business practice (if stern and austere at times, as opposed to quick, entrepreneurial and innovative). He can bring more clarity to when something needs to end naturally, or if we need to swing the sickle ourselves to bring something to a close.

He is often older males in our lives, and those in a position of authority over us. This is not the king or the boss, not the Sun or Jupiter, but someone who has a more primal or longtime power over us. He can be ancestors, doctors, judges in serious cases, morticians, fathers-in-law, or land and property owners with whom we must deal. These people are often necessary facets of our lives, even if they can be unpleasant at times, and Saturn brings forth everything in his own time, irrespective of how we *wish* the timeframes would work themselves out. He is disinterested in what we *want* to happen, and more interested in things such as the right timing of an event, the just outcome, or the needed corrective discipline for the wayward soul.

*.*Saturn in Magic *.*

Saturn, perhaps more than any other planet we work with in astrology, bears the mantle of the reaper. Even though I firmly believe Saturn's influence moves and reaches far beyond the simplistic image of him as Death incarnate, it is true that he is invoked in necromancy. The grimoire tradition links his planetary hours to proper times to call forth the spirits of the dead. This ties into his association in astrology with professions that deal with the dead, such as undertakers and hangmen, and his almost scientific qualities where we can imagine him as working with the raw materials of life, the spiritual "lead" of our existence: cadavers and bodies and dirt. And as much as the reaper bearing a scythe may seem to trivialize the importance of Saturn as a more robust figure (and it certainly can), it is interesting to note that Agrippa does include in his works an image of Saturn as the scythe-bearer, and the image was supposed to help prolong mortal life.[5] Lilly also names him as Falcifer, the Scythe-Bearer.

His negativity was understood, however, as having a strong connection to the Earth, even (interestingly enough) to weather patterns.[6] Pentacles in *The Key of Solomon* link him to powers over the weather, including protection against hail and storms.[7] The same set of pentacles also includes workings to uncover hidden riches in the Earth, which hearkens back to the earthy quality of Saturn. It is interesting to note that *The Greek Magical Papyri* includes an "Oracle of Kronos" (Roman: Saturn) which draws upon the agricultural nature of the deity.[8] He is, in a way, like Pluto or Hades in this sense. Modern astrology has given a lot of this over to Pluto, but in traditional astrological magic, these domains all belonged to Saturn.

It is a fine line between the disciplinary nature of Saturn and the malefic side of him. *The Key of Solomon* says of him: "Although the Planet of Saturn … does not ordinarily have fortunate influences, it is nevertheless steadfast, especially if you can find it in a profitable position in the Heavens."[9] This is a good approach to working with Saturn magically. It all depends on situation, on timing, and on the rightness or wrongness of a working. Saturn is not something to invoke lightly, or for anything easy or gentle. He is a massive planet, and the final gatekeeper to the realms beyond, to the void where God lies. It is Death that opens the door to whatever lies beyond that black veil and Saturn lives at that threshold, toying with the

---

[5] Henricus Cornelius Agrippa, *Three Books of Occult Philosophy*, ed. Donald Tyson (St. Paul, MN: Llewellyn, 1993), 381.

[6] Stephen Skinner and David Rankine, *The Veritable Key of Solomon: Three Different Texts from Those Translated by S.L. MacGregor Mathers* (Singapore: Golden Hoard Press, 2017), 207.

[7] Ibid, 208.

[8] *The Greek Magical Papyri in Translation*, ed. Hans Dieter Betz (Chicago, IL: University of Chicago Press, 1996), 98.

[9] Stephen Skinner and David Rankine, *The Veritable Key of Solomon: Three Different Texts from Those Translated by S.L. MacGregor Mathers* (Singapore: Golden Hoard Press, 2017), 207.

keys that can open and unlock the final frontiers that we may be curious but afraid of when it comes to our magical practice.

The angel associated with him in most magical works is Cassiel, a far lesser-known angel to the masses than Raphael, Gabriel, or the ever-present Michael. Cassiel was a darker angel, linked in the grimoire tradition to the magics of Saturn that one might consider difficult or unpleasant, such as necromantic works, protection against black magic, or binding. His planetary squares in Agrippa are able to (if well aspected) create dignity and protection, whereas their negative versions are able to sow discord and cast people down from dignity, to create quarrels and disperse armies.[10]

Agrippa goes on to give epithets to the celestial spheres, and it is worth quoting his names of Saturn here, to show the varied-but-stern nature of this magical force.

> *Moreover they did call ... Saturn Coelius, Scythe-bearer, the father of the gods, the lord of the time, the high lord, the great, the wise, the intelligent, ingenious, revolutor of a long space, an old man of great profundity, the author of secret contemplation, impressing, or depressing great thoughts in the hearts of men, destroying and preserving all things, overturning force and power, and constituting a keeper of secret things...*[11]

⋆⋅⋆A Rite for Saturn ⋆⋅⋆

To aid in the long-term success of a business, to acquire a piece of property, to finalize an estate or will in your favor.

To be completed on the day and hour of Saturn, during the day.

---

[10] Henricus Cornelius Agrippa, *Three Books of Occult Philosophy*, ed. Donald Tyson (St. Paul, MN: Llewellyn, 1993), 318.

[11] Ibid, 426.

Astrological considerations

Saturn should be well-aspected to the Sun and/or Jupiter. Avoid a poorly aspected Mercury or a Mercury in detriment or fall.

Ritual Preparation

Prepare an altar in the center of your working space, with a black or gray cloth. I prefer an altar close to the ground or on the floor for this rite. Have one dark-colored candle, to the upper center of the altar, in gold or silver. Place four black stones at the corners of the table (jet or onyx are good). Have three long cords of leather or cloth in black, gray, or mixed dark colors. Prepare three sachets of dried herbs belonging to the domain of Saturn. You may also mix in stones or other corresponding items to the planet. Collect images and small items relating to the planet. Good choices include dark dried flowers, branches of willow, the tarot card of The World, etc. In the center of the altar, place a perfectly square piece of parchment with the symbol of Saturn and the following magic square in black ink:

4	9	2
3	5	7
8	1	6

·THE RITUAL

Light the candle and pass it over the parchment, making the invoking pentagram of Earth.

Invoke:

> **"From the North, Cassiel, Falcifer, reaper and ruler. Dis Pater, father of riches, keep pure and holy the work and make right the path."**

Replace the candle and move the four stones from the edge of the table in a clockwise fashion to the four corners of the parchment. As you place each stone, invoke:

> **"To the corners of the world, squared and even."**

Take up the three cords and secure them on one end with a knot. You will be braiding the cords together. Braid slowly and methodically, focusing entirely on the work, envisioning as you go the accomplishment of your intentions. As you braid, begin to work in the images and sachets you have gathered. You can use smaller pieces of cord or twine if needed, as you go. Weave together the work while seated or kneeling in front of your altar. As you braid and connect your working, invoke:

"Seven for the doors, the points of Light, which pass through nine, which is three over itself. One is the soul, the center of All, that brings forth the two: my spirit and the mirror. By winding knot and evening song, the harvest comes and fills the storehouses of the holy. Cassiel from the North, and Chronos in time, turn the wheel of silence.

Shroud of faith and Will of Earth.
Shroud of faith and will of Earth.
Shroud of faith and will of Earth."

Continue repeating the above line as you complete the braid, and all items are worked into your cord. When finished, knot the end of the cord firmly and coil it onto the parchment in a clockwise pattern, creating a spiral. Stand over the altar with left hand extended over the center of the work and right hand pointing down to the Earth. Proclaim:

"It is finished."

Leave your candle to burn down (safely) and keep the work upon the altar for seven days or until the completion of the magic. Dispose of the work only when it is accomplished and on the day of Saturn.

SATURN CORRESPONDENCES
Cold, Dry, Diurnal, Masculine

As Above / So Below

IN THE HOROSCOPE

Domicile	Capricorn and Aquarius
Exaltation	Libra
Detriment	Cancer and Leo
Fall	Aries
House of Joy	12th

THE MAGICAL WORLD

Day	Saturday
Colors	Black, gray, dull browns
Archangel	Cassiel
Sephirah	Binah (Understanding)
Tarot	The World
Divinities	Saturn, Chronos, Set, Kali, Ops, Rhea, The Norns, The Fates, Moros, Janus
Magical Intent	Speaking to spirits of the dead, endings, discipline, time constraints, protection from inclement weather, discerning issues surrounding aging, protection from evil spirits or the wicked dead, wills and estates, invoking a teacher

THE NATURAL WORLD

Mineral	Lead, dust, raw earth, black stones and crystals, sapphire, brown jasper, lodestone
Flora	Wolfsbane, hemlock, poppies (opium), henbane, hellebore, nightshade, willow, yew, sage, rue
Fauna	Jackass, mice, moles, wolf, dog, crocodile, scorpion, tortoises, bats, eels, gnats, flies, owl, crow, hogs, peacocks, lamprey, toad, serpents, all vermin
Fumigations	Myrrh, odoriferous roots

PLANETARY CONDITIONS

Dignities, Debilities, Aspects, and More

Once you have met the seven planets of traditional astrology, it is important to understand how they feel and act within the heavenly spaces they
inhabit on their journeys. Think of them just as you would real intelligences, like people, spirits, animals, or other conscious beings. They can
be just like us, with all our worries, prideful moments, and preferences.
Are we comfortable in every space we enter? Do some houses make us ill
at ease? Have you ever entered someone's home and felt comfortable in
some very real and unexplainable way? Some places just have that innate
ability to make us feel "at home." This is the same with the planets. They
move and act within the heavenly spaces in different ways depending on
where we find them and what their relationships are to each other. The
signs and houses will be explored even further in a later chapter, but for
now just remember that each planet has strong likes, dislikes, attributes,
and associations. And these qualities are affected by the area in which the
planets inhabit (signs and houses). Astrology has many ways of interpreting
how the planets "feel" and operate within their movements. This chapter
will focus on the major tools astrology uses to delineate and understand
these relationships.

The first things are the *dignities* and the *debilities*. These are a set of
situations planets can find themselves in that are crucial in astrology. A
planet in a position where it enjoys being, where its nature is reflected
well, where it has common agreement or comfort, is said to have "dignity."
A planet in a location where its nature is challenged or nullified, where it
feels ill at ease, out of place, or smothered, is said to have "debility." The
logic behind why we label certain areas advantageous or disadvantageous
will be explained as we go along, but for now, just remember that planets
react very differently within the various signs and houses of the horoscope.
This concept of "dignities" was a central factor in traditional astrology

that is sometimes downplayed in more modern approaches. Dignity is so central, in fact, to traditional concepts of astrology that it is one of the first things I teach students to look for and list when they interpret a chart.

Think of it this way: Suppose you are dealing with a group of friends. If you were to never consider these friends' situations and personal environments, would you be able to understand them at all? You label, let's say, Tom as steadfast, strong, and good with money, and Sarah as intelligent and always put-together. Does that mean Tom is always going to be the strong one? He can never change his behaviors? Can Sarah never have an off-day where she is forgetful or frenetic? Of course they can change. Tom might be dealing with a tragedy or a personal challenge. Sarah might have been demoted at work or have moved into a new position where she feels lost and uncomfortable. Even though they will both keep their essential natures, those natures will be heavily affected by the situations they deal with in daily life and in their environment. And, within every good quality is the seed of its opposite. The road to hell is paved with good intentions, as trite as it may sound. Someone good with money and even-keeled can become greedy or cold-hearted in the wrong situation. Someone who is steadfast can also be inflexible if put in a difficult circumstance. The seven Heavenly Spheres are no different. They move and change, and their attributes are colored by experience, time, and location.

*˙*Sect *˙*˙

Sect refers to the play of night and day within astrology. The planets can either be diurnal (preferring the day) or nocturnal (preferring the night). Traditionally, sect was considered quintessential for astrological interpretation, but modern astrology largely avoids talking about sect in most works that teach chart reading. I think this goes to the root of what has been discussed in this book already, about how we approach astrology from our experience here on Earth. As cosmic as astrology is, we must live it through our daily experience. What is more primal and basic than our circadian rhythms of day and night? Dawn, noon, the setting sun, midnight revelries, nighttime escapades, and late mornings. All of these concepts are crucial in our experience as humans. We have mythological and psychological associations with day and night that run very deep within our cultures and our own personal experiences. Therefore, I still think sect is important to consider for any student of astrology. The planets act and move in different ways in our lives depending on their sect. In traditional astrology, sect is given as follows:

Diurnal planets: The Sun, Jupiter, Saturn

Nocturnal planets: Mars, Venus, the Moon

Common: Mercury

⋆⋆⋆Rulership, or Domicile ⋆⋆⋆

The seven planets rule over the signs of the zodiac, and when a planet is within a sign it rules it is said to be in *rulership*, or *domicile*. The rulerships of the planets within the zodiac have a natural and beautiful symmetry in traditional astrology that draws from the cycles of the year. The two brightest lights within our sky, the Sun and the Moon, rule the signs of Leo and Cancer, which are summer months, full of lots of light. Then we move outward, with each planet ruling two signs until we reach the final planet, Saturn, the dread reaper and disciplinarian planet that guards the final gates before the deeper realms of the primum mobile and the highest heaven of the gods. This final planet, naturally, rules the wintry signs of Capricorn and Aquarius.

A planet in rulership is a planet in its own house. It is comfortable, exuding control and measured power. We are always more on our game during home games. We know our own landscapes and hideaways better than anyone else, and the planets are no different. Planets in rulership are given hefty weight in interpreting charts because they are in positions of authority. They are monarchs in their own kingdoms, safe behind walls they are intimately familiar with. A planet in rulership is not going to act in the same challenged way as planets may act when they are in different situations within the chart. Any planet in rulership should be given extra weight and consideration while interpreting a chart, be it horary or natal.

Rulership is considered so important in traditional astrology that we look to the rulers of the signs, even when those rulers aren't located in that sign. Let's say we need to interpret something that is going on in the sign of Aries. Well, we are going to have to look and see what Mars is doing, even if he isn't in Aries. His nature will be important, because rulership is a guiding theme for the Art.

Planetary Rulerships on the Zodiac

*⋆⁎⋆*Exaltation *⋆⁎⋆*

Each planet is *exalted* in one sign. These placements have multiple historical reasonings behind them, but much of the knowledge as to why certain planets were placed in exaltation in certain signs has been lost to us. There is speculation as to whether it was based on agricultural cycles, Babylonian traditions, Hellenistic concepts, or something else entirely, but the truth is that much has been passed down and preserved, but much has been lost as well. As was noted before in the book, it is important to remember that most of the astrology we are dealing with is tied to concepts stemming from Eurocentric worldviews, which means a worldview as it pertains to the Northern Hemisphere and with Northern Hemispheric relationships to seasons and tides of the year. It is up to each individual student of astrology as to how she might want to rectify or change this if working in an area to which this will not apply. There are many resources for more modern schools of astrology that take such things into consideration and provide resources and platforms for those outside the bounds of traditional astrology. Star lore is expressed in many different patterns across cultures, and indigenous systems are just as valid and powerful as traditional astrology stemming from Hellenistic sources.

✦.✦ THE PRECISE EXALTATIONS ✦.✦	
Planet	Precise Exaltation
☾ Moon	3° of Taurus ♉
☿ Mercury	15° of Virgo ♍
♀ Venus	27° of Pisces ♓
☉ Sun	19° of Aries ♈
♂ Mars	28° Capricorn ♑
♃ Jupiter	15° of Cancer ♋
♄ Saturn	21° of Libra ♎

Exaltation means that a planet is in a place where its nature and attributes are comfortable, celebrated, and raised high. A planet in a sign of exaltation will exert its influence openly with grace, dignity, and power. In most resources, the exaltation of a planet is within a whole sign of the zodiac, but in certain traditional sources, it is specific degrees of each sign in which a planet is exalted. I prefer to teach the system wherein a planet is in exaltation in an entire sign, but Dorotheus of Sidon, a titan in traditional astrology, gives the following degrees for the exaltations of the planets. [1] These are also found in other historical sources for the exaltations as well.

For me, the exaltations have a natural and inherent beauty and logic that can be explained when we look at the nature and attributes of each planet. The Sun, hot and dry, would naturally be exalted in Aries, the fiery first sign of the zodiac, containing within it the Spring Equinox, when the Sun seems to be reborn to us again. The Moon, so tied to our earthly experience and exuding control over the cycles of the year and being a resource for centuries to farmers who planted around Moon cycles, makes sense in Taurus, an earthy sign of fecundity. Mercury is exalted in Virgo, a sign that it rules over, a sign of the harvest season and the tides of communication and change in preparation for the winter to come. Venus, a watery and nocturnal planet, finds exaltation in Pisces, itself the most watery of signs: mutable, Water of Water. Love is a fluid thing, after all. Mars is exalted in Capricorn, a wintry sign that is ruled by the second malefic, Saturn, and is dead in winter when calamity might come, and planning was necessary to avoid the harsh realities of the Earth. Jupiter, encompassing so many attributes of beneficence, dominion, expansion, and kingship, seems at ease in Cancer, a sign that is cardinal, directive, containing the Summer Solstice and related to families, fathers, mothers, and household. And finally Saturn is exalted in Libra, the scales, a symbol of weights, measurements, and justice—all things that can tie, at least symbolically, to the disciplined and measured nature of the taskmaster that is the final planet.

I am not saying that the above is not a "stretch" perhaps in determining why the planets are given certain exaltations, but I do believe that the more you work with the planets and the more charts you construct and interpret, you will find a natural flow to the exaltations.

---

[1] Dorotheus of Sidon, *Carmen Astrologicum*, trans. Benjamin N. Dykes (Minneapolis, MN: The Cazimi Press, 2019), 64.

✦✫✦Detriment✦✫✦

A planet is in *detriment* when it is in the sign, or signs, that are opposite of the signs it rules. So, the Sun rules Leo and is in rulership there. When it is in Aquarius, it is 180 degrees away from its rulership and thus is in detriment. A planet in detriment is off-key, it is in a house it does not want to be in, an environment that is not conducive to joy or familiar to the wanderer. Things may seem disorganized in how this planet acts, or seem corrupted in some way. How a planet acts in detriment may come off as scattered, struggling, or weak.

✦✫✦ PLANETS IN DETRIMENT ✦✫✦	
Planet	**Fall**
☽ Moon	♑ Capricorn
☿ Mercury	♐ Sagittarius & ♓ Pisces
♀ Venus	♏ Scorpio & ♈ Aries
☉ Sun	♒ Aquarius
♂ Mars	♎ Libra & ♉ Taurus
♃ Jupiter	♊ Gemini & ♍ Virgo
♄ Saturn	♋ Cancer & ♌ Leo

✦✫✦Fall✦✫✦

A planet is in *fall* when it is in the sign opposite its exaltation. A planet in fall is blinded, unable to be seen or heard correctly. Its value goes unappreciated or silenced by the world. This is a serious debility for a planet and should be given strong weight when interpreting a planet's actions within the chart.

✦.✦ PLANETS IN FALL ✦.✦.	
Planet	**Fall**
☽ Moon	♏ Scorpio
☿ Mercury	♓ Pisces
♀ Venus	♍ Virgo
☉ Sun	♎ Libra
♂ Mars	♋ Cancer
♃ Jupiter	♑ Capricorn
♄ Saturn	♈ Aries

I believe the place of fall for the planets, like exaltation, follows a natural feel and logic to the planetary system. The Moon, a fluid planet of phases and emotional experience, falls in Scorpio, a sign of fixed Water, essentially: ice. Mercury, that planet of communication, logic, mathematics, the real incarnation of the *logos* falls in Pisces, a mutable sign of Water where clarity and logic might not be able to express itself to the fullest. Venus, the goddess of love and the benefic that forgives faults and is gentle, beautiful, and fecund, falls in Virgo, a sign of planning and mercurial logic. The Sun falls in Libra, an airy sign of Venus, where kingship might not feel at ease. Mars, the warrior spirit and red star of rage and revolution falls in the sign of Cancer, a lunar and watery sign that perhaps does not provide a good environment for the firebrand planet. Jupiter, all growth and beneficence, falls in Capricorn, the wintry sign ruled by Saturn, where discipline reigns supreme and constraint is everywhere. And finally Saturn, that cutter and reaper of life that desires boundary, delineation, and finality, falls in Aries, a sign where beginnings should matter, and where fiery creative impulse should be given free rein.

✦.✦ Triplicity Rulers ✦.✦

As we will see when we examine the horoscope later, the classical elements are central to understanding and working with astrology. Another dignity used in traditional astrology is that of *triplicity rulers*. Within this system, planets are given power in certain signs based on *sect* (whether they are diurnal or nocturnal). Each grouping of signs (the elemental groupings) is given three ruling planets: one for the day, one for the night, and a third that participates regardless of sect. Triplicity rulership was heavily used in classical astrological systems, such as those of Vettius Valens and Dorotheus of Sidon. Ptolemy used a differing version of the triplicity system. His system would be further popularized by the popular astrologer William Lilly.

Signs	Day Ruler	Night Ruler	Participating Ruler
♉ Taurus, ♍ Virgo, ♑ Capricorn	♀ Venus	☽ Moon	♂ Mars
♊ Gemini, ♎ Libra, ♒ Aquarius	♄ Saturn	☿ Mercury	♃ Jupiter
♈ Aries, ♌ Leo, ♐ Sagittarius	☉ Sun	♃ Jupiter	♄ Saturn
♋ Cancer, ♏ Scorpio, ♓ Pisces	♀ Venus	♂ Mars	☽ Moon

A planet that has triplicity rulership (determined vis-à-vis day and night, or *sect*) is going to have a stronger influence over the interpretation of the chart. The planet bears more dignity in these situations, just as it does for other dignities such as exhalation or domicile. Dorotheus of Sidon, and other Hellenistic astrologers, gave hefty weight to these situations and believed a planet in triplicity had significant import when interpreting charts. Consider it when assigning dignity to the planets in your charts.

*٭*Terms and Face *٭*

In traditional astrology sources, there are two more areas where a planet may have dignity. The first is called *term*. This can also be known as *limit* or *bounds*. This is perhaps the most complicated dignity to deal with for students because there are multiple systems used to delineate terms and they do not agree. We also have conflicting historical information as to the how and why of this system. I am not going to go into the debates and historical research used to determine the basis of this system, but I do think it is important for students of astrology to be aware of it and able to recognize it within the chart. Within a system of terms, each zodiac sign is divided into sections of five. The Sun and Moon are not included, so we are dealing with just the five planets, hence each sign is divided into an area for five planets.

The first system of terms you might encounter is known as the Egyptian system. The second most common system of terms you will run into is the Ptolemaic system. Things get even more confusing when you realize that there exists more than one system of "Ptolemaic terms." I recommend that you explore the various systems for terms, but as an astrologer I have used the Egyptian system for most of my studies, and it is the system I teach. Below is a table of the Egyptian terms, which breaks down the degrees of each sign by the planets that rule the five "terms" of the given sign.

✦ ✦ ✦ EGYPTIAN TERMS ✦ ✦ ✦

Sign	1st Term Ruler	2nd Term Ruler	3rd Term Ruler	4th Term Ruler	5th Term Ruler
♈ Aries	0-6° Jupiter	6-12° Venus	12-20° Mercury	20-25° Mars	25-30° Saturn
♉ Taurus	0-8° Venus	8-14° Mercury	14-22° Jupiter	22-27° Saturn	27-30° Mars
♊ Gemini	0-6° Mercury	6-12° Jupiter	12-17° Venus	17-24° Mars	24-30° Saturn
♋ Cancer	0-7° Mars	7-13° Venus	13-18° Mercury	18-26° Jupiter	26-30° Saturn
♌ Leo	0-6° Jupiter	6-11° Venus	11-18° Saturn	18-24° Mercury	24-30° Mars
♍ Virgo	0-7° Mercury	7-17° Venus	17-21° Jupiter	21-28° Mars	28-30° Saturn
♎ Libra	0-6° Saturn	6-14° Mercury	14-21° Jupiter	21-28° Venus	28-30° Mars
♏ Scorpio	0-7° Mars	7-11° Venus	11-19° Mercury	19-24° Jupiter	24-30° Saturn
♐ Sagittarius	0-12° Jupiter	12-17° Venus	17-21° Mercury	21-26° Saturn	26-30° Mars
♑ Capricorn	0-7° Mercury	7-14° Jupiter	14-22° Venus	22-26° Saturn	26-30° Mars
♒ Aquarius	0-7° Mercury	7-13° Venus	13-20° Jupiter	20-25° Mars	25-30° Saturn
♓ Pisces	0-12° Venus	12-16° Jupiter	16-19° Mercury	19-28° Mars	28-30° Saturn

The next to tackle is *face*. The system of faces is a system of 10. It breaks each sign down into 10° partitions called *decans*.[2] Each sign, therefore, has three faces. Ten degrees, times three, gives us the full 30° of each sign (12 x 30 = 360, the full circle of the horoscope and its signs). Just like the system of terms discussed above, there were disagreements about face in traditional astrology. Some believe the system is related to the ancient Egyptian system of breaking the year down into portions ruled by starry gods. There was also disagreement as to the ordering of the faces and to how important they were in astrological consideration. Ptolemy, and other authors, ordered the planets in their descent from the furthest (Saturn) to the closest (the Moon). If we start in Aries, we begin with Mars (because it rules Aries) and then move down the line with the Sun, Venus, etc. This is following the Chaldean order of the planets, moving through the Heavenly Spheres continually as we move through the zodiac.

---

2   Also called decantes.

Decans on the Zodiac

Some astrologers, such as Firmicus, gave a lot of weight to this system of faces, and it was held to be crucial in interpreting charts. [3] For the student of astrology, I recommend starting simply by considering the terms and decans as lesser dignities, giving some positive influence on planets that are in their own term or face, but giving less weight than we would for domicile, exaltation, or triplicity rulership (all discussed above). If a planet is negatively aspected, or has debilities, then being in term or face might save the planet from exhibiting the worst of these debilitated characteristics. As you progress in making charts and working with the conditions of the planets, you will explore new ways to interpret these more complex concepts and build a stronger foundation in their use. Do not be overwhelmed by charts, numbers, and glyphs. The language and sacred

---

3 "Faces," Deborah Houlding, *Skyscript*, accessed September 2020, http://www.sky-script.co.uk/gl/faces.html.

geometry of the Art get easier with time, becoming like a comfortable second language. Trust me, you can become bilingual!

✦✦✦Peregrine ✦✦✦

From a term meaning "wanderer" or "pilgrim," a planet that is *peregrine* is a planet with no dignities or debilities. It is essentially lost within the chart. This was not considered a positive thing in many sources. We may be tempted to say, "No news is good news," but we can counter that with the equally trite-but-true, "There is no such thing as bad press." A planet that is peregrine is muted, with little influence, and has difficulty expressing its energy or presence within the chart. Think of the intelligence of the planetary spirit just like you would a person. Someone who is aimless, ill at ease, with no comfortable place to lay their head is not going to exhibit their best selves to the world. There is a strong feeling of being "lost" when a planet is completely unmoored in the chart. Modern astrology students do not often give as much negative weight to a planet being peregrine as the ancients did. I do consider peregrine planets to be in a significant debility and take this into consideration in my charts.

✦✦✦The Almuten ✦✦✦

The planet with the most dignity in a chart is known as the *almuten*, from the Arabic term for "firm" or "strong one."[4] This concept looks for the planet that is the most heavily dignified within the chart, bearing the most positive situations in its placement. This planet should be looked to as a dominant or controlling force in natal charts. The almuten is likely to have a lot to say about a matter at hand or the nature of a person's nativity. As an astrologer, I often find a good pathway to breaking the bad habits of Sun-sign astrology is to look for the almuten in a birth chart. I often

---

4   An important note: In many historical works, there was not just one almuten. The almuten could be for a particular house, sign, etc. For the beginner astrologer, I find that determining the planet with the highest dignity for the entire chart is sufficient. If you wish to calculate the most dignified planet for each scenario as you advance, that is a good practice for the advanced student.

find that the almuten of a person's nativity has far more to say about them than their Sun sign might.

To use a personal example, my Sun sign is Cancer. According to cultural memes and tabloid horoscopes, the qualities I should possess the strongest would be Cancerian traits (and modern interpretations of those traits, at that). The planet with the most dignity, the almuten, of my chart is Mercury, though. Considering I am an astrologer, a language educator, and a professional translator and interpreter in my mundane life, it seems that Mercury exerts more influence than my Sun sign. I highly recommend examining the almuten in your own birth chart and exploring if it resonates more fully with your experience than a simple reading of your Sun sign. It can be a good exercise to understand planetary influence.

A popular way to determine the almuten is with a scoring system, such as that devised by William Lilly in his *Christian Astrology*, which became a popular classic of astrological instruction. Lilly included complicated conditional situations involving aspects, retrograde motion, reception, and other ideas. I think it is best to begin, as a student, with the major dignities and debilities. The table below gives a simple system of scoring you can use to determine the almuten of a chart, assigning values to the conditions that planets can have. If two planets tie, look to other conditions, such as sect, and positive aspects. Once you are comfortable identifying the almuten, or if you have a chart where it is difficult to decide, you can look to further dignities and debilities to qualify the planets.

*. CALCULATING THE ALMUTEN *.	
Dignity or Debility	**Score**
Domicile/Rulership	+5
Exaltation	+4
Triplicity	+3
Terms	+2
Face	+1
Detriment	-5
Fall	-4
Peregrine	-5

*˙*Reception *˙*

Planets can "receive" one another like guests. For example, if Mercury is in Leo then the Sun is "receiving" Mercury, because the Sun rules Leo. Sometimes, this relationship can be quite powerful. There is a system known as *mutual reception* that occurs in times where planets are found in similar situations vis-à-vis each other. This is easier to explain with an example. Let's say that Mars is in Leo and the Sun is in Aries. This is a powerful mutual reception by rulership because the Sun is in a house ruled Mars, and Mars is in a house ruled by the Sun. The relationship between these two planets is going to be strong.

Sun and Mars in Mutual Reception by Domicile

Mutual reception can happen with exaltation as well. If the Moon is in Cancer and Jupiter is in Taurus, then there is mutual reception by exaltation because the Moon is exalted in Taurus and Jupiter is exalted in Cancer.

There are other systems that can create mutual reception, such as face, triplicity ruler, etc. but I have found that reception by the major dignities and debilities (domicile, exaltation, detriment, fall) have the greatest effect on the chart. Negative reception can really hinder planets as well, and the condition of the planets should always be considered. If two planets have mutual reception, but one planet is heavily debilitated, then the reception will not have as powerful of a connection or as positive of an influence as if the planet were unhindered.

The Moon and Jupiter in Mutual
Reception by Exaltation

⋆⋆⋆Retrograde⋆⋆⋆

One of the most common conversations around modern astrology is the
dreaded "Mercury retrograde." Even people who do not follow astrology
have most likely seen references online to this phenomenon and seen or
heard people complaining about how it ruins communication, technology,
or small daily tasks. Believers claim it makes everything just a bit more
difficult. Although there is not nearly the historical fear of this condition
of Mercury as there is in modern astrology, there is indeed a concept of
retrogradation in traditional astrology.

A planet in retrograde is a planet that appears to move backward from its normal track when viewed from Earth. In traditional sources, retrograde planets *could* mean negative influence. There was also, however, a concept that a retrograde planet meant quick change, returning to a starting point (hence the name retrograde: *stepping backward*), or something being cut short. Lilly gives many examples of retrograde planets creating situations of necessary returns, starting over, or things being cut short (even a life, in serious circumstances).[5] In my personal astrology, I often agree with Lilly and find retrograde planets as "going against the grain" in a way, requiring us to step back, to deal with sudden change or unexpected happenings. A planet that is retrograde, in my experience, can exhibit erratic characteristics.

*.*Aspects and Orb *.*

Aspects are the mathematical relationships between the planets in a chart. The planets, traveling in apparently circular motions around the horoscope, relate to one another in angular patterns. These patterns have spiritual and divinatory significance in astrology. In traditional astrology, the aspects were *conjunction*, *opposition*, *sextile*, *trine*, and the *square*. Modern astrology has added many other aspects such as *quincunxes* and *bisextiles*, but these are not found in most traditional sources and are outside of the sacred geometry used in astrological sources from the pre-modern world.

ORB

Orb refers to the areas around a planet and how we use that area to determine relationships between the planets. In many traditional sources, the views toward orb were not as precise as we often see in more modern applications of the Art. For example, if we believe that two planets are in a square (see below) because they are 90° apart, then how exact must that 90° be? There are differing opinions on this, with some astrologers giving complex tables of exactly how many degrees "around" a planet count

---

5 See previously sourced *Christian Astrology*. Lilly gives examples of retrograde influence throughout his aphorisms both for nativities and horary technique.

when it comes to calculating aspects. I have a differing opinion, which I believe was common in many older applications of astrology. I use the signs as my delineators. So, for me, it isn't so much that squared planets are a perfect 90° apart so much as that the planets that are squared are four signs apart.[6] For me, the sacred geometry of the 12 signs and the relationships of the planets within them are more important factors than the precise degrees of orb around each planet.

The only aspect where I take orb into consideration heavily is conjunction, which is described below. I do tend to only consider two planets conjunct if they are within 10° of each other. I also do not consider planets conjunct if they are separated by the boundaries of the signs. This is a controversial position for some astrologers, who prefer to stick to orb as the defining factor of any aspect, not just conjunction. I can only say that through my years of chart reading and experience with the Art, I have found the boundaries of the signs to be demarcations in a very spiritual sense that disrupt the nature of aspects. I believe that this approach goes to what I have repeatedly tried to show throughout this book: Astrology is a spiritual Art based on a holistic and magical view of the microcosm and macrocosm. It is not, for me, a purely causal science. I do encourage my students to explore, however, and determine for themselves how the sacred geometry of the horoscope works for them. There are traditions in astrology, and established practice, but there is room for disagreement as well.

CONJUNCTION AND COMBUSTION

A *conjunction*, according to sticklers for terminology in astrology, is not technically an aspect but instead a unique relationship of planets. I include it here among aspects for simplicity's sake since it is usually assessed as we assess other aspects. Planets are in conjunction when they occupy the same space within the Heavenly arena. We see, from the Earth, the two planets in close relationship. They are in a dance together, united and relating to one another intimately. Conjunction represents working together, a blending and beautiful dance of energy. Sometimes this closeness can be complicated, if the planets are malefic (Mars and Saturn conjunct with

---

6   This four-sign distance is why the square was also called a *quartile*, or *quadrate*.

other planets, for example). Remember, closeness is not always positive. Conjunction is all about the coming together of the influences of the two planets in question.

To give an example, Vettius Valens, when addressing someone who has Venus as a powerful indicator in the chart, tells us that if Mercury is conjunct this powerfully influential Venus, then the person in question might be a musician. [7] Why is that? Well, Venus controls the arts, and public pleasures. Mercury is about communication and is a powerful planet of change and the delivery of information. If we combine the power of Venus' artistic beauty with Mercury's expressionism, then we can easily come to the image of a musician.

There was also a special consideration given to planets that were conjunct with the Sun. This system was called *combustion*. A planet is *combust* when it is conjunct the Sun. From our Earthly perspective, a planet conjunct the Sun would not be visible. The brightness of the Sun would swallow up the brightness given off from the planet. This was usually interpreted negatively, as a planet being suffocated by external influences, by authority figures (the Sun frequently being associated with monarchs and authority figures) or burned up by the heat of the brightest star we deal with in our lives. Some authors gave special consideration to whether a planet was moving toward or away from the Sun, and the exact degrees of the conjunction with the Sun. I will not go into the full systems here, but it can be worth examining further if a combustion places a significant part in a chart you are interpreting. [8]

7   Vettius Valens, *Anthologies*, trans. Mark Riley, accessed June 2020, https://www.csus. edu/indiv/r/rileymt/Vettius%20Valens%20entire.pdf, 27.

8   For more in-depth looks at how combustion works, look to Lilly's *Christian Astrology*, to Vettius Valens' *Anthologies*, or al-Biruni. All are sourced in this work and contain more detailed descriptions of the special considerations around combustion.

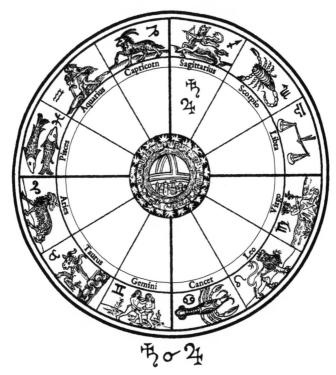

Saturn and Jupiter in Conjunction in Sagittarius

OPPOSITION

Planets are in *opposition* when they are 180° from each other (quite literally: opposed). If the Sun is in Cancer and the Moon in Capricorn, then they are in opposition because those signs are opposite from one another. This is related to the houses of "detriment" as well, as spoken of above. William Lilly describes the state of two planets in opposition as a state of "perfect hatred."[9] These are not minced words. Some classical sources are a bit gentler in describing this aspect, but the struggle is inherent even in the name of this aspect. The planets oppose one another. They work against each other and provide a negative relationship that can present challenges, disagreements, and disharmonies in how the two planets operate in the chart. Consider this a strained relationship, a difficult meeting of two

---

9   William Lilly, *Christian Astrology: Books 1 & 2*, ed. David R. Roell (Bel Air, MD: Astrology Classics, 2004), 106.

minds that are not seeing each other's point of view clearly. The Earth stands between them, so they are blinded to the other perspective. They cannot even see one another, so how could they relate peacefully? This is an aspect of separation.

Mars and Venus in Opposition

TRINE

The concept of the *trine*, as its name indicates, relates to the triangle, a shape that comes up repeatedly in astrology (and many spiritual traditions). The trine is a relationship that *triangulates* the heavenly bodies, with planets 120° from one another. This forms a perfect triangle on the chart. Now, there can be a trine between two planets, or three planets can form the perfect triangle. The central point is that there are 120° between the planets in question. Due to the influence of triangulation in historical spirituality, philosophy, and art, this aspect was given hefty weight as a very benefic situation by most traditional sources. The sacred triangle, used to represent so many spiritual truths (from the divine feminine, to the Trinity, and more) is foundationally important in sacred geometry. Planets in trine have mutual support from each other, and work together. There is facility, and ease of movement. There is understanding, concord, and open pathways of communication. If the planets are intelligent beings, then the trine represents those intelligences working together, understanding, and really *hearing* one another. The conversation is pleasant and guided toward mutual goals and peaceful resolution.

The Sun Trine Mercury

SEXTILE

The *sextile* occurs when planets are 60° apart. The sextile is an angle divisible by three, and so it does have some weight to it within the systems of sacred geometry. Many of my fellow astrologers see the sextile as similar to the trine, but of a weaker degree. My experience has led me to similar conclusions. Planets in sextile influence one another, but not as strongly as they do when we are dealing with a trine. Consider them in communication, but not as openly or frequently as planets in trine. If the trine is a group of friends, or family members, then the sextile is a group of acquaintances. They can work together, even have mutual support and humor with one another, but they are not going to give their entire selves to the union in the way that can happen in the harmonious nature of a trine.

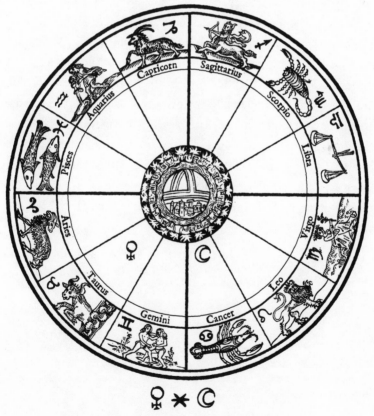

Venus in Sextile with the Moon

Square

Planets are *squared* when they are 90° from each other. Lilly, in *Christian Astrology*, interprets the negative influence of this aspect as weaker than that of opposition, calling it an "imperfect hatred."[10] There is strain in this relationship, but with some hope of working together. The relationship is not in complete disagreement, but there are hindrances to the two planets working together harmoniously. Their influences, when they mingle, will seem forced, uncomfortable, or come with blockages. In my personal readings, I often find that a square represents repeated challenges that come up throughout the situations or associations of the two heavenly bodies in question.

To some traditional sources, squares were only truly negative influences if they involved the malefic planets of Mars and Saturn. There is wisdom in this, as not all squares are quintessentially "bad." Relationships can be complicated, even rocky, without being terrible or destructive. When dealing with a square in the chart, consider the situation of the planets involved and whether they have dignities, or debilities. This will heavily color the nature of the squared planets. In my own practice, this interpretation of the square has led to very meaningful readings. Heavily debilitated planets in a square are going to have a much more negative influence than squared planets that bear a lot of dignity. Think of it as two friends who argue. Are they arguing and debating to help improve the other person? Or are they just fighting? Difficulties can sometimes lead to growth.

---

10   Ibid.

♀ □ ♃

Mercury Squared Jupiter

*˙*Symbols*˙*

All of this information is often recorded by astrologers using a unique set of symbols. Below is a chart of useful symbols for organizing your information when reading charts. These are universal symbols used across systems by most Western astrologers.

. ASTROLOGICAL SYMBOLS *.*	
Condition	**Symbol**
Conjunction	☌
Opposition	☍
Sextile	⚹
Trine	△
Square	☐
Retrograde	℞
North Node (Ascending)	☊
South Node (Descending)	☋

*.*Final Words: Where Are You?*.*

All of this information is a guide to understanding the planets and how they interact in the Art. The question we are always asking is, "Where are you?" What sign are you in? What is happening? Understanding how planets are expressing themselves, due to their environment, will give you the strongest foundation in interpreting charts. Having taught astrology to many different students, I find that introducing the dignities and debilities and making sure students are comfortable with the system leads to the greatest growth in their knowledge of astrology. The planets have many historical correspondences and a real spirit behind them, but they are not static. Their movement through the various houses and signs colors everything about how they act. It is crucial to understand that the planets can display their qualities in both positive and negative ways, based on their circumstances. They are similar to us in that way. We may be a steadfast person but have all had to change and adapt based on our situation. Knowing this will guide you in appreciating how to interpret and work with the seven wandering stars.

THE FIXED STARS

⋆⋆⋆ The Old Gods ⋆⋆⋆

Keeping with our theme of beginning from the Earth and moving outward, an elevation and emanation in our approach, we move from the spheres of the planets into the realm of the fixed stars. The fixed stars include those in the constellations of the zodiac as well as those that exist in the constellations outside of that belt of signs. [1] These stars do not wander the way that planets do, and they are seen as above the seven Heavenly Spheres, part of the "Firmament" which by its definition means *fixed*. They are closer to God, to the higher intelligence and divine will manifested in the universe. Working with them in terms of the constellations of the zodiac can be tricky, since Western astrology is not *sidereal* (solely star-based) but *tropical*, meaning that the seasons and times of the signs we use do not match the constellations as they once did due to the Earth's actions on its axis. [2]

That does not mean, however, that they should be ignored or avoided by the serious practitioner. They play an important role in traditional astrological divination and magic. It is also true that we grow up knowing certain constellations, and even young stargazers with little experience can often point out the Big Dipper, or a favorite constellation they learned in school. These stars are part of our experience of living on this planet and what we see when we look up into the night sky. They have a quite different influence compared to the wandering planets that we

---

[1]   Some sources separate the stars of the zodiac constellations from the stars of other constellations. The zodiac exists in the *primum mobile* in some systems, whereas the fixed stars of the constellations outside of the belt of the zodiac are in the firmament, the Empyrean Heaven or one of many other terms associated with the highest heavens that exist beyond the seven Heavenly Spheres.

[2]   We will explore this further in chapter 11.

know—thanks to modern astronomical imaging, in a different and more varied, visual way. We can imagine the red and desert-like Mars or the stormy and multicolored face of Jupiter because we have all seen them in textbooks, but the sheer empty light of the enormous stars that populate the universe comes to our imagination and our spirit in a different way. They are also more tied to our location, as where we are on the Earth determines for us what the starry sky will look like and what we might find therein. The astrologer must know where she plants her feet before she can determine what stars are going to shine above her head.

In terms of spirituality, the fixed stars have a unique feel compared to the planets. The fixed stars are, well, *fixed*. By that very nature they have a strength and timelessness to them that provides a constant source of inspiration. In a way, they are higher in the spiritual chain, closer to a philosophical concept of the divine than the more human and evolutionary figures of mythology that we have given over as archetypes for the planets. When we imagine the god Mars (the war deity) or Venus (the Roman goddess of love), we are conjuring personalities, art, temples, and stories. When we look to the fixed stars we are dealing with a more primal concept of light, heat, and creation. They are not as personable as the planets, not as causally related to the mythologies we know and understand. They are beyond that, harder to grasp, older gods with stories told in ways beyond the narrative paths we are accustomed to as finite beings. Even though stars themselves are born and die, the timeframes in which they act out their drama are so enormous as to bewilder us mortals here on our ever-changing and quickly evolving planet.

This primal egregore of the stars goes to the very heart of creation and the makeup of the universe itself. The elements that make up the planets, including our own, were originally created by the nuclear fusion at the heart of the stars of our universe. This power to create all other lower forms of existence is a good window through which to view the fixed stars. They are like the utter *is-ness* of the universe, being-itself that first comes into manifestation from the nothing, and the elements these stars create become the planets and, eventually, biological life as we know it. All this chain of power and magic begins in the stars. Whether we look at it through the lens of science and the creation of the base elements of existence or we see it through the Platonic or theurgic lens of the stars as the first manifestation of the divine and the created planets coming later, being more mutable and evolutionary, we are still seeing the silver chain of astral light that flows from God through the fixed stars to the planets and down to biological existence. Creation is a cosmic dance of being and nothing, ever flowing in and out of coming-into-being and non-being and the fixed stars are the fountainheads of that experience, crucibles that work with light and heat to breathe out matter into the void—matter that changes, shapes other matter, and evolves.

And these fixed stars did play into the spiritual and religious frameworks of past astrologers, magicians, and believers. In the Greek world, there are references to divination based on the rising of stars, such as found in Euripides. [3] There are hymns to the stars as deities. A particularly moving version of this devotional literature is the *Orphic Hymn to the Stars*. Thomas Taylor's classic translation captures it quite well.

> *With holy voice I call the stars on high,*
> *Pure sacred lights and genii of the sky.*
> *Celestial stars, the progeny of Night,*
> *In whirling circles beaming far your light,*
> *Refulgent rays around the heav'ns ye throw,*
> *Eternal fires, the source of all below.*
> *With flames significant of Fate ye shine,*
> *And aptly rule for men a path divine.*
> *In seven bright zones ye run with wand'ring flames,*
> *And heaven and earth compose your lucid frames:*
> *With course unwearied, pure and fiery bright*
> *Forever shining thro' the veil of Night.*
> *Hail twinkling, joyful, ever wakeful fires!*
> *Propitious shine on all my just desires;*

---

3 Benson Bobrick, *The Fated Sky: Astrology in History* (New York: Simon & Schuster, 2007), 19.

These sacred rites regard with conscious rays,
And end our works devoted to your praise. "[4]

The constellations were used to tell myth and story, and they were known by Homer and Hesiod. In Egypt, monuments were often tied to stars, not planets, and the fixed stars played a crucial role in spirituality and religion. The star Sirius was centrally important to Egyptian religion and associated with the gods Isis and Anubis. Egyptian artwork is rife with the image of the starry heavens, often painted on the body of Nut, the Sky-Mother, and decorating the ceilings of temples and tombs. And the Christianization of these lands did not remove the fascination of the stars in art and imagery. The Virgin Mary became herself the "Queen of Stars" and the "Star of the Sea"[5] and countless woodcuts, paintings, and mosaics were created where she bore a crown of the stars, a reference to Biblical texts.[6] Saints, images of Christ, and other divine figures in the Christian milieu were also decorated with the stars, all linking back to that primeval fascination with the fires of the sky.

We tend to forget how important star lore was to ancient cultures because the planets of astrological texts have eclipsed the central power and importance of the fixed stars. This needs to be remedied in any real approach to astrological magic, and we should always remember the power behind these stars, so lauded in Egyptian prayer and architecture, Greek myth, Medieval magic, and more. In Celtic lands, stars were given spiritual weight as well, such as the linking of the *corona borealis* with the castle of Arianrhod. In Greece, the *corona borealis* was the crown of Ariadne, seduced by Dionysus.[7] It is across cultures that the constellations spoke to us and gave frameworks for our magic.

---

4   *Hymns of Orpheus*, trans. Thomas Taylor, 2015 E-book ed., Loc: 868-878, Kindle.

5   A common incarnation of the Blessed Virgin is *Stella Maris*: literally, "Star of the Sea."

6   "And there appeared a great wonder in heaven; a woman clothed with the sun, and the moon under her feet, and upon her head a crown of twelve stars. And she being with child cried, travailing in birth, and pained to be delivered." Revelation, 12:1-2.

7   Carl Kerényi, *Dionysos: Archetypal Image of Indestructible Life*, trans. Ralph Manheim (Princeton, NJ: Princeton University Press, 1976), 109.

Modern astrology tends to downplay the fixed stars. In the Medieval and Renaissance worlds, the fixed stars were still central to astrological divination and magic. Marsilio Ficino wrote that the stars were the highest of a spiritual "chain of being" that linked the stellar worlds to the planets and then on down to earthly correspondences in natural magic such as stones and herbs. [8] The stars rest at the very top of this chain and act as the sources for the power that flows down through the celestial hierarchies. Ideas on the fixed stars permeate Agrippa's occult works as well, and many of the writers of this era drew on texts claiming to be Hermetic (read: written by Hermes Trismegistus, for their information).

The fixed stars are deeply associated with religious and magical practice. Stars were godly entities to many cultures, signs and omens of divinity made manifest in the night sky. They are used for navigation, with the invention of the astrolabe having an indelible effect on human history. Grimoires and magical treatises do not forget their power, even if the seven Heavenly Spheres of the planets eclipsed the fixed stars in popularity. *Picatrix* contains a spell to avenge an enemy, employing a star in *Ursa major*. [9] Agrippa writes of a system of creating talismans using the fixed stars for various magical purposes. All of these texts saw the fixed stars as an integral part of astrological magic. Without them, our experience of the Heavens is limited.

⋆⋆* Within the Zodiac *⋆*⋆*

As mentioned above, and addressed in our chapter on horoscopes, it can be confusing to work with the stars of the zodiac. The reason for this is that they no longer line up with the signs themselves. This should not, however, discourage the practitioner from using the fixed stars, both in

---

[8] "Fixed Stars and Constellations," Christopher Warnock, *Renaissance Astrology*, accessed August 2020, https://www.renaissanceastrology.com/fixedstars.html.

[9] *The Illustrated Picatrix: The Occult Classic of Astrological Magic Complete in One Volume*, trans. John Michael Greer and Christopher Warnock (Renaissance Astrology, 2015), 173-4.

chart reading and magic. It did not discourage ancient astrologers, even though they were aware of the progression of the equinoxes. Astrologers in history often associated the stars in the signs with the natures of certain planets. This makes it easier for the student to get a feel for these stars, as we have already examined the individual planets and can make strong correspondence-based connections in our mind for each planet. This is the best way to begin with the fixed stars, because once we know the power and energy of each planet and then correspond that with the stars, we can get a coherent grasp on what these stars do and how they act within divination and magic. If a star has "the energy of Saturn" and we have a good understanding of Saturn's influence, then we can see how that star might engage with our astrological work. The stars have lore far beyond a one-to-one correspondence to the planets, but I think starting with this concept is a good foundational introduction. Stars bearing the "nature of a planet" gives us good ground from which to work. [10]

⋆⋆⋆ The Behenian Stars ⋆⋆⋆

In Medieval and Renaissance astrology, drawing from many Arabic sources, a system of 15 stars became popularized and repeated throughout magical works. These were known as the *Behenian* Stars, from the Arabic word *Bahman*, meaning 'root.' Agrippa's works made these 15 stars centrally important in works on magic, and his influence was everywhere in later writers. Agrippa is drawing in his work from popular texts claiming to be from the hermetic tradition. [11] This system is a useful introduction to the fixed stars and the magic within the constellations. Agrippa gives instruction on the creation of stellar talismans using these stars. Their

---

[10] A full layout of the zodiacal stars would be less useful here than our discussion of the other fixed stars. To see a complete breakdown of planetary correspondences that share natures with the fixed stars of the constellations of the zodiac, see Ptolemy's *Tetrabiblos*.

[11] Hermetic texts are work that claimed to be written by Hermes Trismegistus and were quite common in occult circles. Many are forgeries, and many are simply copied bits of other works cobbled together into popular magical treatises. Despite this, many do contain legitimate pieces of classical works on philosophy and magic. They can be a remarkably interesting rabbit hole to explore for someone interested in the history of occult ideas in Europe and their proliferation and development.

power can easily be worked into astrological magic by looking to them by their nature and correspondences. We can use their images and correspondences in the natural world not only for talisman creation, but sigil magic, candle inscription, and more. We can time our magics using not only the planets but the conjunctions or aspects of these stars with other heavenly bodies. Learning to incorporate the fixed stars gives a new plane to work with, a new level to astrologically guided magic and divinatory practice.

★ ★ ★ THE BEHENIAN STARS ★ ★ ★

Star	Agrippa	Image	Mineral	Plant	Sigil	Planets
Algol	The Head of Algol	Head of a man with a bloody neck	Diamond	Black Hellebore, mugwort		Saturn, Jupiter
Pleaides	The Seven Stars	Small virgin, or a lamp	Quicksilver	Frankincense, fennel		Moon, Mars
Aldebaran	Aldeboran	Likeness of God, or a flying man	Carbuncle, Ruby	Milky thistle, woodruff		Mars, Venus
Capella	The Goat Star	Man with musical instruments	Sapphire	Horehound, mint, mugwort, mandrake		Jupiter, Saturn
Sirius	The Great Dog Star	Hound and little virgin	Beryl	Savin, mugwort, dragonwort		Venus
Procyon	The Lesser Dog Star	Rooster, or three maids	Achates	Marigold, pennyroyal		Mercury, Mars
Regulus	The Heart of the Lion	A lion or cat, or an honorable person in a chair	Garnet	Mugwort, mastic		Jupiter, Mars
Alkaid	The Tail of the Lesser Bear	A pensive man, a bull, or a calf	Lodestone	Succory, mugwort, periwinkle		Venus, Moon
Algorab	Wing of the Crow	A raven, a snake, a man in black	Black onyx	Burr, henbane, comfrey		Saturn, Mars
Spica	Spica, The Spike	A bird, or a man with merchandise to sell	Emerald	Sage, clover, mugwort, mandrake		Venus, Mercury
Arcturus	Alchameth	A horse, a wolf, or a man dancing	Jasper	Plantain		Mars, Jupiter
Alphecca	Elpheia	A hen, or a man in a crown	Topaz	Rosemary, clover, ivy		Venus, Mars
Antares	The Heart of the Scorpion	An armed and armored man, or a scorpion	Sardonyx, amethyst	Aristolochia, saffron		Venus, Jupiter
Vega	The Falling Vulture	A vulture, hen, or a traveler	Chrysolite	Succory, fumitory		Mercury, Venus
Deneb Algedi	The Tail of Capricorn	A hart, a goat, an angry man	Chalcedony	Marjoram, mugwort, nip, mandrake root		Saturn, Mercury

The Arabic influence in astrology is particularly strong when it comes
to these fixed stars. As learning and science flourished in the Arab world,
treatises on astrology and astronomy (not yet differentiated in our human

minds) proliferated. These texts would be used by later European Christian writers and magicians to expand their knowledge of astrology and its magics. Muslim and Jewish writers in the Muslim-ruled lands became the premier stargazers of their time, outperforming their European counterparts for many years. Hence many of the stars are still known by their Arabic names, while the planets are known to us by the names of Roman deities. The Arab writers furthered the study and thus gained naming rights for the stars. It is important to recognize and appreciate the Arab influence on astrology and just how prolific and influential these Muslim and Jewish writers were, even if we have often read them filtered through the writings of later Christian authors who drew heavily from their works.

The following is a chart of the Behenian stars, with correspondences drawn from Agrippa.

*˟*Starry Talismans *˟*

The Behenian Stars can be used in talismanic magic, when planets are in conjunction within a horoscope with the stars, or when they are well aspected within a chart. Each star also has many powers and abilities that bear similar correspondences to the planets that are associated with each star in Agrippa and other occult works. Albertus Magnus, in his *De Mineralibus*, gives formulae for the creation of talismans using images of the constellations, both of the zodiac and beyond.[12] His talismans are used for a variety of interesting purposes, from endearing the wearer to others to protection against certain tragedies. His correspondences are often quite literal, pulling from natural magic's belief in the interrelatedness of all things (As Above, So Below). For example, he recommends a talisman with the Serpent-bearer (Ophiuchus) to protect against snakebites, and an image of Pegasus is good for those who fight on horseback. Agrippa's correspondences for talisman magic and the stars are quite similar, such as using the constellation Hercules for victory in battle.

---

12 "Albertus Magnus on Talismans," *Renaissance Astrology*, Christopher Warnock, accessed September 2020, https://www.renaissanceastrology.com/albertusmagnustalisman.html.

⋆⁖⋆Fixed Stars in a Chart ⋆⁖⋆

Fixed stars can be read within charts as well, adding to the strength of certain planets and giving them an added influence, or adding to their detriment if there is a conflicting relationship present between a planet and a fixed star. We will examine how planets and other things within a chart relate to one another mathematically in a later chapter, but for now it is important to remember that the fixed stars can add to the interpretation of a chart. They are important players in any chart that you will draw up or interpret. Consider incorporating the fixed stars into your magic and divination. I have always experienced a deeper, fuller, and richer divination or natal chart interpretation when I incorporate the fixed stars and their influence on the horoscope. I often find they have a unique, lasting impact on how a planet acts within a chart when there is a strong aspect between the fixed star and a planet in question.

It is also amusing to note that William Lilly devoted a portion of his writing on astrology to teach his would-be students about how the fixed stars can portend violent deaths. One example of Lilly's reasoning here says, "If Saturn be with Cor Scorpio and Moon with Oculus Taurus the native will be hanged, or killed with the stroke of a Sword: say the same when Mars is so posited."[13] Lilly did not mince words when it came to death, and he highlights a certain morbid fascination with natal charts and death popular in many traditional astrological works. This only hammers home the more dread aspects of the fixed stars, their older, deeper magic that can speak to our fears and preoccupations with mortal existence.

⋆⁖⋆A Ritual for the Old Stars ⋆⁖⋆

Working with the fixed stars is a powerful magical practice. The use of starry talismans has been discussed above, and it is an exceptionally good way to incorporate these spirits into your practice. I am including here a different style of ritual for the Old Stars, something to focus energy

---

13   William Lilly, *Christian Astrology: Books 3*, ed. David R. Roell (Bel Air, MD: Astrology Classics, 2004), 649.

and strengthen any working. This ritual can be used for any working, so I recommend consulting the table of Behenian stars above or the stars within the zodiac to determine what links, spiritually, with your desired outcome and specific situation. I also believe it is crucial in this work to be able to see your star, so choose one that is visible from your location and choose a night for working this rite that is clear of cloudy weather or hindrances to your vision (it might warrant a trip out of the city, to avoid light pollution).

Ritual Preparation

Choose your star, locate it with a star atlas or technology. Make sure you know where you're going to be focusing.

Have a clear space outdoors to work in, with no distractions and with as much privacy as possible. Simple ritual clothing is all that is needed, as we will not be working with an altar or specific tools in this ritual.

The Ritual

Begin with your breath. See the star within the sky and focus on it. Unclench your fists, relax your muscles, stand firmly with your feet apart and breathe in deeply. Fill the bottom of your lungs and then exhale completely. Repeat this until you feel centered, with calm and even breathing.

Visualize a clear and strong light descending from your specific star, keeping it in your line of vision. See this piercing light highlight your body, a pillar of light as you look up and focus on your breath and this moment. Have your intent strongly in mind, preferably having done a working beforehand more specifically attuned to your desired outcome. Visualize it as complete, finished, and compliant to your will. It is done. This work is done, here and now, beneath this star that will aid you. With these thoughts firmly in your mind, invoke:

"Son and Daughter of the First Fires, I am here. Spirits of [name the star], I call you from dread night. Open the gates of horn and ivory. Spend the power of the crucible that makes the worlds. Your bright and streaming rays speed across the ether and bring down boons from the One. In the beginning, the middle, and the end of days you are the shining circle of Mind. I send forth the Work that it may be accomplished in your palace."

Place your hands into the form of a square, using thumbs and index fingers. Frame the star and focus on the light framed in your line of sight.

"So mote it be."

Astrological Points Beyond the Stars

Astrology considers more than the fixed and wandering stars in the Art. Along with the more commonly known planets, there are also important mathematical situations and phenomena in the sky that carry weight in astrological reading and magic. Primarily, these include the nodes and the lots (also known as Arabic Lots, or Arabic Parts). The nodes relate to the Moon, and the parts are mathematical relationships between celestial bodies. This sacred geometry goes to the core of the astrological world-view. Relationships in sacred forms represent deeply spiritual principles of the divine unity behind Creation and the interconnectedness of all experience. Over time, the use of the lots diminished in astrology. By the time of William Lilly, one of the primary sources for traditional astrology in the English-speaking world, it was really only the part of fortune that was heavily considered. Depending on where an astrologer goes for her sources, many more parts may become influential. Arabic sources tend to give them hefty weight. Whatever our approach to the lots, they are part and parcel of the Art and are still due their rightful consideration.

⋆ ⋆ The Lunar Nodes ⋆ ⋆

The nodes of the Moon are the places where the Moon's path around the Earth coincide with the path of the Sun's apparent travels around the Earth.[1] Again, it is important to remember that we are not denying the Copernican model of the solar system, only looking up from our earthly experience and witnessing the phenomena of the stars from the ground.

---

[1]   There are differing calculations used to determine the placement of the nodes. The two most common that you will encounter in astrological works or software are the "mean node" and the "true node." Examine both systems and experiment, but I use the true node in my personal charts.

When we watch the movements of the luminaries, we notice these two intersections. The north node is where the Moon's path intersects with the Sun in the northern ecliptic hemisphere and is also called the ascending node. The south node is where the path intersects at the southern ecliptic hemisphere and is also called the descending node.

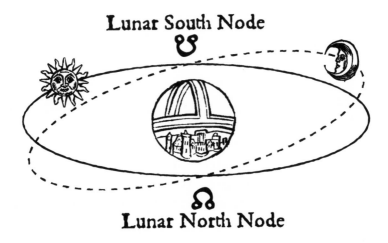

Lunar South Node

Lunar North Node

In European astrological texts, we often find the north node referred to as the *caput draconis*, the *head of the dragon*. The south node is referred to as the *cauda draconis*, or *the tail of the dragon*. This dragon is the great line that runs from the ascending and descending nodes, an imaginary line we can envision in the Heavens. It is no surprise that a dragon image was used given the historical link to serpent imagery in religion and esotericism. We see countless examples of dragons, serpents, and the ouroboros in traditional texts on magic and religion. Whether it is the dragon of Genesis and Revelation, or the ouroboros swallowing its own tail in alchemical texts, the imagery is everywhere.

Interpreting with the nodes has had some disagreement across traditions, but many correspondences and shared natures do arise within the literature. Lilly, for example, gives the *caput draconis* the nature of the benefic planets of Jupiter and Venus.[2] Drawing from traditional

---

[2]   William Lilly, *Christian Astrology: Books 1 & 2*, ed. David R. Roell (Bel Air, MD: Astrology Classics, 2004), 83.

sources, many from the Arab world, astrologer Lucia Bellizia gathers the following associations:[3]

☊ **Caput draconis** *(north node): Masculine, hot, fertile, diurnal, aggrandizing and growing*

☋ **Cauda draconis** *(south node): Feminine, cold, infertile, nocturnal, diminishing* [4]

Using this information, we can interpret the influence of the nodes within the chart as strengthening or conflicting with planets that may come into relationship with the nodes. A benefic planet in a good position is only going to be strengthened by the presence of the *caput draconis,* whereas a planet in serious debility may have an even more restrained voice in the chart if it couples with the *cauda.* On a personal note, I have noticed in my own work how important it is to remember that the nodes are really about the luminaries. We see the symbol of the nodes in the chart and forget that what is being represented is a very powerful union of the two most luminous objects in our lives: the Sun and the Moon. The Sun, that monarch of the sky, and the Moon: the eternal mother, goddess, and emotional storehouse, are coming together at these points. Thinking of the nodes in this way, as the place of union between the divine masculine and the divine feminine, has helped me to interpret their influence on planets that relate to them. Ego and emotion may be coming together beautifully, or in conflict, and that is going to color the planets. I realize that this is a unique approach to the north and south node, but I have seen it bring clarity to interpretation and often pass it on to my students as one way to look at this that might break through the disagreements and conversations

---

³ Luzia Bellizia, *Of the Judgments on the Lunar Nodes,* trans. Margherita Fiorello, accessed October 2020, http://skyscript.co.uk/pdf/nodes.pdf.

⁴ Note: noted Arab astrologer al-Biruni disagrees with giving such stark correspondences to the nodes, preferring to consider their relationships to all other planets and situations present in the chart. I believe it is important to take all relationships into consideration, but I do agree with the general natures of the nodes I have given and sourced here.

from historical texts. Remember: Astrology thrives in practice. It is an Art, not just a collection of aphorisms that we take as dogma.

⋆⋆⋆The Lots ⋆⋆⋆

The *lots* (also known as *parts*) are points that exist in the celestial environment based on the relationship between certain heavenly bodies. They were influential in historical astrology, but they are lesser known than other astrological concepts in modern practice. They are often called *Arabic parts* due to the weight of history we must give to the practitioners in the Arab-ruled lands of antiquity for preserving and expounding upon their usage. We can suppose that the lots predate the Arab conquests, though, having their likely source in older astrological knowledge. But it was in Arab lands that much information was gathered around the practice of these special configurations. In modern practice, many readers may have read about or encountered the *part of fortune* but are less likely to have encountered or explored the other parts.

And the Arab writers placed a significant weight on the sacred geometry and mathematical nature of these tools of the Art, tying it all in with deeply religious philosophy inspired by Pythagoras. [5] This concept of sacred geometry, or the spiritualizing of mathematics, is something found across cultures among traditions. We can see the influence of this concept in the *yantras* of Hinduism, or in the numerological practices of Kabbalah. Numbers and basic forms are part of the underlying nature of our experience with the world. The golden ratio, repeating patterns in nature, fractals, and more are all part of our vision in this earthly existence of the harmony sometimes visible within the works of nature. The parts play into this experience we all share of finding meaning in the mathematical beauty of the world, the ability for our eye and our mind to draw connections and notice patterns. Philosophy, art, and mathematics have existed in a complicated dance across time, and the lots explore and work within that framework of sacred numbers and heavenly configurations.

---

5 Robert Zoller, *Arabic Parts in Astrology: A Lost Key to Prediction* (Rochester, VT: Inner Traditions International, 1989), 9.

Bonatti, one of the most influential traditional astrological sources, devotes a large treatise to the lots, including some that are rarely (if ever) discussed today—such as the *part of olives*.[6] We find the parts in other sources as well, but by the time of William Lilly, it seems that the part of fortune was the only dominant lot used in many astrological considerations. This is a shame, since the lots offer a deep and spiritual look into charts for the astrologer and the client. Many traditional astrologers I have worked with and discussed with over the years seem to view the lots as more *spiritual* than other configurations in astrology, holding within them the possibility of deeper appreciation and understanding of a nativity or a horary reading.

The calculation of the lots also differs in one key aspect across sources. For most, there is a separate calculation used depending on whether the chart in question is a day chart or a night chart. For some, this distinction did not matter, and the same formula is used throughout. As an astrologer, I have always looked at sect[7] as crucial to understanding a chart fully, so I do respect the different calculations for the parts.

The lots are calculated with three points. This triangular calculation should not be surprising, given the historical significance of triangular concepts in Pythagorean and later philosophies. Triangulation itself is used with the stars in more mundane aspects, so it is natural to think of elevating that concept to the Heavens, engaging in our *As Above, So Below* framework of viewing the world. Triangulation comes up frequently in astrology, for example in the trine aspect discussed in our chapter on planetary condition, as well as the triplicities, or elemental rulerships, associated with signs. Since it is the most common, we can begin with the *pars fortunae*, the part of fortune, and move on to the others.

---

6 Ibid, 128.

7 See chapter 8.

THE PARS FORTUNAE
(Part of Fortune, Part of the Moon)

Calculating: Day Chart: Ascendant + Moon – Sun
Night Chart: Ascendant + Sun – Moon

Bonatti writes of the *pars fortunae*, "This part signifies the life, the body, and also its soul, its strength, fortune, substance and profit, i.e., wealth and poverty, gold and silver, heaviness or lightness of things bought in the marketplace, praise and good reputation, and honours and recognition, good and evil, present and future, hidden and manifest; it has signification over everything..... if this part and the luminaries are well-disposed in nativities or revolutions, it will be notably good."[8]

THE PARS FUTURORUM
(Part of Things to Come, Part of the Sun, Part of spirit)

Calculating: Day Chart: Ascendant + Sun – Moon
Night Chart: Ascendant + Moon – Sun

Bonatti writes of the *pars futurorum*, "The pars futurorum signifies the soul and the body, after the pars fortunae and the quality of these, and faith, prophecy, religion and the culture of God and secrets, cogitations, intentions, hidden things and everything which is absent, and courtesy and liberality, praise, good reputation, heat and cold. ... The significations of the pars fortunae appear more during the day ... the pars futurorum appear more at night."[9]

OTHER LOTS

There are many lots given in traditional sources, including ways to calculate lots for houses, for each planet, and even specific lots for political, agri-

---

8 Robert Zoller, *Arabic Parts in Astrology: A Lost Key to Prediction* (Rochester, VT: Inner Traditions International, 1989), 85.

9 Ibid, 87.

cultural, religious, and personal questions. An exhaustive examination of each calculation is beyond the scope of what we want to achieve with this work, so I have given the two most commonly used above, and I am going to include, here, a table with the lots given to each planet with simplified information that I believe would be useful to a student of astrology. The part of fortune and the part of things to come are the parts associated with the Moon and Sun, respectively, so the following planetary lots do not include the luminaries, having been dealt with above.[10]

PLANETARY LOTS

Lot or Part	Calculation	Significance
Part of Mercury, Part of Poverty, Ordinary Intellect	Day: Ascendant + Pars Fortunae – Pars Futurorum Night: Ascendant + Pars Futurorum – Pars Fortunae	Cunning, wit, intelligence, buying & selling BUT ALSO war, strife, poverty, fears, and hatredsv
Part of Venus, Part of Love, Part of Concord	Day: Ascendant + Pars Futurorum – Pars Fortunae Night: Ascendant + Pars Fortunae – Pars Futurorum	Pleasure, desire, licit and illicit wants, delights, unions, sex, games, joys and delights
Part of Mars, Part of Daring	Day: Ascendant + Pars Fortunae – Mars Night: Ascendant + Mars – Pars Fortunae	Armies, wars, battles, worth of the soul, resolution, bravery, impulse, haste, improper relationships and incest
Part of Jupiter, Part of Happiness, Part of Assistance	Day: Ascendant + Jupiter – Pars Futurorum Night: Ascendant + Pars FuturorumJupiter	Honor, the attainment of things, being celebrated, faith, belief in God and religion, wisdom, participating in good and righteous things
Part of Saturn, Heavy Part	Day: Ascendant + Pars Fortunae –Saturn Night: Ascendant + Saturn – Pars Fortunae	Memory, depth, moderation in religion, constancy, durable things, matters and items lost or stolen, the dead, dying, buildings and land, transportation, old age, incarceration and confinement and liberation thereof

---

[10] All information from Zoller's work and his interpreting of Bonatti.

*⋅*Using the Lots *⋅*

The lots can seem intimidating, since they add another layer onto the astrologer's interpreting. With the planets, houses, aspects, and other considerations, it may seem daunting to add another mathematical system into the Art. I always teach my students to approach the lots differently than they do the main planetary conditions and chart conditions that form the basis of most astrological interpretation. The lots, for me, are secondary sources of information to probe specific areas more deeply. They carry with them a unique fatalistic flare and spiritual egregore that is not as straightforward and visible as the actions of the planets.

When we are examining a nativity, or an election chart, we can use the lots to probe a question that is of particular importance to us. If we are almost entirely focused on a question of love, then we can bring in the *pars veneris* to gain a deeper understanding of the question and see what might be the true *destiny* of love for the person. If the planets and their interactions with houses, aspects with one another, and other considerations are a celestial play, then consider the lots a deeper backstory for each character, an analysis of the play, a guiding hand or a particular train of thought in the director's mind. They are mathematical relationships, and thus bear that arcane and mysterious power that exists in all mathematically driven philosophy.

Robert Zoller, cited throughout this chapter, wrote a lot to bring back the lots as part of astrology and was the premier voice for their renaissance in the Art. In his work, he does mention that the lots can be used as a secondary decision-making application (relying on Guido Bonatti) and I agree with him. When an issue seems to have two influencing planetary answers, the lots can be used to "break the tie" so to speak. If the question is about communication, and the planets seem contradictory or too difficult to unknit, then looking at the part of Mercury might serve to open a clearer answer to our question. The same could go for a question of a disagreement or calamity, and the part of Mars. Or it could be said for a question about the purchase or inheritance of land and the part of Saturn.

*.*The Outer Planets and Beyond*.*

I have written about why the traditional forms of astrology speak to me and why I choose to practice and teach this system. I do want to address the outer planets, however, because they have entered the conversation of the Art, and for many astrologers, they are an integral part of prediction and astrological magic. Some astrologers choose to work with a traditional system but still take into consideration the outer planets of Uranus and Neptune as well as other celestial bodies such as Pluto and the asteroids (Ceres, Lilith, etc.). I do not use them in my workings at all, so I cannot speak to what they mean for the practitioners, but there are countless resources of modern systems available to the student who wants to investigate.

For me, as I've written, astrology must begin from a terrestrial perspective. The outer planets are so removed from our experience and take so long to move through their orbits, that to consider them influential in our framework is difficult from my point of view. The seven planets are visible from Earth, and we can watch their movements without much difficulty or the need for advanced technology. We experience their full orbits in one human life.

Saturn, the furthest planet in the system, orbits the Sun in a little under 30 years. Uranus, the next planet, if we accept the outer bodies, takes 84 years. This is a massive jump. Neptune is even more extreme, completing its orbit in around 165 years. These numbers are so large, so removed from a lived human life, that I believe it is difficult to comprehend their relationship to our own timeframes. Other bodies, such as asteroids, are also complicated to understand since astronomy is constantly updating its understanding of these bodies. Chiron, for example, was classified as an asteroid, and many astrologers still write about it as such. Astronomers, however, have continually reclassified and updated information about this body. It has also been called a "minor planet" as well as displaying comet-like traits. So, what is it? Well, astronomy will have to define that as it receives new information. Until then, it seems premature to assign an entire worldview or spirit to a body we do not fully understand.

For students interested in incorporating these bodies, I have seen astrologers consider them for larger questions than a single human life or a question in a horary chart. Perhaps they can be used to ask and interpret questions of political eras, movements, and large swaths of our history as a species on this planet. We could, as some astrologers do, consider the discovery of each of these planets or asteroids and assign ideas and concepts based on the period of that discovery. We can see this with Uranus, which many modern astrologers associate with revolutions in ideas and information because of its discovery time—an age of change and revolution.

All of that being said, I do believe that the inclusion of the outer planets and the asteroids as well as shifting to a more heliocentric, solar system-based approach, has actually made astrology *more* superstitious, not less. Modern astrologers want to communicate with astronomy and science, to accept new discoveries and integrate new concepts. This is admirable. There is an insidious effect, however, in this practice. Traditional astrology operates within a framework of spiritual principles and sacred geometry. There is a balance in the elemental rulerships, aspects, and correspondences. When we wreck that system of numerology and balance by shifting rulerships (giving Pluto to Scorpio, for example, and Neptune to Pisces—thus altering the entire system to where it is almost unrecognizable), we are unmoored from these foundational ideas.

In the new system, we must rely on a much more unscientific worldview. We have to believe, as some did in the past, that the planets must have some measurable, scientific pull on us or emit some kind of special ray or beam that influences us. We enter some very bizarre and, frankly, hokey territory with this system. We also must account for massive time frames that are difficult to apply to human experience. This may be an extreme statement to some astrologers, but I do not believe astrology is purely a sister-science to astronomy. I am not sure I even like describing astrology as a science *at all*. For me, it is a spiritual worldview, a divinatory practice, and a way of touching the Fates and their machinations. It is not purely causal. And so, for this, I leave the dread lords of the outer planets to the astrologers who feel called to that practice, while I continue to work with the traditional, Chaldean order of the stars.

Now that we have met the wandering stars, fixed stars, and other players of the heavenly game, we can begin to understand how we represent them and interpret their relationships and movements using horoscopes. This chapter should serve as a foundational overview of what exactly a horoscope is, and how we interpret it. The language can be complex, but once mastered, these tools can become second nature to the astrologer and the magician, opening the entire system to the reader and seeker. Once you have learned the tools, the following chapters will lay out systems of interpreting these charts for different needs that the astrologer might have. For now, focus on mastering the foundational tools needed to understand what exactly we are looking at when we look at a map of the heavens in the astrological Art.

⋆⋆⋆ The Horoscope in Astrology ⋆⋆⋆

Astrology's central imaging tool is the horoscope, literally: an observation of the hours, of time. A horoscope is a complex snapshot and can be daunting to the beginner, so we will break it down and examine each part. The bones of astrology may seem many, but once mastered you can interpret most of the crucial information in a chart with a glance. We will examine what influence this architecture has on the planets we have experienced and worked with so far later, but for now we need to get a good look at the palace of the sky and orient ourselves to the astrological chart.

Astrologers cast horoscopes for particular reasons. The most common form that most readers are familiar with is *natal astrology*, which is the reading of birth charts, also called *nativities*. This is where we read the chart for a person's birth. There is also *electional astrology*, in which we prepare charts to determine a beneficial time for an activity, a magical working, or an event. This is particularly useful for magicians who want to draw upon certain astrological frameworks for their practice. Electional astrology is often used in readings concerning weddings, starting business ventures, or making important decisions. There is also *horary astrology*, a form of divination in which we cast a chart at a specific time when asking a question and determine the answer from the chart. It can be a simple yes-or-no situation, or we can gather complex information and further insight. Historically, horary astrology was immensely popular as a form of divination, and major works on astrology such as William Lilly's *Christian Astrology*, the works of Ibn bin Sahl, Vettius Valens, al-Biruni and other major influential astrologers, poured out much of their ink in setting up and answering specific questions with horary techniques.

For many seekers, this form of astrology is less well-known than natal astrology, but it really is a central tool for the Art. While tarot cards, palmistry, and other forms of divination have come to dominate the scene, horary astrology was, for many centuries, the premier form of divination in the learned world. In horary astrology, the seeker asks a question, and the chart is drawn up for the moment the question is asked. The astrologer will examine the chart with the question in mind. For example, if the question is about a seeker's love life, then we will play close attention to Venus, to the 7th house, and other associations with love. If the question were to be about a person's pet, then we would examine the 3rd house. For death, the 8th house, and perhaps the 6th if it's a question of illness, and so on and so forth. This technique allows us to answer any question, using the planets, fixed stars, and other aspects of the horoscope to give a fully fleshed-out answer to any querent. When you have a strong foundational knowledge of the planets, the fixed stars, and the other players in a horoscope (particularly houses and signs), you can use horary astrology for divination in any situation and with regard to any question. It can be an incredibly powerful tool for the psychic and diviner, and I have often found that once students get a taste for horary charts, other forms of divination don't provide the same depth or scope.

Luckily, the architecture of the horoscope is the same regardless of whether we are trying to create a natal chart or cast a chart for divination in horary astrology. Once you have learned the foundations of the Art, you can begin to move forward with your own interpretations and rely less on tables, charts, and glossaries. The horoscope is a map of the stars, and once you get your bearings, becoming oriented with the visual language of the Art, then you can fully engage with the system and explore all the facets of astrological divination, natal interpretation, and magic.

Creating charts from scratch is a difficult but often rewarding endeavor. Using an ephemeris, the astrologer can cast a chart for any time and lay out the placement of the houses and planets. This is a delicate art, and I do recommend that an astrologer learn how to read an ephemeris and create a chart from scratch. Many professional astrological organizations require that students be able to create charts in this manner in order to pass exams or get certifications in their organizations. It is a process that naturally teaches the student a lot about how the heavens are organized in horoscopes, and I always like to have students learn the system for themselves. Constructing charts from scratch is no longer a necessary step, however, given the development of technology in recent times. The information age has made astrology much more accessible, and I do not think there is anything wrong with using digital resources to help construct charts. You should understand how a chart is created and verify digitally created charts, but I do not think it is necessary to start from the ground up with every single instance of horoscope creation. It can be tedious. Once you have learned the art and math behind chart creation, using an ephemeris, you can trust and rely on technology to help you. Creating a chart from scratch using an ephemeris is beyond the scope of this work, but there are many astrological works that detail the steps, and all students of astrology should investigate this system as part of their education.

*⁕*The Chart *⁕*

Horoscopes have been visually represented in different ways throughout history. Before the use of circular charts like those that are common today, the Medieval and Renaissance astrologer would use a square that was broken into the 12 houses of astrology in a regular pattern. This form of horoscope was common throughout systems and is still used by many Vedic astrologers in the East. Some traditional astrologers in the West will prefer this chart because of its long historical usage.

16th c. horoscope showing the traditional pattern. The
12 houses are marked around the center, with the
degrees and minutes of the signs and planets.

This form of horoscope is beautiful, and with a strong background knowledge, it is easily readable by any astrologer, though it does have its dis-
advantages. The circular charts employed by the majority of astrologers
today have a much stronger visual link to how we experience the stars,
and it can really help us to understand what we are seeing when we are
examining a horoscope. As a teacher, I have learned that most modern
students are very visual learners. This makes sense given our consumption
of visual media and the advancements we've made in pedagogy by using
visuals. Because of this, I highly recommend circular horoscopes in lieu
of the more traditional form simply because it makes life easier. Even
though I teach traditional pre-modern astrology techniques for a lot of
my practice, I still believe that the Art can develop and evolve. It must,
if it is to remain meaningful to us in any real way. When we look at the
circular chart, we can orient ourselves quickly and begin to notice patterns
that might be more occluded in the previous models used by astrologers.

In the circular chart, which we will use throughout this book, the center of the chart is the Earth, and the Heavens move around it. This is where we begin. We place the Earth at the center, and then we have the Heavens above us (the daytime) and the Heavens below us (the night time).

The Sects of the Heavens

If we are standing on Earth at the center of this chart, then the line through the center is the horizon. What is above the line is daylight, and below it is the darkness of night. The planets will move around the chart. In astrology, the working of day and night are referred to as *sect*. [1] Planets all have a relationship to sect. Some planets are diurnal, others nocturnal. This orientation lets us look at a chart and know, at a glance,

---

[1]   See our chapter on planetary condition.

if someone was born at day or at night. If the Sun is located anywhere above the center bisecting line, they were born at day. The inverse is true if the Sun is below the line: they are a child of the night.

We can even make guesses at a person's birth time. If the Sun is barely above the Eastern horizon, then the person was born at dawn. If it is right above the Western horizon, they were born at dusk, close to night. This visual cue is the benefit of the circular chart. It gives us an orientation from which to work, one where we can begin to literally *see* the Heavens reflected in the horoscope. We are looking at a snapshot of the Earth and the celestial spheres around it.

⋆⋆Is the Zodiac Wrong?⋆⋆
Tropical vs. Sidereal Astrology

So, with the horizon, we can start to understand the signs of the zodiac and the house system of astrology. We need to begin, though, with an important discussion of what the zodiac is and isn't in traditional astrology. One of the things detractors of astrology will bring up is that the zodiac signs are "wrong." What they usually mean is that the 12 signs of the zodiac do not correspond directly with the constellations from which they draw their names. For example, if you are born with the Sun in Cancer, it does not mean that the Sun is literally appearing in front of the constellation of stars that we have historically called Cancer. This used to be true, but axial shift in the Earth (basically, the wobbling of the Earth in its movements), causes the alignments to be off and the constellations to no longer correspond to the signs that bear their names.

What detractors do not understand is that this has long been known to astrologers who use the zodiac system. This is not new information, even though every few years it is published in a sort of "gotcha!" way to shame those interested in astrology. The fact is, there are different systems of astrology and interpretations of the zodiac. The form of astrology I teach and use, and that which is traditional in the West, is *tropical astrology*. That means that it uses the seasons of the Earth and precise dates to determine the boundaries of the zodiac signs, and not the literal constellations. In *sidereal astrology*, the signs are corresponded to their constellations, and axial movements of the Earth are factored in. Vedic astrology, and other forms as well, is sidereal and will use different dates for the signs.

The rationale for using traditional zodiac placements goes back to the argument that astrology is essentially geocentric, even though it is a heavenly Art. We experience everything in the heavens from our home on Earth, and the seasons and experiences we have here on Earth are going to influence our reading of the heavens. We place Aries with the Spring Equinox as the beginning. Just as the seeds are planted, and life springs forth from the Earth, so do we place the first sign at that time. The rest follow suit, associated with seasons, weather, temperature changes, and all of the subtle and not-so-subtle changes that Earth experiences based on our human timekeeping. Ptolemy, Manilius, Valens, Masha'allah, al-Qabisi, and countless other traditional astrologers poured out a lot of ink on conversations about seasons, weather patterns, moistness, dryness, and the distribution of daylight and nighttime. This is because they were breaking the year down by the experience of us earthlings, and not merely as parts of the sky belonging to groups of stars. As we have continually said in this work: begin from the Earth.

This is why the constellations are not still used as the only demarcations and why we maintain the traditional placement of the zodiac signs. The 12 zodiac signs do not correspond directly to the constellations, even if they once did. We used the constellations to mark the sky out into segments and to understand the passage of seasons and time, but we are not bound to the starry configurations as literally as our detractors think we are. The magic of the fixed stars is its own thing, and fixed stars *do* play an important role in astrology (which we discuss in a separate chapter), but do not let this confuse you. There are 12 zodiac signs, corresponding to seasons and time periods here on Earth. There is not a mystery "13th sign"[2] and astrologers are not lying about the Art. We know about axial shift, thank you, and we have for a very long time.

So, tropical astrology divides the sky into segments. These segments and degrees of space and time were once marked by constellations, true,

2 Ophiuchus is given as the 13th sign by those that do not understand the difference between tropical and sidereal astrology.

but it is disingenuous to mock the Art because of axial shift when even the ancients knew of it. We really are demarcating our human experience here on Earth, so we do not need to answer any questions about the "wrongness" of the zodiac. The zodiac is about time: what rises, what falls, what we experience here on Earth as we watch the lights move across our sky. This allows the seeker to tie her astrology into the cycle and rhythms of life. From the changing of seasons and the agricultural cycle, to the major festivals and historic holidays of our cultures, the zodiac taps into the holistic experience of the human soul as it grows and changes here on Earth. This may mean that astrology looks and feels very different depending on where one is located on Earth. Most of the astrological knowledge presented in this book is very Eurocentric, and we have to keep that in mind when we approach nativities from places far-flung from where astrological knowledge was codified in Europe. Each astrologer will have to determine how important these differences are and how to account for them. So, having addressed this, we can begin to look at the zodiac.

✦˙✶˙The Zodiac ✦˙✶˙

The word *zodiac* comes from the Greek word for animal or living thing. This makes sense considering the original constellations were considered to have represented just that. The zodiac was often given a special place in the Heavenly Spheres, above the seven planetary spheres but not quite yet the Firmament of God, or the *Empyreum*. This area was called the *primum mobile*. [3] The 12 zodiac signs are placed around the wheel of the horoscope and move in a counterclockwise fashion. They each inhabit 30 degrees, making the complete circle of 360 in their 12 incarnations.

The 12 signs of the zodiac are broken into different groups that teach us about their natures, and the nature of the times they control and take their associations from. I like to begin by teaching about the zodiac sign

---

[3] Separating the zodiac from the rest of the fixed stars is a standard practice in many traditional texts. The nature of the fixed stars in the zodiac were given separate consideration than the other constellations. For more information, see chapter 9.

of Aries, for it is the Spring Equinox, time of beginning, the fiery sign.[4] The signs are organized and grouped in many ways, including feminine/masculine dichotomies, cold/hot, moist/dry, and more. Keep in mind how very *earthy* the ancients were, how tied to the experience of agriculture, weather, and the seasons. This mindset is very important for any seeker approaching traditional astrology. Words like "moist" and "drying" and "vernal" may not be as popular in modern astrology, but they were quite important in the old ways of the Art. The two most central groupings of the zodiac for most practitioners now, however, are the *triplicities* and the *quadruplicities*.

THE TRIPLICITIES

The triplicities, or *trigons*, are when we organize the signs by the four classical elements of Earth, Air, Fire, and Water. The signs are all assigned to an element and, being 12, create a group of three signs per element.

Element	Signs
Fire	♈ Aries, ♌ Leo, ♐ Sagittarius
Earth	♉ Taurus, ♍ Virgo, ♑ Capricorn
Air	♊ Gemini, ♎ Libra, ♒ Aquarius
Water	♋ Cancer, ♏ Scorpio, ♓ Pisces

The classical elements are the building blocks of creation, much more than a rudimentary attempt at pre-chemistry. Although they have roots in attempts by natural philosophers to understand the base of matter, they have a spiritual thread running throughout them, and they bear certain connotations and correspondences with all aspects of Creation. The elements are a way of understanding the foundational *is-ness* of the

---

4 Historically, there was a practice of beginning with the sign of Cancer. This was called the thema mundi, which was believed to be an image of the horoscope at the exact moment of Creation. In this system, Cancer was the original sign in the Ascendant position, as Cancer was such a maternal sign. It is, I admit, more "modern" to begin at Aries, but I find it such a useful approach that I have stuck with it over the years.

world, the heart of materiality and how we interact with it. The signs are all manifestations of this power. They tie everything into the cycles of nature. Their cyclical nature is a dance of generation, dissolution, and regeneration that speaks to the inner dynamism of the world. The zodiac signs, bearing these elemental natures, work in that rhythm of forces that is at the heart of life.

Triplicities on the Zodiac

The four elements are all about coming into being and the dissolution of being. Fire, the progenitor of creation, the divine spark, is hot and dry. Earth, the maintainer of fixed reality, the very earthy *realness* of materiality, is cold and dry. Water, the giver of life, the necessary womb for biological existence, is cold and moist. Finally Air, the breath of life, the movement across the worlds, is hot and moist. These relationships are important to understand magically and spiritually for the student of the Art. A "drying" effect might have a very different effect on your magic than one that is "moist." What combinations might you need for a working that was for fertility? What would you need for one that was designed to stop an unfortunate incident from occurring? Using these traditional relationships of the elements, and of dryness, moisture, coldness, and heat, can be very useful for understanding both magical workings and to gaining a deeper understanding of the zodiac signs within chart reading and interpretation. Traditional magic gave a lot of weight to these concepts, with a worldview of interconnected balances that could become unhinged and in need of repair. Use this in your interpreting and your magic, and understand the areas of our lived experience that might need a second glance, or a rebalancing.

QUADRUPLICITIES

The quadruplicities (also called *modes*) are more about the nature of the signs. In modern astrology we encounter three terms used for this organizational scheme: cardinal, fixed, and mutable. In traditional astrology, these were moveable, fixed, and common, respectively. This can create some confusion since "mutable" and "moveable" sound similar but, in fact, are two separate modes. I use the more modern vocabulary, even though I practice traditional astrology, simply to avoid confusion. The language is so ubiquitous now that I find trying to revive the older terms an unfulfilling and difficult endeavor.

Cardinal signs are associated with matters being quickly resolved, with action, and beginnings. These are initiators.

Fixed signs show firmness and stability. These are maintainers.

Mutable signs are useful for bringing things together, for fraternity, and for adaptability. These are changers.

There is a natural flow to this if you meditate upon it. We begin with the "Cardinal" because all things must begin with action. This is the *fiat lux* moment—the act of creation. Once a course of action has been taken, it must be grounded. This *groundedness* is within the fixed signs that lock down choices, that solidify and make real our ideas and attempts to create. Finally, nothing can continue existing if it does not participate in creation and have relationship with other aspects of reality. Thus, the mutable signs. They bring harmony and accord with creative principles. So, the quadruplicities are like a cosmic cycle of creation, maintenance, and growth, repeated throughout the zodiac in a very real way. These natures help us to understand how we act in creation, and they can be powerful lenses through which to view magic.

❋ ❋ ❋ QUADRUPLICITIES ❋ ❋ ❋	
Quadruplicity	Signs
Cardinal	♈ Aries, ♋ Cancer, ♎ Libra, ♑ Capricorn
Fixed	♉ Taurus, ♌ Leo, ♏ Scorpio, ♒ Aquarius
Mutable	♊ Gemini, ♍ Virgo, ♐ Sagittarius, ♓ Pisces

I find that we can use the quadruplicities in astrology in unique and varied ways, but I always find them underutilized in a lot of modern works on astrology. Using the quadruplicities is so useful when interpreting how a planet is acting or what influence a certain area of the chart has. For example, if we are examining a course of action in a chart and we are dealing with almost everything in question (major planets, nodes, etc.) in cardinal signs, then we know that we are dealing with something that is going be impulsive, go-getting, directive, managed, etc. If it were all in mutable spaces, it might be that this is going to be constantly changing, difficult to pin down, quickly evolving, and perhaps shapeless if taken too far.

Quadruplicities on the Zodiac

The elements and quadruplicities make up an intricate and beautiful unity within the chart. Three signs per four elements and four signs per three natures gives us a beautiful mandala within the horoscope, a system of interconnecting relationships that we can draw on for our divination and planetary magic. The nature of each sign creates a unique environment in which a planet can act, a coloring of various hues of meaning from the elemental correspondences to the relationships between signs. Each planet can act in a unique way. Venus in Libra is going to act very differently than Venus in Scorpio. The signs are the backdrop, the scenery to the majesty that is the celestial theater. Each one sets the stage in a unique way, influencing the planets and the seeker who interprets them. They costume the planets, powder the planets, influence them, and cajole them.

And we continually come back to our Earth-centered approach when we engage with the chart like this. We remember that the "cardinal" sign of Cancer, again associating moveable with initiation and change and the power to begin something, contains the Summer Solstice. We remember that the fiery sign of Aries rules the beginnings of spring, and the Saturn-ruled signs of Aquarius and Capricorn are in the dead of winter. All of these interconnections are based in our experiences here on Earth, connected with the natural cycles of time and place that we experience while journeying on our own rock.

Terms and Face

The breaking down of the zodiac signs into term and face is also shown on the chart. These areas were used to determine planetary dignity. The *decans* (faces) were believed to come from older, Egyptian systems that broke the yearly progression through the signs into smaller chunks ruled over by stars (or stellar gods). This system will also be represented around the chart, and a fuller explanation of term and face is found in chapter 8, referencing planetary condition.

The Attributes of the Zodiac

The signs have been used, historically, along with the houses discussed below, to reference body parts (in medical astrology), nations, ethnic groups, major historical areas, religions, and more. The lists in traditional sources can be endless. These lists can be wonderful ways to explore the zodiac more fully and to continue to build our connections to each piece within this astrological architecture. I often recommend my students to review William Lilly, al-Biruni, Ptolemy, Vettius Valens, Dorotheus of Sidon and others regarding correspondences made with the zodiac. Doing this can help flesh out the feel and influence of these areas. For the student interested in traditional astrology, or Hellenistic in particular, this exploration can really help to reset our brains to think the way traditional astrologers thought. When we have learned certain correspondences from modern sources (such as Cancer always being emotional, or Scorpio being heavily associated with sex), then we can really be shocked to discover how much ink the elders of the Art poured out to associate the signs with geographical areas, illnesses, and religious philosophies. It changes our perspective of the signs, tying them into the seasons and the realities of life here on Earth. It gives us a new vocabulary and a wider vision.

✦ ✦ ✦ THE ZODIAC ✦ ✦ ✦

Sign	Dates	Ruler	Light	Gender	Element	Mode	Body
♈ Aries	Mar 21 - Apr 20	♂ Mars	Diurnal	Masculine	Fire, hot, dry	Cardinal	Head, face
♉ Taurus	Apr 20 - May 21	♀ Venus	Nocturnal	Feminine	Earth, cold, dry	Fixed	Neck, shoulders
♊ Gemini	May 21 - Jun 21	☿ Mercury	Diurnal	Masculine	Air, hot, moist	Mutable	Throat, lungs, arms, hands
♋ Cancer	Jun 21 - July 23	☾ Moon	Nocturnal	Feminine	Water, cold, moist	Cardinal	Chest
♌ Leo	Jul 23 - Aug 23	☉ Sun	Diurnal	Masculine	Fire, hot, dry	Fixed	Heart, upper back, spine
♍ Virgo	Aug 23 - Sep 23	☿ Mercury	Nocturnal	Feminine	Earth, cold, dry	Mutable	Abdomen
♎ Libra	Sep 23 - Oct 23	♀ Venus	Diurnal	Masculine	Air, hot, moist	Cardinal	Kidneys, navel
♏ Scorpio	Oct 23 - Nov 22	♂ Mars	Nocturnal	Feminine	Water, cold, moist	Fixed	Genitals
♐ Sagittarius	Nov 23 - Dec 22	♃ Jupiter	Diurnal	Masculine	Fire, hot, dry	Mutable	Thighs
♑ Capricorn	Dec 22 - Jan 20	♄ Saturn	Nocturnal	Feminine	Earth, cold and dry	Cardinal	Knees
♒ Aquarius	Jan 20 - Feb 19	♄ Saturn	Diurnal	Masculine	Air, hot, moist	Fixed	Lower legs
♓ Pisces	Feb 19 - Mar 21	♃ Jupiter	Nocturnal	Feminine	Water, cold, moist	Mutable	Feet

You may have noticed I refer to the signs as places, or stages, more than independent actors. This is a crucially important approach when you are learning astrology. In modern language, many people will say things such as, "That is such a Taurus thing to do!" or something along the lines of "Virgo in my chart is doing a lot!" This seems to suggest that the signs *do* things in the chart. It insinuates that the 12 signs are the main players here. This is a mistake that stems from Sun-sign astrology's popularity. The signs don't necessarily *do* anything. They are places where things may be done. The planets and the other players of the celestial game are the real actors. The signs of the zodiac provide environments for our actors. Keep this in mind whenever you are studying the signs. They carry a lot of correspondences, but those correspondences, rulerships, and associations are only activated or acted upon by the stars and other players.

⋆⁂⋆The Houses ⋆⁂⋆

Aside from the zodiac, astrology also has 12 *houses*. Houses are not the same as the zodiac signs. They are a separate division of the heavens. There are multiple house systems in use in astrology, but I use and teach what is known as *whole sign houses*, which was common practice in Hellenistic astrology and for many Medieval and Renaissance astrologers. Other systems include Porphyry, Placidus, Reigomantus, Koch, and others. These systems divide the circle around the Earth in different patterns, using varying calculations that are too technical for this work. Not all historical astrologers I use in my research used whole-sign houses. William Lilly, for example, drew up natal charts using the Regiomantus system. Other astrologers preferred the Porphyry system. But whole-sign houses were the standard for many practitioners of the Art during the Hellenistic period and into the Medieval and post-Medieval European world. I find that they create an easy-to-work-with chart with a natural harmony and simplicity that has worked well for me and my students. Astrologers might have very passionate arguments for using specific systems, be it house systems or anything else in the Art, but the real test is if we can connect with a system and incorporate its symbolism and experience into our lives. For me, whole sign houses connect beautifully and simply with the Art and my study, while use of other house systems has not yielded the same fruitful results.

Whole signs work in a different way than other systems. In the whole sign method that I use, I assign the first house to the sign that is rising in the East (the *Ascendant*) and then each sign afterward takes a house. They are evenly distributed so that every house is 30 degrees (30 x 12 being 360, the full circle). This also means that my system is an equal system. I give the Ascendant entirely to the 1st house and continue around the circle in an even pattern. Each degree of a sign has 60 minutes. This is written out using an apostrophe and a closing quotation mark in print. Consider this a shorthand for where a planet is, a directional system that lets you know exactly where on the map a certain item is located.

Example: Sun in Leo 3'52" means that the Sun is in the third degree of the sign of Leo and at 52 minutes.

Houses and signs in astrology mean different things, and the two systems are not interchangeable. Many modern astrology works will associate the signs, in order, with houses and their meanings. So, for example, Aries is the first sign, so they will assign the things associated with Aries to the 1st house. This is not a historical practice. The 1st house and Aries are two separate entities, and we use them differently in interpreting charts. The best practice, for a student new to the system, is to consider them for what they are: two different tools within the Art. Trying to create deep links between the signs and the houses often leads to confusion, and it has led to an almost complete rewriting of what many of the houses meant in traditional astrology.

Houses were defined, historically, in three groups that helped us to understand their influence. The first group is the *angular* houses. These are houses 1, 4, 7, and 10. These are all at the angles of important astrological placements such as the Ascendant, the *imum coeli*, the descendant, and the Midheaven[5]. These houses are largely positive, with strong influences on the person or situation in question. The second grouping is the *succedent* houses (literally, *the houses that follow*). These are houses 2, 5, 8, and 11. These are houses dealing with steady, fixed things. We can think here of the 2nd house's association with estates and income, the 8th house's association with death, etc. The final grouping is the *cadent* houses. These are houses 3, 6, 9, and 12. Cadent means "falling." These houses tend to deal with more negative or difficult aspects of life such as illness, bondage, or enemies. Grouping the houses in this manner is a way to organize our thoughts about their placement and how to interpret using them when we work the Art.

---

[5]   The Midheaven is an important point within a chart, associated with profession, public life, and the person we are when we interact in the wider world. Aspects to the Midheaven are taken into consideration, as well as what sign the Midheaven is in, what planet rules that sign, and what its condition is in the chart. You will see more about this in our chapter about natal chart reading.

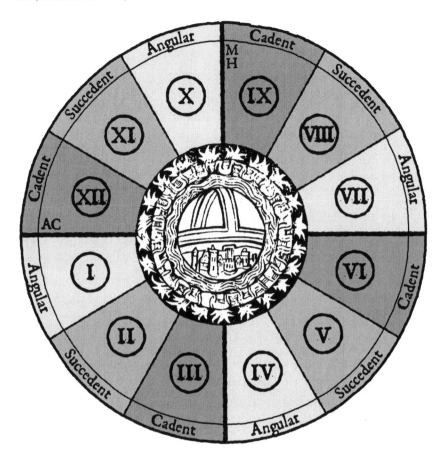

The Twelve Houses of Heaven

There is also a system known as the houses of planetary joy. These are the houses where each of the traditional planets have increased comfort and where they "rejoice" to be. These are associated with the natural correspondences of each planet in relation to that which is ruled by certain houses. I tend to consider a planet in its house of joy more at ease and exerting a good influence. If a planet is debilitated, the house of joy may provide a bit of reprieve. If the planet is dignified, being in the house of joy will only increase the benefic nature of the planet in question.

* .* .* PLANETARY JOYS .* .* .*	
Planet	House of Joy
☿ Mercury	① First House
☽ Moon	⑪ Third House
♀ Venus	⑤ Fifth House
♂ Mars	⑥ Sixth House
☉ Sun	⑨ Ninth House
♃ Jupiter	⑪ Eleventh House
♄ Saturn	⑫ Twelfth House

The above system related back to the central idea I always come back to when it comes to astrology: a holistic approach. We always take into consideration the *spirit* behind the stars and then relate it down to our earthly experience—as above, so below. Mercury, which is the communicator of the stars, is joyful in the 1st house, which speaks so clearly to our ego, to our sense of self and how we communicate it to the World. The Moon is in the 3rd house, the house of the divine feminine, of siblings, of early maternal education. In the 5th house, which is pleasure and mirth, games and friendships: we find Venus at home. Mars, with its malefic and tragic powers, finds joy in the 6th, where disease and calamity can strike at our hearts. Like a powerful god, the Sun is in the house of religion and philosophy—the 9th. When we look to the house of good fortune and friendship, 11, the great benefic of Jupiter, is in joy. And finally, the disciplinarian of the stars, the controller and reaper, is in the 12th, where enemies, imprisonment, and difficulties arise.

✳ ✳ ✳ ✳ THE HOUSES ✳ ✳ ✳ ✳

House	Associations	Grouping
First	Physical appearance, the head and face, self and sense of self, the general life and personality of the querent or the heart of the situation	Angular
Second	Estates, money, the wealth or poverty of a person, properties and ownership	Succedent
Third	Siblings, neighbors, short journeys, letters, messengers, rumors and gossip, education in youth	Cadent
Fourth	The father, inherited land or money, ancestry, the motherland, large structures, houses, dwellings and buildings, agriculture	Angular
Fifth	Children, games, hobbies, joyous endeavors and happy places, luck and games of chance, alcohol/drinking	Succedent
Sixth	Servants, drudgery/labor, disease, ill health, extended family (primarily uncles)	Cadent
Seventh	Marriage and weddings, love, relationships, duels, lawsuits, peace or victory in a war	Angular
Eighth	Death, wills, legacies, estate law, dowries, fear and anguish, mental disorders	Succedent
Ninth	Long-distance travel, religion, clergy, philosophy, dreams, visions, prophecy, higher education and spiritual teaching, foreign lands	Cadent
Tenth	Earthly rulers and authority figures, trades, careers, public persona, ministerial and administrative issues, public record	Angular
Eleventh	Friends and friendship, hopes, confidence, good counsel, allies, our chosen family of associations over our given blood family	Succedent
Twelfth	Enemies, malefic magic, beasts of burden, sorrows, troubles, prison and imprisonment, spies, informants, traitors, self-destruction	Cadent

The houses are the realms of the world, and what must be experienced in a lived human life. They are the tribulations and glories that we all must face. If the signs influence the actions and nature of the planets, the houses are where those planets are going to act out and what they are going to influence. We can think again of that concept of microcosm and macrocosm. The celestial spheres, so macrocosmic and distant in their enormity, interact within the houses that are a little more micro-cosmic—dealing with human lives, society, expectations, and the cycle of our experiences here below.

The 12 houses are interpreted quite differently in traditional astrology than they are in modern astrology. And here is where we should highlight a major difference in approach from traditional to more modern schools of thought on astrology. Traditionally, the 1st house (the Ascendant) was about the person for whom the chart is cast, in a nativity. It contains much information on ego, sense of self, and even physical appearance and background. The rest of the houses were seen as external. Modern astrology has become heavily influenced by psychoanalysis, particularly that of Jung. This influence has led modern astrologers to often use a very different language when discussing a horoscope, particularly the house, than a traditional astrologer would have used.

For example: the 2nd house is about assets, estates, money, etc. (We'll go over the houses soon). For a traditional astrologer, this would be where we would find information about one's inheritances, monies, estates, and literally what was going to happen for the person. In modern astrology, a different language is sometimes used. So, a modern astrologer might look for "how one approaches money" or "what is your relationship to money." The difference here is that the traditional astrologer was externalizing the reading, looking at the person's relationships and experiences in the World. The modern astrologer is often looking more into the internal, sometimes entirely internally, making the chart about one's personal psychology in different spheres of life. Therefore, traditional astrological texts can sometimes be shocking to those trained only in modern techniques. They can seem fatalistic, dark even, with death predictions, illnesses, statements about physical appearance, and the blessings and calamities that may be coming. To a modern astrologer, the language is completely psychologized and personalized, made about how one feels or experiences these things much more than exactly *what* they will be experiencing.

This is a differing worldview. Modern and postmodern thought is ego-centric, whereas more traditional philosophies were community based and deeply religious. Traditional approaches to reading a horoscope are rooted in a holistic framework of the human soul in the midst of other souls, in connection to family, legacy, aspiration, calamity, and luck. Destiny and fate need not be dour or depressing. They can also be viewed as more beautifully connected, more deeply human. If everything in the chart is simply "what you think about something," a mere condensed and ego-locked rendition of "it's all in your head," then this can seem liberating at first and deeply insightful—only to turn out to be a gilded prison. Traditional astrology looks more to what we are going to experience *with others*. It looks to what is going to happen, not just what we might think about. To put it more bluntly: *you are not the center of the universe.*

READING NATIVITIES

The goal of this chapter is to make you comfortable with reading a natal chart. So far you have met the major "players" of astrology, the agents that act with will within the system. There are the planets, the fixed stars, the nodes, lots, and more. All of these have been introduced to you as well as the architecture with which we read the heavens: the horoscope. Our goal now is to put this information into practical use in nativities. Although some see a sharp distinction between interpreting horoscopes and doing astrologically guided magic, I do not. I believe firmly that planetary magic such as the rituals you've been introduced to in the previous chapters on the planets and fixed stars are powerful tools in themselves which can help the student of the Art to become a better astrologer, even if the astrology we are doing is reading horoscopes by casting nativities. I believe astrology has the power to inform many aspects of our lives, and weaving the magic of the planets and stars into our practice as well as the divination aspect of horoscopes means we are creating something deeply meaningful with which we can work. Too often, forms of divination are divorced from any real connection to the bigger picture of magic, religion, and spiritual practice. They become parlor games or hobbies. I always hope my students approach working with nativities with the same sense of power and enchantment as they would approach magical working or the more esoteric aspects of astrological systems.

*∗*Before the Beginning*∗*

Natal charts have become the dominant form of astrology that most people interact with in the modern age. The question of "What's your sign?" has become ubiquitous, and even nonbelievers can answer it with relative ease. Many people even know base information about the signs, such as compatibilities that they have heard, or the importance of the "rising sign" or the "Moon sign." This interest in astrology from the deeply personal level of one's birth has led to nativities dominating the scene for quite some time. It is important to remember, however, as we have discussed before, that there are other very good reasons to create a horoscope as well, and we will explore the most important of these non-natal horoscopes, the horary chart, in the following chapter. But for now, let's indulge in our love of birth charts and go over how to interpret a nativity with good, solid foundational skills.

⋆⋆⋆What is a Nativity?⋆⋆⋆

A nativity, or natal chart, is a horoscope cast for the moment of someone's birth. We try to be as exact as possible in working with someone's birth date and time so that we can accurately calculate the placement of the Ascendant, the planets, and everything else that goes into building the horoscope. Birth charts created when birth times are unknown are difficult to engage with since the rising sign (Ascendant) cannot be accurately determined, and we will be unsure of the placement of the planets when it comes to aspects. There are astrologers who predominately work with rectifying birth charts for people who do not know their exact birth time and cannot get access to it, but that is beyond the scope of this chapter. With this chapter, we will assume that you know the date and birth time, as near to exact as possible, as well as the location of birth for whomever you wish to create a natal chart.

⋆⋆⋆The Interpretation Process⋆⋆⋆

I always recommend a systematic approach to getting all the information you can from a chart before you begin to interpret. Have a notebook with you, plus the chart, and go through everything in a systematic way so that you can have everything you need to interpret. As you progress, you can interpret in a more "as-you-go" method, but in the beginning it is a good idea to write everything down and come back to it, looking for important aspects and relationships in the chart so you can give a solid interpretation. I recommend the following system:

★ Look at Ascendant and 1ˢᵗ House

Start out by looking at the Ascendant and the 1st house. Who rules it and what is that planet doing? What is going on in the 1ˢᵗ house? Then, look at the houses in terms of angular, succedent, and cadent. What are the trends?

My first step is to look at the Ascendant. In traditional texts, the Ascendant and the 1ˢᵗ house told us a lot about the person's physical appearance, their placement in the world, their ego, and who they are as a person. Guido Bonatti says, "The 1ˢᵗ house, whose beginning is out of the direction of the east, is called the Ascendant. And this house … signifies the life and body of any native, or even of a querent."[1] It can give us vital information as to who they are and how they are going to appear to the wider world. Any planets within the 1ˢᵗ house are going to have influence on the person's ego and personality. Also, the planet that rules the sign of the first house will have heavy influence so note what that planet is doing and use its relationships and placement to help determine personality traits, ego, and physical appearance.

Also, look at the houses. How many important players are in the angular, succedent, and cadent houses? Note this.

★ Triplicities and Quadruplicities

Make a list of every planet and write down the element and mode (triplicity and quadruplicity) of the planets in the chart. Notice any imbalances or relationships here. Is the nativity full of fire? Completely drowning in water? A good balance of all four elements and modes? Are the fixed signs predominately where the planets are? Look for these relationships, as this can color the interpretation of the entire chart. It may be that a person is severely lacking in a certain element, or that they are completely fixed in their mode of being. Noting all of this will help give you a fuller picture of the chart.

---

[1]   Benjamin N. *Dykes, Bonatti on Basic Astrology: Treatises 1-3 of Guido Bonatti's Book of Astronomy, Theory, Signs, Houses, Planets, Configurations* (Minneapolis, MN: The Cazimi Press, 2010), 95.

⭐3 Planets: Dignity and Debility

My next step is to make a list of dignities and debilities for each planet. Are they exalted, in rulership, in detriment, in triplicity rulership, or in fall based on the signs they occupy? Note this. This is basically a way to see what condition each planet is in within the chart. Are some planets in an awfully bad place? Are some happy and cozy where they've been seen? Note all of this down so that you can determine the inherent nature of what the planet is doing within the chart. Note what sign each planet it is in and the house. Look for trends, houses that seem over- or underpopulated, or if entire regions of the chart are blank. Notice these trends as you write. Use this information to find the *Almuten*, the planet with the most dignity, which will have a hefty influence on the client. A chart for calculating this is found in our chapter on planetary condition. It is also important here to note any mutual reception between planets based on domicile, exaltation, detriment, fall, triplicity, etc.

⭐4 Consider Sect

Is this a night chart or a day chart? How are the planets affected by this? Are there diurnal planets below the horizon? Note that. What if every planet is in the wrong sect or the correct one? Note this all as well. It will give you an idea of how "comfortable" the planets are and how easy or difficult their experiences might be in the chart.

⭐5 Note All Aspects

Next, note all aspects: conjunctions, oppositions, trines, sextiles, and squares. By this point, you will notice certain planets having a much more prominent place in your notes. Some planets may already have significant dignities, plus sect issues, as well as strong aspects. This lets you know which planets are influential in this chart as you go through this process and which ones you may want to spend extra attention on while interpreting.

⭐ Consider the Others

Next, write down the placements of the major fixed stars that you choose to use, if you choose to use them, as well as the lots and nodes. Notice trends with elements, modes, and relationships here as well, just as you did with the planets. In this chart we are going to be using the nodes and the part of fortune, to keep it simple. We won't be using the fixed stars. If you want to examine this chart further, using the fixed stars, you may add them and consult our chapter on the fixed stars as a reference.

*∴*Analyzing a Sample Chart *∵*

We are going to go through an interpreting session for a nativity drawn up anonymously, but who we will refer to as "Pat." Pat's chart is below. We are going to first go through and get the information we spoke of above, getting a clearer image of this chart and the information it can give us about Pat. I am going to start by just getting the major information from the chart, with a few insights along the way, but not a full interpretation yet. This should show the student how to notice trends, to be a good note-taker and notice what needs to be noticed throughout the process.

Example Chart for "Pat"

✠ Checking Ascendant and 1st House

The 1st house, or Ascendant, is in Gemini. There are no planets in the 1st house. The part of fortune is here, though. The ruler of the Ascendant, Mercury, is in Taurus in the 12th house. This gives Mercury no major dignities, but it is in *term*. This is a minor dignity.

Angular Houses: Part of fortune

Succedent Houses: Venus, Mars, Jupiter

Cadent Houses: The nodes, Midheaven, Saturn, Mercury, Sun, Moon

That is a lot of energy in the final, cadent house, and the only thing in an angular house (outside the Ascendant, which is always in the 1st, and thus angular) is the part of fortune. There are three planets in succedent houses, though, and two of them happen to be the two benefics. This might be helpful to counter all that 12th house, cadent nature.

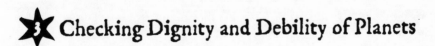

2 Listing Triplicities and Quadruplicities

Water: Venus

Earth: Sun, Moon, Mercury, Saturn

Fire: Jupiter, north node

Air: Midheaven, Ascendant, part of fortune, south node, Mars

Mutable: Ascendant, part of fortune

Cardinal: Jupiter, Mars, Venus

Fixed: Nodes, Midheaven, Sun, Moon, Mercury, Saturn

So, I notice immediately a predominance of fixed nature here, followed by cardinal, with mutable a distant third (but with the Ascendant there, a crucial aspect of a chart). The elements are relatively balanced but lacking in water.

3 Checking Dignity and Debility of Planets

Moon: Taurus, 12th house. Exalted.

Mercury: Taurus, 12th house. Term.

Venus: Cancer, 2nd house. Term. Face.

Sun: Taurus, 12th house. Peregrine.

Mars: Libra, 5th house. Detriment.

Jupiter: Aries, 11th house. Peregrine. House of joy.

Saturn: Taurus, 12th house. Peregrine. House of joy.

Other planetary notes: Lots of peregrine planets. Only one strong dignity, the Moon (in exaltation in Taurus). Jupiter and Saturn in their house of joy, so impact these houses a bit more positively. Mars in detriment.

Moon and Venus have mutual reception by rulership (Moon in Taurus and Venus in Cancer). This is a powerful relationship.

Now let's look for the Almuten, using our chart from chapter 8.

Planet	Conditions	Score
☾ Moon	Exalted (+4)	+4
☿ Mercury	Term (+2)	+2
♀ Venus	Term (+2), Face (+1)	+3
☉ Sun	Peregrine (-5)	-5
♂ Mars	Detriment (-5)	-5
♃ Jupiter	Peregrine (-5)	-5
♄ Saturn	Peregrine (-5)	-5

The Moon and Venus carry good dignity, and this will only be helped by their mutual reception. There are a lot of planets with debility, due to their peregrine nature and the detriment of Mars in Libra.

★ Checking Sect

All planets are in their proper sect except for the Moon, which is right above the horizon in this chart. Looking at this chart, I wouldn't necessarily consider the Moon being "out of sect" as a major negative influence on this chart considering the Moon is exalted in Taurus and is very close to the horizon as it is placed. She is only just coming into daylight here, and in a sign in which she is exalted. So perhaps the out-of-sect nature will not have as much influence here. These are thoughts to note as you interpret and trust your intuition here. At this stage, we're only getting a feel for everything and letting ourselves be guided by our knowledge and relationship to the tools of the Art.

⭐ Listing the Aspects

Aspect: The Sun and Moon are in conjunction.

Aspect: Mercury and Saturn are in conjunction

Aspect: Jupiter and Mars are in opposition.

Aspect: Venus is sextile to the Sun and Moon (which are in conjunction) and to Saturn and Mercury (which are in conjunction).

Aspect: Venus is also squared to Mars and Jupiter.

What am I noticing? Two major conjunctions, one major opposition, and some positive sextile aspects. There are also a few minor trines in this chart, but since they are not directly affecting planets, the above aspects are going to be the most influential, I believe, and so I am not focusing on them. The squares with Venus will also be worth investigating.

⭐ Checking the Others

Part of fortune in the 1st house in Gemini. The nodes seem disconnected from other heavenly bodies, although the south node is near the Midheaven. The south node is in the airy sign of Aquarius. The north node is in the fiery sign of Leo. The south node may give added positive influence to questions of career, but the nodes are not heavily influencing any major heavenly bodies here.

⋆⋅⋆ Weaving it Together ⋆⋅⋆

Pat's rising sign is Gemini. The 1st house has no planet within it, however, and the planet that rules his rising sign, Mercury, only has the minor dignity of term, and it is within the 12th house—a house associated with imprisonment and negative fortune. Given this information, Pat may struggle with finding himself, perhaps feeling out of place in many public situations or when answering personal questions. The 12th house is just so restrictive, and there is so much activity in it for Pat. The fixed nature is *strong* here. Saturn is with Mercury here, which we will look at later, but the saturnine nature lends a heaviness. My reading is that the native may be prone to introspection, over-thinking, and grow dour at times.

We do not have to read this as entirely negative, however, since Saturn here is in its house of joy and is in its proper sect (diurnal). There is also the part of fortune right there in the 1st house, bringing in a positive force. Inward thoughtfulness is not always a negative, after all! And the Moon is exalted, even in these difficult circumstances. So, even if Pat deals with an inwardly turned nature, it does not necessarily portend serious unhappiness. The Sun is conjunct the Moon, a possible combustion scenario, but the two luminaries are very powerful, and the Moon is not so easily stamped out by the Sun as the other stars. The Moon is carrying the dignity here, so I believe it can overcome. A serious-minded person is not a bad thing.

The planets have a lot of peregrine situations across the chart, with lesser dignities in many cases, which drives home the difficulty in easy living or expressing oneself openly. Things will come in small ways—difficult, but doable. Mars is in detriment, in Libra and the 5th house. The 5th house speaks a lot about the social sphere, so interpersonal relationships will not be easy. Friendships and relationships with children will take time to grow, not flowing easily. This ties in with Pat's thoughtful, perhaps taciturn nature. Interpersonal relationships will be easier with women, however, since the sign of the 5th house is ruled by Venus and Venus is in Cancer, with an exalted Moon in the chart. Female energy is strong here, with positive implications. Pat might just relate to women better than men.

Saturn and Mercury are conjoined in the nativity, in Taurus. Saturn is in the house of joy here, the 12th, and this combination of planets is a good omen for business, although it will be restrained in the 12th, perhaps coming later in life or in difficult circumstances. The path is solid, but not necessarily easy. The working together of Saturn and Mercury is described by Valens, who says of the two, "[They} are allies and productive of activities/employment ... these stars make men who are not without resources and not unintelligent, with much experience and awareness, and who are curious, far-seeing scholars, seekers after mystic lore, revering the gods, but with much on their consciences."[2] With our knowledge of the native's Ascendant being so empty and a little-dignified ruler of the Ascendant, this combination leads me to believe that the native will have an effective and sane approach to money and work, but with a heavy proneness to worry over and keep those worries to himself.

I'm even more confident about work and money being ordered by this Mercury and Saturn relationship due to the Moon. Why? Well, Pat's 2nd house is in Cancer, and the Moon rules Cancer. The Moon is exalted in Taurus here, which is a major dignity. Venus rules Taurus, where the Moon is located, so there is a positive relationship here. Given the influence of Venus here, it might be that Pat has money from his mother's side of the family, or a wife. Whatever the situations is, it is solid. Female influences are going to be crucial to Pat's success. The Moon and Venus are doing a lot here!

The Sun and Moon are closely related, in Taurus, a house where the Moon is exalted. This major dignity does give clarity to the native, and Pat will have a sense of purpose tied to work. Saturn is the planet that rules the sign of the Midheaven (Aquarius), which ties to work-life and public persona, and Saturn is in its house of Joy. The peregrine nature here, to me, signifies that it may come later in life (as we thought before). This is driven home by the fact of it all being so strongly centered in the final house. Given what we have said about the relationship with Mercury above, I do believe that work will be a strong place of importance for Pat and a place where he draws meaning and purpose in his life. The strong saturnine influence here, and the restrained Mercury, would lend

---

2   Vettius Valens, *Anthologies*, trans. Mark Riley, https://www.csus.edu/indiv/r/rileymt/vettius%20valens%20entire.pdf, 17.

itself to careers in estate law, agricultural business, or insurance. There are, of course, other options here, but I do believe it will be something more inwardly turned and without a strong, lively component. I couldn't see this chart as a party planner, or a club promoter, for example. Tying something together from the Earth with business makes a lot of sense to me here. Saturn is in Taurus, in its house of joy, tied to the Earth, to closed spaces and confinement.

We can look a bit at love for Pat, moving away from the work discussion. The 7th house is with Sagittarius here, ruled by Jupiter. Jupiter is in its house of joy in a strong sign: Aries. It is, however, in opposition to Mars, which is in Libra, and it is squared to Venus. This can portend a marriage with a strong-willed person, someone who pushes, perhaps even argues, but with that strong, cardinal Aries energy. The partnership will be one where Pat is pushed to grow. This is strengthened by the square between Mars and Venus. It may be an attraction to strong-willed individuals who are opposite to his inward nature. I don't consider anything here heavily debilitated for long-term partnerships or marriage; I simply see it as strong-willed and sometimes strained.

Venus is in some dignity here, in Cancer, due to term and face. Venus in the 2nd is often a marker of a wealthy spouse, or a marriage that involves money being taken into consideration, or a good working relationship. I do not believe Pat will enter a marriage with financial difficulties. I also believe there may be a similarity of work between Pat and his spouse. Venus is in Cancer, a sign ruled by the Moon, and the Moon is in Taurus, a sign ruled by Venus. There is mutual reception by rulership here! This is a major positive influence. The spouse will be strong-willed, but the marriage is very secure, particularly in the aspects of money and work and it is a long-lasting, purposeful relationship.

Jupiter is in the 11th, a place of allies, and is in its house of joy which speaks to me. It may be in opposition to Mars, which we spoke of above, but I still see a bit of strength here in terms of friends. Jupiter squaring Venus in relationship to the 2nd and 11th houses may portend a bit of over-indulgence when it comes to friends or partners. I believe Pat will enjoy the company of strong-willed individuals, perhaps even enjoying a debate or a positively adversarial nature in personal relationships. It could also mean that Pat has good connections with people in power, such as judges, lawyers, or business leaders. This could work to Pat's favor, balancing out his inward nature. We thrive when we are open to new experiences and people who challenge us. I can see Pat doing that, and perhaps it would be good advice to encourage this. Seek the outward and the free, even if you are rooted in the inward. Balance is always the key.

⋆⋆Literal or Figurative ⋆⋆

It is important to restate that traditional astrology can be very straight-forward and literal at times. This contrasts with many modern techniques that prefer to rely on more interpersonal, psychological explanations for phenomena in a chart. We have discussed this before, but it is important to reexamine it here, when dealing with a nativity. I have been a little open in my interpretation above, because I want students to begin to notice trends and relationships and draw conclusions based on their knowledge of the planets, signs, houses, and other players in the Art. I do want, however, to reiterate that there is nothing wrong with giving a more point-blank interpretation sometimes.

What do I mean by that? Well, let's look at Pat's 12th house. It is the most active house in the chart, with four planets, including both luminaries. The 12th house is a difficult one, with many historical sources linking it to imprisonment, enemies, and restriction.[3] If we wanted to be more direct and accept the chart for what it is, we might ask Pat if he has ever been to prison or if one of his parents was imprisoned. We might also ask if Pat works in a corrections facility, or in a legal profession tightly tied to one. This may seem very literal, but that's OK! Traditional astrology technique often is.

Keep this in mind when reading a chart. If the house of marriage (the 7th) and Venus had been heavily debilitated, we may have been tempted to ask Pat if he has a difficult approach to love, or if it has been hard for him to find a mate. The more traditional approach, however, would be to say that Pat is *in a difficult relationship* or that his partner is unpleasant or

---

3 Some sources even link it to malefic magic and Witchcraft.

challenging. This may be shocking, but it is probably more honest. The tendency to make everything egocentric is not necessarily a helpful path in divination or astrological counseling. Don't be afraid to be direct. Don't always make everything about how someone *feels* about a certain aspect of life. Sometimes, how we feel isn't what is being addressed. What is being addressed is what we are experiencing or will experience—whether we like it or not.

✦✲✦ Taking it Further ✦✲✦

The above case with Pat is a slimmed-down example of a nativity reading. Beginning to read nativities is a skill that only improves with further practice and reading. In the above chart, we did not go into every single detail of the chart, but instead focused on the largest tendencies we saw within the stars. This is a good place to start, but natal charts are always open to further investigation and a honing in on particular aspects we want to explore.

Working with another person means that we often have a guide for where we want to go. A client may want to know more about their love life or their spiritual path (the 9th house will matter here!) than they do work or family matters. Some clients will want to probe the issue of children further, or marriage prospects. A nativity is meant to represent the life of a living human being. It isn't just a random collection of symbols and numbers. Remember that in your divination and understand that each session with the stars will be different.

There is also the question of timing and progressions in a chart. Many astrologers specialize in examining transits and moving charts forward throughout the life of the person in question. This can be a powerful tool in divination, but it is a more advanced technique. I recommend that students begin by reading nativities and getting comfortable with the system before they move on to this.

Also, don't forget that you can always hone your Art to focus in on what really matters. If you are doing a nativity for someone on a spiritual path who is heavily focused on what their religious life will bring, don't be afraid to focus more heavily on the aspects of the chart that speak to that.

A workaholic is going to want to know more about how her investments or promotions are going to go and if she is in the right career that aligns with her soul. And if you need to probe these areas deeper, don't be afraid to go beyond the basics. You can bring in the fixed stars or the Arabic lots or the nodes to give more information on areas of the chart that matter to the person in question.

Finally, you may have noticed that I never said that Pat *is a Taurus*. It is true that Pat's Sun is in Taurus, but is this the most dominant force in his chart? The Sun does not bear a lot of dignity here, and the ruler of Taurus (Venus) is in Cancer. Traditional astrology does not look at charts solely based on Sun sign. I have tried to give a holistic approach to Pat's chart here, and I hope the reader will use that as a guide for interpreting any nativity. The Sun sign is not the center of natal chart reading unless the Sun is the most central player in the chart. Pat is not a Taurus. Pat is his entire chart, with every aspect bringing something to the table. We bear all the stars of Heaven within our souls, and the Art must reflect this.

When we encounter historical references to astrology, we often do not realize that we are reading about a form of situational divination. Most people who encounter astrology today approach it from the perspective of natal chart reading. Not only do they approach it from the perspective of an astrology only existing to read nativities, but they are usually only introduced to Sun-sign astrology, which is a modern incarnation of the Art that places heavy influence on the Sun sign to the neglect of almost every other aspect of the astrological tradition. This is a very recent practice that owes more to the tradition of tabloid journalism and easily repeated horoscopes than it does to anything that was practiced, historically, with astrology. It is interesting to note how this evolution has completely eclipsed the central role horary astrology played in the history of Western civilization. Astrologers were frequently called up to perform divination for potentates, and the systems of horary astrology were once the reigning form of divination for the learned and powerful classes of the world. When people wanted to probe the numinous for answers to the mundane, they looked to the stars.

Many of my students are actually surprised that astrology was and is used to answer questions or probe a difficult issue in a similar way to more popular methods of divination in the modern world such as cartomancy, runes, or spirit boards. But the fact is, this is exactly how astrology was used for many centuries across cultures. Horary astrology was probably more common than natal astrology, given that precise birth times might not have been accessible for large swaths of the population given the re-cord-keeping standards of the times they inhabited. Horary astrology, on the other hand, only requires a competent stargazer with an understanding of how to use an ephemeris and how to map the stars on her own.

The method was relatively simple. A question was asked, and the chart was drawn up for the exact moment the question was asked, observing the relevant aspects of the horoscope for the question at hand. The practice was so common that many of the central personalities of astrology wrote entire treatises on how to interpret horary questions. Horary guides, usually organized by groups of questions around similar themes, were quite common in the premodern world. There is a treasure trove of astrological information for any student who wishes to practice this form of divination, and the system is heavily documented with examples that we can use to help us get a foothold in the tradition.

In horary astrology, our knowledge of the planets, signs, and houses guides our interpretation techniques and narrows our field of vision to the most relevant facts revealed in the chart. At the simplest level, this means a system of intelligent associations. Questions of war will pay attention to Mars. A lover's quandary will take Venus into consideration, and the 7th house, if marriage is an issue. The natural correspondences between signs, houses, and other astrological considerations are easy to connect once you begin using the technique and become familiar with the tools of the Art.

Beyond the simple act of finding logical correspondences between questions and the horoscope, I think it is important to investigate the *why* of horary astrology. Before we can begin to actually engage with the art of horary divination, we might want to ask why we should even bother to look to the stars to unknit our anxieties, answer our questions, or help us to make difficult decisions. The fact is, the *why* is going to depend a lot on your worldview and spiritual practice. For those who believe that the universe is essentially a material thing, with no guiding principles to it beyond the laws of nature (physics, biology, and so forth), then any form of divination is going to seem spurious and superstitious. Astrology is going to be relegated to the dustbin, along with phrenology, and physical mediumship, and a host of other practices that the post-scientific revolution world regards as debunked.

This can be a hurdle for many who would approach astrology, or any form of divination, in the modern world. For some practitioners, the answer is to double down on the scientific quality of astrology. I have read many astrologers pour their hearts out defending astrology on the ground of physical science. These well-meaning astrologers are convinced that science and astrology are on the same path. They cling to studies produced by paranormal and psychical research committees. They link astrology to quantum physics, psychology, and sociology. I have even seen some astrologers try to make arguments about the "gravity" of the planets pulling on our bodies, since we are made mostly of water. [1] I have to say that I think this is a completely wrong approach to astrology and to the wider questions of religious experience, spirituality, divination, and magic. I do not believe that the physical sciences and the spiritual practices handed down through the ages are speaking the same language, and any attempt to translate one of these languages to the other is going to cause problems. The French have a saying: *Traduire, c'est trahir.* This means, "to translate is to commit treason." We can apply this to a lot more than working from one language into another.

I teach my students to go beyond the created dichotomy that separates physical experience from religious and spiritual practice. Divination, and astrology as a part of that larger umbrella, is answering a separate set of questions than science. Astrology is operating with a different set of foundational principles. The two worlds are axiomatically different. Astrology, at its highest spiritual level, is rooted in a belief that the human spirit is participating in something larger than itself. It does not operate solely on linear, physical experiences. We are all part of the same cosmic practice, coming and falling out of being. For those who believe the world is mechanistic and operates solely in materiality, they are not going to feel or understand these connections. And even if they did, they would

---

[1] I have seen my fair share of odd arguments trying to "science-up" the Art of astrology. I've never cared for this approach and actually think it does more harm than good.

be quick to dismiss them as delusion or wishful thinking. We, as spiritual practitioners drawn to divination and magic, must learn not to play some back-and-forth game with our hecklers. It isn't going to benefit either side. Learned discussion and debate are great, but when two people disagree on the fundamental experience of the human soul, there is not going to be a lot that can be agreed upon with regard to the meaning of life or the tools we use to discover that meaning for ourselves.

*ː*Horary Technique *ː*

The first task to cast a horary chart is to ask a question. Sounds simple enough, but it is important to realize what we want or need to know before we begin any divination technique. Horary is prepared to answer many different styles of questions, but if we do not know what we are really looking for, the chances we'll find anything are slim. Questions can be intensely specific, or more general, but they should have a purpose behind them. We can ask a yes or no question, an open-ended question, or ask to get more clarity on an event or decision.

Examples can be as simple as:

- What will happen if I take this new job offer?

- Is this person going to take the initiative in our relationship and propose?

- What is my best path forward with school: should I change majors or stay the course? Where are my strengths going to come out the most and benefit me, later?

- Should I buy the new house that came on the market, or wait until next year?

These are just examples, and you can get more in-depth or more specific with your focus, but what matters is setting your mind on what it is you really wish to know. The next step is to cast the chart for the moment you are setting down to do the divination. I prefer to do a simple meditation before this, focusing on my question, or the client's question, with some simple deep-breathing exercises and a calm, ordered space that is free from distraction or interruption. Once you feel you have centered and are ready, create the chart.

This centering is quite important. Classical astrologers did not take horary divination lightly, and any attempt to approach it frivolously was akin to temping the gods, or Fate. Vague questions, silly or dishonest questions, or a flippant approach was *dangerous,* according to classical sources. The reason for this is simple. We get from magic, divination, or spirituality what is put into it, and if we approach something as heady as the stars themselves without a sense of wonder, we might find ourselves lost in ramblings, or even worse—guided poorly. Horary astrology is a serious form of divination that is an attempt to take our mundane lives and place them into a much larger framework of divinity and cosmic consequence.

And we cast for the moment the question was asked, so that we can attune ourselves to the entire tapestry of the lived life that has worked up to the moment of this divination. Every action, thought, night of kvetching or wrestling with God on the mountain, has led to someone coming for guidance to the highest concepts of light and starry magic. The moment is *sacred,* precisely because someone has chosen to consider his or her life from a higher perspective. We are setting this moment apart from the purely terrestrial. So really consider the question, its merits and difficulties, and approach this work as a serious endeavor. Once you are sure that you are ready, or your client is ready, then cast the chart for the moment.

Now we interpret for our question. There are many ways to do this, but I find that two over-arching styles dominate horary readings. For very pointed, singular, yes-or-no, or simple questions, I will often med-itate on what planet, house, signs, or other players most causally relate to that question. Then I will examine those things in the chart, focusing almost all my interpretation on what is going on with those players. If the question is more in-depth, open-ended, or complicated (such as involving multiple players, or a longer time frame), I will interpret the entire chart, taking more of the players I see into consideration. There are benefits to both broad approaches, but I think the question should guide the choice here. As an astrologer, it is up to you to determine what really relates to the question. It is your consciousness engaging in this process, and you need to follow that. The reason I stress this is because it is amazingly easy to get lost in a horoscope. There is so much going on that we can get overwhelmed and read into every detail of the chart. This often leads to murky, and frankly pointless, readings that are unsatisfying to both the reader and the client (and doubly painful if you are reading for yourself).

⋆⋆⋆Keys to Beginning⋆⋆⋆

One of the simplest and most effective ways to begin is to determine the condition of the client, or *querent*. To look for what is going to represent your client, look to the planet that rules the Ascendant, or 1ˢᵗ house, in your horary chart. For example, if the 1ˢᵗ house is with Scorpio, then we will look at Mars and its condition to determine the state of the querent regarding his or her question or conundrum. If the 1ˢᵗ house has Pisces, we will look at Jupiter, etc. Any planets or serious situations with the 1ˢᵗ house should be taken into consideration as well about the person in question. Their attitude and situation will be heavily demonstrated in this area.

We will also take the Moon into consideration as it relates to the querent. In traditional astrological systems around horary charts, the Moon was heavily associated with situations pertaining to the querent. I always look to both the ruler of the Ascendant and the Moon in determining how the querent is doing with regard to the matter at hand. A heavily debilitated ruler of the Ascendant and a heavily debilitated Moon will spell a troubled or misguided querent. Both figures having a lot of dignity in the chart may spell the opposite. A mixed bag is often more common, and we must use our knowledge of the chart to determine the truth.

Now, knowing what is going on with the person himself, or herself, we will look at the question. The matter at hand is called the *quesited*. My first place to look is always the house that most intricately links with what is being asked. You can refer to our chapter on the architecture of astrology for an overview of houses. Think about what is really being asked by your client. What realm of life is this question considering? Who in the client's life is involved with the question? Some determinations will be quite easy: a question about a sibling will be in the 3rd house. A question about death will look at the 8th. A marriage will take into consideration the 7th, etc. Some will be more complicated and require some time to consider all angles. [2] Take your time with this, because once you decide, you will begin to interpret with what is given from the chart. You will want to consider all planets, and conditions, relating to the house in question.

These two foundational beginning areas, of querent and quesited, are the backbone of good horary astrology. We will, of course, take into consideration the signs, major aspects, and other players in a chart, but starting with a strong grasp of what is going on with the significators of the querent (ruler of the Ascendant, the Moon) and the quesited (the house in question, and everything going on with it), we can really begin to give a clear and meaningful answer to any matter or question brought forward to the Art.

⋆˙⋆Keeping a Holistic View ⋆˙⋆

One of the powers of traditional astrology is that it is a holistic, internally coherent system. The spiritual force behind the Art is what makes it a useful tool for divination. When reading a chart becomes too bogged down in pure mathematical relationships, with no consideration of what the entire chart is *saying* to us, then I think we run the risk of not seeing the forest for the trees. What I mean here is that every sign, planet, house, fixed star, or lot has a certain *spirit* behind it. The correspondences are

---

2   For example: if a question of money is at hand, we would naturally go to the 2nd house. However, if we are looking for money from a sibling, we might need to move to the 3rd. And if the question is about money from a lover, or a marriage, then the 7th will be our focus. Questions will often involve a bit of thinking to determine where the quesited really is located within the chart.

powerful and meaningful, and we need to take the entire system into consideration when we interpret for a horary client.

A way to ensure that you are engaging with the system in this way is to remember the traditional correspondences of signs, planets, and the rest of the architecture of the Art. Remember that signs and planets can be masculine or feminine. They can be hot, cool, dry, or moist. They can be diurnal or nocturnal. All this colors the spirit of the astrological reading and must be taken into consideration. Do not forget the elements, either. Ask yourself what it would mean if a chart was completely masculine or feminine. What would it mean if a chart is entirely in hot and moist areas, with no coolness? What if a chart is entirely dry with much fire and no water? Is every planet we are focusing on in a fixed sign? If so, this will be saying something important that we need to consider. These are meaningful groupings that help us make sense of the intricate cosmic language we are using.

And the houses are no different. As we discussed in our chapter on the architecture of astrology, the houses have associations and groupings as well. The angular houses are strong and powerful, and they will speak louder than the succedent houses. The cadent houses (meaning *falling*) are more difficult, and a chart completely falling in cadent houses is going to be a unique situation: the message that comes through will be heavily colored by this. Keep notes as you read and notice the patterns that appear in your charts. These repeating patterns will help you build up your knowledge as an astrologer and give more nuanced, impactful readings.

⋆⋆⋆Example⋆⋆⋆

A client has a question about her marriage. She believes that she and her partner are drifting apart and worries that poor communication will ruin their relationship, possibly leading to a split. She wonders where the relationship is headed, as of this very moment. She desires further guidance on what to do and hopes to save her relationship. So, taking this into mind, you cast the horary chart and begin to divine.

To begin, we need to find out the state of the querent. We are going to look to the ruler of the 1st house, the Ascendant, as well as the Moon.

Then we need to find out about her husband and his relationship to the marriage. We will look to the 7th house since this is the house of marriage. Whatever planet is ruling this house will signify a lot about his feelings on the matter and where he is, emotionally and spiritually. We can also look to the Sun and its position to get a stronger feel for how he is, given that the Sun is traditionally the planet of men and husbands. Venus will come into play as well, considering she rules marriages, love, and questions about these areas.

So, we begin with the querent. The Ascendant is in Aries. We know that we need to look for Mars in the chart, since Mars rules this sign. We find Mars in Aries, so it is in the house of its domicile, a major dignity. There is no other major planet in the 1st house. Let us look at the Moon. We find the Moon in Libra, which means it is peregrine. We don't see any other major dignities at all, so the Moon is truly peregrine. The only planet in the 1st house, Mars, is in opposition to Venus. Given all this information we can begin to understand the position of the querent.

Frankly—she is probably angry, and rightfully so. The ruler of the 1st house is in domicile, giving it a lot of power. Mars is a powerful planet, a planet of strength and fire. She wants something to change, having this strong significator in a cardinal sign that it rules. It is in opposition to Venus, showing the discord brewing here. Mars is well-dignified here, so it is angry for a just cause, with prudent understanding. She is not flying off the handle or reading into the situation. She sees it for what it is and is responding accordingly. They are butting heads. She is not timid at all and has been clearly expressing her frustrations.

The Moon is in the 7th house, in Libra. It is peregrine, with no major dignity. But it *is* in the house of marriage, the house that most relates to what we are investigating. Emotionally, she is still attached to the marriage. Despite her worry, the Moon shows that her emotional investment in the marriage is still high and tied to her husband. This is not an indicator that she wishes to dissolve the relationship just yet, despite the difficulties.

Let's look at the 7th house and its ruler to determine the husband. We can also look at the Sun to get further information. The 7th house is with Libra, containing the Moon and Venus. The ruler of the sign of the 7th house, Venus, is in domicile, so it has a lot of dignity. The husband does love his wife. There is no conjunction or major aspects, so I don't believe he is seeing anyone else. I see no affair here. I simply see a butting of heads and a strong opposition where both sides are "in domicile," which signifies to me strong emotions and a sense that both parties constantly feel they are right—and this leads to intense arguing. The Sun, as a significant planet for the husband, is in Scorpio in the horary chart, bearing no major dignity. He is as lost as she is as to what to do. They both think they are right. They both love each other. They both aren't budging.

Looking at Mercury, as ruler of communication, might help us here. I find some minor dignity, perhaps, but nothing major. There's not a lot of communication help coming anytime soon. With all of this information, I believe that the relationship is gridlocked until they seek outside help. Counseling is definitely the best option for the marriage since both parties are strongly convinced they are in the right, perhaps unable to see the other side of the situation, but they are both still invested in the marriage. No significators in the chart lead us to believe an affair is happening or that either party has disinvested from the relationship. This sort of communicational gridlock and oppositional natures would benefit from a calm, reasonable outside source that can break the tension and help heal the marriage.

The Condensed Version: *You both think you are right, but you love each other. Communication is oppositional. You need counseling to break the gridlock. There isn't anyone else or a longing to leave from either of you. Get help and heal in a respectful, supportive way. Do that, or you will keep arguing with no sign of relief.*

✦✦Considerations✦✦

The above is a condensed reading, looking at the major players involved in the question. We began with the significators of the querent: ruler of the Ascendant and the Moon. Then we looked at the person and question at hand: 7th house and its ruler, plus the Sun in this case. We concluded the reading with little else (a bit of Mercury, but nothing much more). This is a perfectly fine way to begin horary reading. You do not need a massive undertaking to get meaningful readings with this system. I often find that a clear approach with a few key details is often enough to get an answer for a client.

But some questions will not be so simple. As you progress with the tools of horary astrology, you will begin to find exactly what you need for each reading. The chart will reveal itself. There is always an answer. If you

find that one is lacking, or that a reading seems murky, ask the querent to redefine his or her question. Probe deeper. There is a touch of counseling required in any form of divination. Sometimes more information will come out. I have often done charts for clients that have business questions, and when I cast the chart, shady or unclear messages come through. Often, when I probe the querent, there is more information that they are uncomfortable sharing, and the lack of openness is making the reading difficult. This is also true of relationship questions. Sometimes, a client will have a relationship question about a communication issue in a relationship when what is really going on is an affair from one or both parties. This often comes out in horary readings, so be prepared to redefine, ask, and truly get to the core of what is going on in a consultation. Not everyone who has a question has fully worked out what the consequences of what getting an answer might truly be.

This is not to say that you need to grill your clients. The truth is that when people are coming for a reading, it usually means they are worried about something. Something just *isn't right* in their lives, or they are anxious about an important aspect of their experience. This can sometimes mean that clients are not sure of what the real question is. Sometimes they are afraid to come out and ask what is really going on because they are scared of the answer. Sometimes they are afraid that they are not being fully honest with themselves. All of this is completely natural, and being a good astrologer often requires you to talk with your clients (and yourself!) when casting charts. Communication is key here, so that we can get to a serious and meaningful question and approach the stars with it, confident that we are looking in the right place and at the right time.

And never stop learning! You can begin with classical sources such as the ones used throughout this book, but you can investigate modern astrological teachers who work with horary or have written on the technique. These include John Frawley, Deborah Houlding, Benjamin Dykes, and others. The field is still full of astrologers working with the Art, many teaching classes or translating classical works on astrology so that we all have access to them in our native language. Online forums, astrology workshops, and conferences continue to grow. Look into the community and find the voices that speak to you, learning what you can and continuing to grow your skills. Everyone must begin somewhere, and I have found that the community is often very good at teaching newcomers and welcomes the excitement that novices can bring. There is nothing wrong with asking questions, or even making mistakes as you begin. Learning and honing the Art takes time, so do not be afraid to look for good teachers and fellow stargazers.

MAGICAL ASTROLOGY

We've discussed the planets, stars, and correspondences so far and provided a taste of ritual magic with each planet. What I want to do for the reader now is provide a framework for really delving into astrological magic. This should be a series of tools and recommendations that apply to any and all magical practices, truly. Deciding to work with planetary magic and engage in ritual is not something that should be taken lightly. All magical work has effects on the mind and spirit of the practitioner. It has become very popular to approach magic as something one tries out for a bit of time, a hobby, something to pick up as a quirky spiritual experiment. The fact is, discipline and commitment were always central to the Arts, whether it was astrological magic, spirit-summoning, divination, or any other form of magic. To approach magic with no sense of grounding, no purpose or plan, is to begin something that will most likely garner little result, or even be harmful. For many seekers, beginning a new path or training is done with little investment, and the practice is dropped almost as quickly as it is picked up, with nothing truly gained. This does not have to be the case. Discipline and sustained practice are possible, and the results they produce can be incredible, powerful, and they can transmute our lives.

There is such a palpable difference of approach between many modern New Age guides to magic or ritual versus more traditional sources. The grimoires, occult treatises, and magical textbooks we have inherited were quite stern in the intense preparation and discipline needed to engage in truly transformative magic. Fasting, fully realized ritual spaces, special clothing, tools, and more were all part of what it meant to approach and engage with serious magic. The rites in the *Abramelin*, for example, include intense periods of isolation, fasting, purity rites, and ritual along every step of the processes described in the work. [1] I am not saying any of this to be off-putting or make the Art seem daunting or difficult to approach. I am only saying it to highlight the real discipline that magic takes. It is, on some level, no different than any other serious undertaking. If someone wanted to learn a language and studied a few minutes every other day, forgot their lessons, avoided difficult vocabulary, and generally only approached it when they were bored or slightly curious, then the chances of them learning that language are slim to none. The same would be true for learning a musical instrument, mastering a visual art technique, or building muscle or bodily fitness.

We get from our workings what we put into them. If we approach magic as pure, unadulterated superstition, then we are going to feed the worst parts of our psyche. We are going to feed our paranoia, our egotistical desire to feel more powerful than others, and our credulity. If we, instead, put into our workings a sense of spiritual progression, a desire to reach the higher planes of ourselves, then we can expect to grow with our ritual and our practice, to gain new insight and new tools for acting in the world and reacting to what we encounter. When we approach our magic like this, the discipline seems worthwhile. There is no drudgery in it, and we begin to get excited by the results we see. We see the tools and rituals as extensions of ourselves and our practice, not simply as bygone, esoteric bric-a-brac that we created out of whimsy or boredom with traditional religion. Real magic engages mind and body; it takes the full enthusiasm and commitment of the practitioner.

So, this chapter is a guide to the person who is interested in approaching astrological magic as a real and living practice, something that can be worked into an already-existing spiritual path or provide a foundation for one. This guide is not a dogmatic list meant to be taken as a final word on the subject, but it is going to suggest a disciplined and serious approach to the Art, because I know that this is the only approach that truly transforms the practitioner and helps the seeker reach higher states of development in his or her practice.

---

[1] The *Abramelin* is a decidedly non-astrological work of magic, but it is an excellent example of the seriousness with which many occult texts approach ritual and magic.

⋆⋅⋆Belief⋆⋅⋆

❝ Lord, I believe; help my unbelief!❞ – Gospel of Mark

The primary struggle I see with many seekers in the beginning is the question of belief. For many, the modern and largely materialistic worldview is so ingrained that they want to see even magic as nothing more

than cause and effect, a series of gestures and actions that garner a desired outcome. There are no spirits, no divine apparatus, no true mysticism in the work. They aren't trying to elevate the soul, they only want to "make something happen." The irony in this is that many people think they are avoiding "superstition" in their magic or practice by avoiding divine names, god-concepts, angelic workings, or whatever else they deem "too religious," when, in fact, the opposite is true. There is nothing more superstitious than a pure cause-and-effect approach to magic. *If I put the right stone down at the right time, this thing will happen that I want.* This is just as superstitious as the basest supplicant's prayer. It robs magic of its truly transformative power *within*. We are not only working our will into the world around us, but we are transforming the deepest parts of ourselves. As Above, So Below is mirrored in the concept of As Without, So Within. What we are acting out in the world takes place within us as well, and we are truly working these rites to progress and reach a deeper place within ourselves, not merely affect the material plane.

Because belief *does* matter. If we do not believe that we can change our circumstance or that ritual, rites, prayers, or meditation can actually do anything, then we are not going to get very far. We should put the books down, break the tools, and just move on with whatever mundane distractions we can find to numb our senses. We have to believe that a path can help us, that what it says is even possible, before we can ever truly be touched by it. This is not to say that we should be credulous. We should hold judgment and have our reservations about any serious undertaking in our lives, but if we begin every single path we try with deep-seated cynicism and a refusal to commit to the precepts or possibilities within that path, then we are never going to make progress. We have to know, in the deepest part of ourselves, that we truly can change our circumstance and elevate our experience, or we are not going to get anything from magical practice.

It is also important to realize that divinity suffuses almost all magical practices. The two are not enemies, as seems to be the belief of some modern practitioners. Magic can be, and was in many systems, a divine act. The Greek Magical Papyri are spells that are essentially based in prayer and supplication to divine beings. The grimoire tradition is deeply spiritual and religious in nature and views magic as essentially contracted with higher and lesser spirits. Witchcraft and folk magic have a long history of working with "familiar spirits." Historical astrological texts, as discussed in this work, for example, are linked to concepts of gods, angels, and the Divine Will. The divine nature is *everywhere* in magic. It is not some "religious intrusion" to bring the gods or the angels into our magic. They have always been there. It is their world. It has always been my experience that stripping magic of its divinity, casting out all forms of belief that we find "antiquated" or "delusional," leads to a sterile magic, a mummer's play that accomplishes nothing more than passing the time when someone is bored or serving as a small rebellion against a seemingly religious world.

The Christian theologian David Bentley Hart strikes a powerful chord when he describes the deeply anti-religious and secular sentiment of modernism: "It is a diverting alternative to thinking deeply. It is a narcotic. In our time, to strike a lapidary phrase, irreligion is the opiate of the bourgeoisie, the sigh of the oppressed ego, the heart of a world filled with tantalizing toys."[2] This is not to say that we must have the same dogmatic approach to belief as traditional theologians would often have us think. It is only to say that belief is a powerful tool, and that the ecstasy of spiritual practice can be a challenge and a true rebellion against a world of chrome and steel, a world of nihilism and brute force.

So, I teach my students to approach astrology, magic, or any spiritual practice with real vigor of belief. I cannot stress, even in fear of repeating myself, that this is not cheap credulity. I want the seeker to question. I want the seeker to doubt. I also, however, want the seeker to actually believe that change is possible. Without that initial spark—that little seed of belief in the power of our will and the divinity present and flowing throughout the world and throughout the body—then magic is a dead Art. I know the power it has, and what it can do to change a person's experience and station. I know the seed can be watered, so I always bring it back to belief. Let us believe. And then let us do the work.

*˙.*Discipline and Cycles *˙.*

    Often also man is changeable, and while beginning a thing well, finisheth it badly, being in no way firm and stable in resolution. Ponder the matter then well before commencing, and only begin this Operation with the firm intention of carrying it out unto the end." –Abramelin

As I mentioned in the preface to this work, astrological magic is a wonderful tool for learning discipline. Being rooted in timekeeping and repeatable, predictable cycles, this Art can give us a framework for ordering ourselves toward progress and spiritual elevation. For the seeker, I recommend developing a cycle of good habits that will aid your magical workings and provide spiritual fruits on their own as well.

---

2   David Bentley Hart, *The Experience of God: Being, Consciousness, Bliss* (New Haven, CT: Yale University Press, 2014), 312-313.

The first is to keep a journal. This may seem like trite advice, but very few people keep them faithfully. Keep notes on all that you experience when you do a ritual, on the effects you experience internally and externally. You can also begin to journal how you feel during certain astrological phenomena, how you begin to see patterns of repetitions, fruitful times for creative pursuits, or times that would be better for reflection or internal work. Keep this journal faithfully, even when you're tired, even when you feel that there was not much to say. Going over what we have learned and experienced and seeing it laid out before us in a chronological way can do amazing things for our practice. It holds you to a practice as well, stops the mind from going lazy or from imagining things that *might* have happened during a magical working or ritual. A journal keeps you honest. We are very forgetful creatures sometimes, and we also have a nasty habit of remembering what we want to remember. Confirmation bias is a very real thing, and a poison for the magical practitioner. Faithful record-keeping provides a cure for a lot of bad habits.

A second piece of advice for habits is to keep up with purifications. This may sound antiquated, even churchy, but it has a rich history in magical and esoteric practices. Ritual bathing, purification rites, and prayer

work was central to keeping the mind and body ready to engage in higher practice. Egyptian priests only spent part of their time serving the temple, often having regular professions and responsibilities during much of their time. Before they entered temple service, they would shave their bodies, clean themselves, and purify. Jewish tradition places utmost importance on purity rituals such as the *mikveh*, which is deeply woven into traditional Jewish practice. Grimoire traditions recommend fasting and ritual purification before all magical undertakings. For the reader, it does not have to be as intricate as what was required for temple service in ancient cultures. I recommend a weekly purification bath as well as a small rite of purification before beginning any major magical undertaking or spiritual work.

A purification bath can be simple. Consecrated water and salt are all that is needed. Traditional herbs for purification, should you want to add them, include rosemary, hyssop, fennel, sage, vervain, lavender, and mint. You can include a purification prayer or exorcism prayer, such as those found in *The Key of Solomon* or other grimoires. Allow this to be a time of reflection, of meditation or prayer. It should act as a purifying and centering reset during the week. Sunday is the traditional day for purification such as this, but the more important thing is discipline, setting aside this time every week to reflect and readjust.

Before magical workings, purification rites are often already worked into the magic. The grimoires contain simple exorcisms and water purifications, but the act of starting out this way is a good practice. Develop the habit of always starting your works out by a small act of purifying, sanctifying your space and self. This is most commonly done, just like the bath, with water and salt, consecrated and blessed by the practitioners. Herbs are often added as well, just as mentioned above. This small act begins to train our minds to set our working space and time apart from our mundane experience; it sanctifies and elevates the experience, creating the spiritual muscle memory we need to draw the most out of our ritual and magical practice.

Along with these more practical habits, I also stress to students the importance of learning to appreciate cycles. Astrology is a cyclical magic. Planetary magic is related, deeply, to timing. Begin to learn and work with the planetary days and hours. You can consult the chapters on the individual planets as well as the chapter in this book on magical timing and the planetary hours. Once you've gotten a foothold in the system, begin working it into your practice. Choose auspicious times for certain endeavors, avoid negative timings, and keep a mindful eye on the stars and their patterns. Remember the agricultural cycle of the year, when times are ripe for planting and outdoor work, or when it may be a time of inner reflection and quietude.

A simple beginning step is to keep track of the Moon's cycle. Modern online applications make this very easy. We do not need to consult an almanac or an ephemeris like we once did. We can find planetary hours, Moon phases, and astrological information almost effortlessly now. This practice will teach you patience. When you need to wait for an auspicious time, it gives you time to plan, to think, and to be conscious of your decision-making. You aren't just mindlessly going into an operation, but instead you are planning it out diligently and considering it from different angles. By the time the hour arrives, you might find you need something entirely different, or that it has worked out a different way.

This is not just about magical timing, either. I was taught, and teach others, to use the Moon cycles to determine decision-making as well. If you have a major life decision to make and you feel overwhelmed, wait a Moon cycle before making any rash decisions. Allow the lunar phases to wax and wane before you jump headfirst into something or you do something that could have far-reaching consequences. This ability to utilize the natural and visible cycles of nature removes the constant anxiety that modern living tends to create in the mind. We are tapping into much larger cycles than the tedium of our everyday lives, and, in doing so, we are powerfully altering our perspective. We are learning to look "from above," from the place of the stars, and not get mired in the terrestrial worries that make progress difficult. Timing our magic, and mundane, experiences with the Heavens is a tool that we can use to improve our discipline, calm our minds, and order our practice.

*.*Sacred and Profane *.*

One of the strongest pieces of advice I give to anyone interested in practicing magic is to begin to separate the sacred from the profane. This can be a little off-putting to many students who read more and more how important it is to do what "feels right" and to be guided solely by intuition and to avoid anything that smacks of spiritual snobbery or elitism. There is also a very strong movement in many circles to stitch the mundane and the spiritual together, to evaporate the difference that exists between sacred space and lived space. "Kitchen Witchcraft" and other movements have worked to teach students how to use everyday objects in very everyday ways to craft magic and create ritual. There is nothing inherently wrong with this practice, but I still see the spiritual wisdom and power in creating separate sacred space and treating our magic and spiritual practices as something set apart and holy. For me, it has nothing to do with elitism or some appreciation for antiquated and stuffy practices. It is much deeper than that.

Setting apart your sacred work and space is a form of training for the mind and body. It is not about being better than someone else who uses a more mundane setting or ritual structure. No. It is about making *yourself* better. It is about improvement and elevation. Creating a ritual space may be difficult, particularly if living situations make it tricky, but it is still important. Some things on the path are going to be difficult, and trying to bypass anything that does get tricky is not going to help you. It isn't going to challenge you—and if it isn't challenging you, or moving you, or inspiring you, then how is it going to do anything to make you grow? There is a reason we tend to get a better workout at a gym with a trainer than at home on our own. There is a reason that a trained dietician might create a better diet for us than we can create at home with a few hours of Internet research under our belts. There is a reason many serious artists struggle to maintain a studio, even when it's difficult, so that they have a place in which to create art that is not their home. The temple, the church, the dojo, the potter's studio, the rehearsal hall: these all exist for a reason. When we enter a space that is set apart, it shifts our consciousness. We are entering a different space, physically, and it creates a different space, mentally. We know the feeling of awe and reverence certain buildings or spaces that are important to us can bring about. We know what it feels like to be on "holy ground." For the practitioner and the spiritual seeker, we need to know how to create that holy space for ourselves. We need to be able to create that *othering* that enables us to experience the numinous, the uncanny, the wild and free. Creating a separate space with separate tools for our practice means that we can suspend the cynical disbelief that infects so much of daily experience to engage in ritual and spiritual practice in a fresh and liberated way. We can carve out our own temples and meet the gods face-to-face.

You can also begin a regular practice of beginning with a cleansing or banishing before setting up your ritual space. The Lesser Banishing Ritual of the Pentagram, available in multiple sources, is one such ritual. You can develop your own as well, using the rituals in this work or others as a reference point. Repeated use of this ritual helps to build up the sacredness of space I have been writing about in this chapter.

So, this all means that ritual space and ritual items can become tools of discipline, mental training, and consciousness. Be mindful of your space and your tools. Although I can understand why some systems might suggest using everyday items for magic, I believe strongly that creating a separate set of working tools for your magical practice is an inherently spiritual act. Forging, creating, or even just supporting artists who make beautiful items and, thus, keep beauty in the world, as well as valuing a creative soul, are all holy acts. I recommend that the practitioner develop a relationship with the tools, curating and keeping clean and ready all instruments they might need for the Art. This can include ritual knives, wands, herbs, stones, pentacles, parchment, ink, writing instruments, or anything else that is needed. The beginner does not need every single instrument mentioned in certain texts, but a good starting arsenal includes:

- A sacred blade, small enough to use easily.
- A wand, usually made from the wood of a flowering tree.
- An altar and different colors of altar cloths for different rituals.
- A censer or cauldron for burning resin-based incenses on charcoal.
- An offering plate.
- Candles of differing colors with good holders.
- Parchment, ink, and writing utensils.

You will develop your own tools, and this list will change, grow, or diminish as you experiment and work through your own practice. As for where to use these tools, that is up to you. I firmly believe that carving out a space in your home, if at all possible, that is reserved for spiritual work, is a very powerful act. It is a show of commitment and seriousness that encourages engagement and discipline. When we put effort into our space, we are more apt to use it, to cherish it, and to feel a shift in our consciousness when we enter the space. Keep it clean and simple in the beginning, and develop a relationship with each item you use within this space. When sacred items are not being used, keep them out of sight and kept holy. Purify items and use them with care.

A final note on sacred space and separation from the mundane is clothing. I am a stickler for not performing magic or ritual in street clothing or anything I use regularly. This may seem like an excessive or a trivial point, but it is not. It is linked to the same sense of *othering* that we have mentioned above in terms of tools and space. When we enter our sacred space, we are engaging in work that is deeply transformative and is there to elevate us. If we are entering that space in the exact same way that we would enter our jobs, a restaurant, a friend's house, or any other mundane place, then we are not triggering our minds to shift our consciousness to a higher level. Working nude is perfectly acceptable for many rites, and is the norm in some traditions, but a simple white robe is the easiest and most traditional garb for magical workings. It is not ostentatious, difficult to obtain, or make (if you can sew, it is a very simple pattern), and it is easy to clean and maintain. As you develop your workings, you may use different-colored robes, sashes, cords, or magical jewelry items, but in the beginning a simple white robe will suffice for ritual and sacred work.

✦˙✦Mindfulness and Meditation ✦˙✦

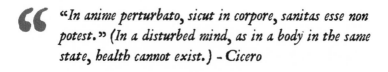

> "*In anime perturbato, sicut in corpore, sanitas esse non potest.*" (In a disturbed mind, as in a body in the same state, health cannot exist.) - Cicero

Ritual magic is not just about objects and words. It is a state of mindfulness and consciousness. We must always be mindful in our practice. This is true of any magical practice, from the highest Solomonic rituals to the simplest folk magic practices. The intent and will behind magic is the guiding thread that tugs at the warp and weft of destiny to create change.

We cannot begin to work magic, to truly change our world, if we cannot change our own mind. We must be able to change habits, challenge thoughts, rework our pathways of thinking, and more if we are ever going to be able to make an impact in the world through our practice. Mindfulness is at the core of all magic, astrological or otherwise.

The practitioner should be able to meditate. The simplest beginning meditations are calming meditations, centering the mind, focusing on the breathing, and not grasping onto the random thoughts that arise and fall within our minds. Practice this regularly. Discipline is key, like I mentioned before, so try to develop a schedule for calming meditation. Twenty minutes, twice a week, may suffice in the beginning, but try to keep it at the same times and in the same place if possible. You can grow this practice as you see fit, returning to breath-centered meditation as needed. Being able to calm your thoughts and feel at home in your own headspace is crucial for any spiritual seeker or magician. This style of meditation is similar to *samatha* meditation in the Buddhist tradition, but it does not belong to any one religious group. Calming the mind by focusing on the breath is a central technique for many practitioners. It is also found in *pranayama* practices and other calming and meditative techniques. Explore these different paths openly, but always keep it a regular and sustained practice. A simple, repeated and meaningful practice is better than a collection of rabbit holes we explore with no discipline.

In the occult and esoteric traditions, visualization meditations are very common, and I do recommend them. For more modern pathworkings, you can explore the visualization pathworkings of esoteric writers such as Dolores Ashcroft-Nowiki's *The Shining Paths*[3] or the meditative practices of Franz Bardon in *Initiation into Hermetics*.[4] The "Middle Pillar Ritual" of Israel Regardie is another useful meditation for frequent use and development. Explore these, and other visualization techniques and meditation practices freely, but the key is to find one that works, and stick with it. The discipline of coming back again and again to a meditation

---

[3] Dolores Ashcroft-Nowiki, *The Shining Paths: An Experiential Journey Through the Tree of Life* (Loughborough: Thoth Publications, 1997).

[4] Franz Bardon, *Initiation* into Hermetics, trans. Gerhard Hanswille and Franca Gallo, ed. Ken Johnson (Merkur Publishing, 1999).

technique is richly rewarding. Each time, you will begin to notice new aspects of the meditation, new truths will become evident, and you will gain a fuller understanding of the techniques and teachings inherent in these systems. Explore as much as you need when you are first starting out, but begin to develop good habits and repeated practice. It is only with this repeated practice that you will begin to see real results.

There are two meditations I want to give here that I think are excellent for beginners. The first is the psychic shield, and the second is the private astral temple. I am drawing from both traditional and modern sources for these meditations, but I have worked with and developed them on my own and recommend them to all seekers. Both of these meditations can be kept up regularly and developed by the practitioner through time and repetition.

Psychic Shielding

The psychic shield is a protective barrier we create and maintain around us at all times. It is strengthened through regular visualization and practice, and it serves as a constant reminder that we are in control of what we are going to allow into our mental space. It is a useful tool to calm anxieties, refocus our efforts and will, and to avoid the influence of negative thoughts and mundane pettiness. When we shield ourselves psychically, we are curating what we are going to allow into our headspace. We cannot be mindful if our entire track can be thrown off by any and every intrusive thought or negative experience in the world. We need a reminder, a tool that can teach us to control our thoughts and tame our mind.

To begin, sit in a comfortable position in your space. Incense is useful here, a clean and pure scent like frankincense or copal. Begin with focusing on your breath. Feel it move across your philtrum, under your nose, and feel each breath fully, entering and exiting your body. When thoughts come, don't fight them, but also don't latch onto them. Allow them to come and go easily. They can swim right past your stream of consciousness, but do not engage. Continue focusing on your breathing until you feel centered, free of any nervousness in the muscles, or tension in the body. If you cannot reach a relaxed state, stop and wait to try again.

It may take a developed practice of calming breath-centered meditation before you are ready to move forward with more.

When you have reached that centered state where you do not feel compelled to grab at thoughts and you are not distracted by tension or anxieties in the body, then you can create the shield. You will begin by visualizing a piercingly bright white light at the base of your body. Focus on it with your entire will, seeing the white light move across your body, growing, covering your body from the bottom and moving upward. It envelops and encases you, like a large silkworm cocoon or a blanket of light. Keep visualizing this light encasing and surrounding you, protecting you from all outside influence. You are safe and comfortable within it but very alert. When you feel that you have truly sustained the shield around you, you are going to choose a watchword. Your watchword can be anything, but it must be something that resonates with you on a deep, spiritual level. I recommend names of divinities, angelic names, Hebrew God names, or a simple word of power that holds meaning to you. Resonate the word within you. If you are able to, and the space is private, you can resonate the word vocally. Visualize the sound filling up the space of your shield, vibrating with the light. Echo it as many times as needed until you feel the complete protection of the shield around you. Continue focusing on your breathing now, the light around you, the word in your mind. You can leave the meditation when you are ready, and the shield will stay.

You can recreate the shield whenever you need to and strengthen it with meditation. The watchword is there for you to be able to use the shield in your daily life. When situations feel stressful, you feel you need more protection, or you feel something unnerving in your mind, you can resonate your word within, reminding you of the created barrier you are maintaining, reminding you that you carve your own protection when needed and cannot be disturbed. It is a trigger, an easy way to build a neural pathway for your magic so that your protective shield is available whenever you need it.

The Astral Temple

Creating an astral temple is something many traditions practice, but I have developed a technique that I believe is very useful for the seeker, particularly for the magician who is going to work with astrological magic. The word "astral" has many meanings in New Age thought, but it literally means "of the stars." The astral world is the starry world. Because

of that, we are quite simply going to use the stars to construct our temple. I recommend having a strong meditation practice before creating an astral temple. If your mind is not able to focus easily, and you are still struggling to maintain your meditative mindset during practice, then wait to begin this one until you feel surer of your ability.

The beginning of the practice involves stargazing. This may be difficult if you are in a city with light pollution or if the weather is cloudy for a long stretch of time, but as I have said before, some things are worth waiting for, and discipline is key to the Art. Either research what stars are visible where you live or buy a stargazing guide. There are many reasonably priced and informative guides for stargazers at your local bookstore and online. You are going to choose a star that is bright enough to be visible on most clear nights from where you live, as well as one that you can locate easily with practice. This will take time. I recommend choosing two nights a week to go out, find your star, and spend some time memorizing the look of it, journaling about it, and trying to locate it on your own by using other markers such as constellations that are easily recognizable. Eventually you will know where it is and recognize it easily.

Once you have built up the habitual location and link with the star, you are going to begin to construct your temple. In your sacred space, sit comfortably and begin your calming meditations. Make sure your psychic shield is engaged and your mind is alert but calm. Do not engage with passing thoughts or move too quickly here. Begin to visualize the fixed star you chose. See it clearly as a point of light in a dark void. See it brighten and grow. The light expands, extending into all directions. It takes up the field of vision. You are within the starry light, freely moving and calm.

Now you will begin to construct a visual space within this starry light. Begin with the simplest shapes and structures. Is it a square or a circle? What are the walls like? The ground? What images come to your mind? Build a simple space to begin, but you can add details as you feel comfortable. Keep them consistent. This is a process, and journaling is very helpful if you are prone to forgetting visualizations during meditation. Keep up the practice, as often as needed, until you can easily enter the starry space and see your temple clearly and easily, the same each time. This will take a different amount of time for each practitioner, but you will eventually reach a place where your astral temple is quick to appear within your mind, and it will serve as a spiritual refuge and place of calm, contained power.

You can return to stargazing as well, visualizing your temple in the Heavenly Sphere of the fixed stars, actually focusing your willpower on the chosen star. Continue this practice and use your temple as a place to do visualization meditations, magical workings, or calming practices such as breath-centered meditation. The more you use this mindfulness technique, the more powerful it can become. You will find yourself returning to the temple frequently, effortlessly. It is one of my favorite tools to combat stress-based blockages in my practice, external influences that are hindering my progress, or the onslaught of toxic people in life.

*˙.*Conclusion *˙.*

I use the word *practice* a lot when discussing magic, as well as *Art*. I like these terms for the work because they imply a certain learned discipline and commitment to progress and creation that I believe are central for any serious-minded person who is working on spiritual progression. I want to stress that my recommendations here are only the beginning. A strong foundation is crucial to any path, but every person will grow and find their interests in different ways. There is a myriad of paths in the esoteric traditions, and in astrological magic itself. You are not bound by any single one, but I do recommend sticking with something before moving on to a new idea. So many students end up aimless in their work because they keep switching things up, never returning to the same ideas and principles that can be developed through a continued application of will. The work is done incrementally, and with focus. Astrological magic has a strong sense of ascension in it, a passage through the Spheres, and a belief in our ability to elevate our experience here on Earth. Keep those key ideas in your mind as you move forward with your own path. Climbing the stars is going to require a sturdy and reliable ladder, so take your time when building yours.

ASTROLOGICAL TIMING

Timekeeping is such a part of our everyday life that we forgot how difficult it was, historically. We also forget how completely uninform it has been. Even today there are lunar calendars still in use to calculate important aspects in the lives of millions, despite the solar calendar dominating the business, education, and digital worlds. The Jewish and Muslim calendars are still lunar, as well as most calendars used in East Asia. And it isn't just the whole year that can be difficult to measure, but even the concepts of weeks and hours within the day varied across cultures and time. We think of time as so rigid, but we've never really agreed on exactly how to measure it out in the world.

The Moon was used to measure the year out into segments, which gives us lunar months. Weeks come later. And how to name or dividing those weeks produced different systems. This was not just an ancient practice, either. During the French Revolution, revolutionaries attempted to create an entirely new calendar with new months and a different system for the weekdays and weekends. This was, eventually, a colossal failure, but it was eagerly enforced by many who wanted to remake France after the fall of the *ancien régime*.[1] All of this speaks to our fascination with the marking of time. How do we measure the passage of our lives? What does it say about how we live our lives and what we choose to give meaning to? Each system is going to address these questions differently.

For the major passages of time, the cosmic order was the most natural tool to use. The Moon, moving through her even phases, gave a clear and universally recognizable measurement for time. Her name gives us the word *month* for a reason. Observing the heavens gave humans the ability

---

1 The French Republican Calendar is a hilarious example of hubris and poor planning. It is also an example of how completely secular, contrived, and forced changes to more holistic systems that we have developed over time tend not to inspire real change in people.

to share a common language around time. We could say to one another, "We will meet again when the Moon is Full." Or we could measure how long an activity took by how many phases the Moon passed through.

Measuring time was not completely the purview of the Moon. The stars were used to demarcate time in Egypt, with the year broken down into portions ruled by starry gods.[2] Egyptians named the 12th month of their year the "Coming forth of Sirius," a star of the goddess Isis.[3] The Egyptians had a strong connection to the stars in their religion, with special significance given to this star, Sirius, and to the appearance and disappearance of certain constellations and starry configurations in the night sky. This method of stargazing would leave an indelible mark on spiritual and astrological traditions throughout the ancient world. Egyptian tombs and temples often figure starry imagery, either as stand-alone figures, as hieroglyphs with particular meanings (phonetically or semantically), as well as the ever-present figure of Nut, the starry Sky-Mother of Egyptian religion. Her blue body is literally painted in the stars.

And beyond the Moon and Stars, the Sun was crucial for marking agricultural seasons. For temperate climates, the ability to understand the seasons was a question of feast or famine, life and death. In modern Witchcraft practice, the celebration of the Eight Sabbats is drawn from

---

[2] Nicolas Campion, *Astrology and Cosmology in the World's Religions* (New York, NY: NYU Press, 2012), 87.

[3] Ibid.

solar festivals, created to mark out the seasons of the year. We become very aware of the Sun's presence (or lack thereof) as we move through the year in temperate climes. We know that the days get darker, the weather more bitter, and we mark that with the dying light of the Sun. In summer, we can celebrate his return, with longer days and increased heat and light.

All of these celestial methodologies tie our souls into something greater. With the presence of digital timekeeping, divorced from the natural order for convenience, it is easy to forget what it is we are really measuring. The passing of the clock's hands should not just be about some materialist, meaningless concept of "time." It should be about the changes we experience as living beings in our environment. Remembering the passage of the stars, the phases of the Moon, the growing and dimming light of the Sun, all ties our souls into the cosmos we inhabit. We are *participating* in time, instead of watching it pass us by.

And time itself is not our enemy. The modern world seems to have a relationship with time based in pure dread. We have a terror of aging. We view things too linearly. We are fearful of "wasting" time. Reconnect with the heavenly bodies and begin to unknit these fears. Undo them by choosing to see the cycles as something you are truly a part of, and not merely a victim of, or a bystander to. The passage of time is not something foreign to your soul, some hateful god that watches and waits. Time is your *experience*—right here and right now. The heavens are moving through time with you, helping you to understand and give meaning to the journey. You are not in the audience of a play over which you have no control. Instead, you are as much of an actor within the work as anything else, even the stars.

⋆⁖⋆ The Planetary Week ⋆⁖⋆

Using the planets to mark a seven-day week can be found in Hellenistic times. It became common practice in antiquity, spreading through the world as a standardized system using planetary names. In magic, this became a common tool to focus intent and work with certain spirits associated with the stars. If we desire to work with Michael, then we will work on the day of the Sun. If we want to connect with the spirits of Air, particularly those ruling communication and speed, then we need the day of Mercury. We bring together these correspondences to tap into the great reservoir of belief, power, and intelligence that has been built up by tradition, practice, religion, and magic.

The days of the week in many Western languages have kept their planetary origins. For example:

French for Moon: Lune

French for Monday (day of the Moon): Lundi

Spanish for Mars: Marte

Spanish for Tuesday (day of Mars): Martes

Welsh for Jupiter: Iau

Welsh for Thursday (day of Jupiter): Dydd Iau

The exception to this is the weekend. Saturday became named for the Sabbath in some languages, and Sunday became "the Lord's day." The Latin word for "Lord" is *dominus,* and we can see that influence in many languages.

French: Dimanche

Spanish: Domingo

Italian: Domenica

This planetary weekly system still carries weight, and most grimoire-based magical systems instruct practitioners to take the day of the planet into question for astrological-based magical workings.

⋆⁺⋆Planetary Hours ⋆⁺⋆

The use of planets to delineate time periods is not limited to the days of
the week. The planetary hours make up a system used throughout many
astrological and magical texts and traditions. They follow the same Chaldean
order of planets found across most systems we've discussed so far: Saturn,
Jupiter, Mars, Sun, Venus, Mercury, Moon. There are differing systems
of ordering the hours, depending on if we begin the day at the night of
the preceding day, or at sunrise of the day in question. This decision of
when the concept of *a day* begins or ends is present across traditions. In
Catholicism, attending Saturday evening Mass counts as meeting your
holy obligation to attend Sunday Mass because Saturday evening "counts"
as the next day. The Jewish Sabbath begins on the evening before the
full day. Whether or not to count sunrise as the beginning of the day is
a question of culture, practice, and religion.

The system of planetary hours I use and teach counts the hours around
the actions of the Sun, instead of arbitrarily breaking the day into two
parts based around midnight. The first hour of the day is the hour that
begins at sunrise. Twelve "hours" are allotted to the daylight time, and 12
"hours" are allotted to the nighttime, after the sun has finally set. This is the
most common system encountered in Western magical treatises. Modern
technology has made calculating the planetary hours much easier, given
that there are apps available that will give the hours. Just like I warn with a
digital ephemeris, or digital chart-creating software, I always recommend
the student learn how to delineate the system on her own, so she is able
to double-check technology-assisted practice. But I see nothing wrong
with using a little help to calculate the hours for workings.

So, in this system, the first hour after sunrise is ruled by the planet
of the day. For example, the first hour of Monday belongs to the Moon.
The hours then move down from that planet toward Earth, following the
Chaldean ordering. The following table gives the planetary hour system,
but precise calculations will depend on when the Sun rises and sets.

✴ ✴ ✴ PLANETARY HOURS ✴ ✴ ✴

✴ ✴ ✴ HOURS FROM SUNRISE TO SUNSET ✴ ✴ ✴

Hour	Sunday	Monday	Tuesday	Wednesday	Thursday	Friday	Saturday
1	☉ Sun	☽ Moon	♂ Mars	☿ Mercury	♃ Jupiter	♀ Venus	♄ Saturn
2	♀ Venus	♄ Saturn	☉ Sun	☽ Moon	♂ Mars	☿ Mercury	♃ Jupiter
3	☿ Mercury	♃ Jupiter	♀ Venus	♄ Saturn	☉ Sun	☽ Moon	♂ Mars
4	☽ Moon	♂ Mars	☿ Mercury	♃ Jupiter	♀ Venus	♄ Saturn	☉ Sun
5	♄ Saturn	☉ Sun	☽ Moon	♂ Mars	☿ Mercury	♃ Jupiter	♀ Venus
6	♃ Jupiter	♀ Venus	♄ Saturn	☉ Sun	☽ Moon	♂ Mars	☿ Mercury
7	♂ Mars	☿ Mercury	♃ Jupiter	♀ Venus	♄ Saturn	☉ Sun	☽ Moon
8	☉ Sun	☽ Moon	♂ Mars	☿ Mercury	♃ Jupiter	♀ Venus	♄ Saturn
9	♀ Venus	♄ Saturn	☉ Sun	☽ Moon	♂ Mars	☿ Mercury	♃ Jupiter
10	☿ Mercury	♃ Jupiter	♀ Venus	♄ Saturn	☉ Sun	☽ Moon	Mars
11	☽ Moon	♂ Mars	☿ Mercury	♃ Jupiter	♀ Venus	♄ Saturn	☉ Sun
12	♄ Saturn	☉ Sun	☽ Moon	♂ Mars	☿ Mercury	♃ Jupiter	♀ Venus

✴ ✴ ✴ HOURS FROM SUNSET TO SUNRISE ✴ ✴ ✴

Hour	Sunday	Monday	Tuesday	Wednesday	Thursday	Friday	Saturday
1	☉ Sun	☽ Moon	♂ Mars	☿ Mercury	♃ Jupiter	♀ Venus	♄ Saturn
2	♀ Venus	♄ Saturn	☉ Sun	☽ Moon	♂ Mars	☿ Mercury	♃ Jupiter
3	☿ Mercury	♃ Jupiter	♀ Venus	♄ Saturn	☉ Sun	☽ Moon	♂ Mars
4	☽ Moon	♂ Mars	☿ Mercury	♃ Jupiter	♀ Venus	♄ Saturn	☉ Sun
5	♄ Saturn	☉ Sun	☽ Moon	♂ Mars	☿ Mercury	♃ Jupiter	♀ Venus
6	♃ Jupiter	♀ Venus	♄ Saturn	☉ Sun	☽ Moon	♂ Mars	☿ Mercury
7	♂ Mars	☿ Mercury	♃ Jupiter	♀ Venus	♄ Saturn	☉ Sun	☽ Moon
8	☉ Sun	☽ Moon	♂ Mars	☿ Mercury	♃ Jupiter	♀ Venus	♄ Saturn
9	♀ Venus	♄ Saturn	☉ Sun	☽ Moon	♂ Mars	☿ Mercury	♃ Jupiter
10	☿ Mercury	♃ Jupiter	♀ Venus	♄ Saturn	☉ Sun	☽ Moon	Mars
11	☽ Moon	♂ Mars	☿ Mercury	♃ Jupiter	♀ Venus	♄ Saturn	☉ Sun
12	♄ Saturn	☉ Sun	☽ Moon	♂ Mars	☿ Mercury	♃ Jupiter	♀ Venus

✴ ✴ Magic ✴ ✴

The planetary hours were not quintessential to predictive astrology. They really shine in magical practice and ritual. *The Key of Solomon* and other traditional grimoires give specific associations for each planetary hour and what work is best accomplished during that time. Mundane decisions *could* be taken into consideration with the hours as well, such as we find in Henry Coley's 17th century work the *Clavis Astrologiae Elimate*.[4] But, usually, we encounter the hours in discussions of magic and not simple decision-making in daily life. We look to the hours to give weight and connection to our working, to be amenable to certain spirits, or to order and project our will in accordance with a more cosmic system of timekeeping.

The image of the planetary week and the hours can be placed on a seven-pointed star, or septagram, that ties the system up neatly. Drawing out the septagram, and following the lines, we discover the planetary week. For example, if we start with the Moon (Monday), then we move to Mars (Tuesday), and then Mercury (Wednesday), and so on until we finish. If we move around the septagram clockwise, then we discover the planetary hours in the Chaldean order. For example, we can start again with the Moon (the closest sphere) and move clockwise. If we do that, we will be following the traditional Chaldean order for the hours: Moon, Mercury, Venus, Sun, Mars, Jupiter, Saturn. It is an especially useful visualization tool.

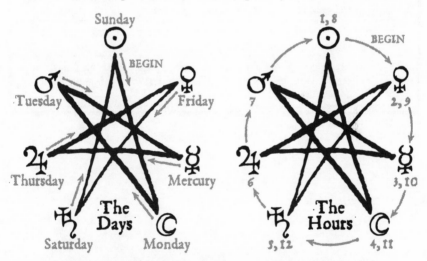

Calculating the Days and Hours of the Planets With the Seven-Pointed Star

---

4   See Christopher Warnock's *Renaissance Astrology* site for an accessible version:
https://www.renaissanceastrology.com/coleyplanetaryhours.html.

The natural flow ties in our thinking and ritual to the journey through the seven Heavenly Spheres. If you are inspired to use the planetary hours for magical workings, the following table gives associated works for each:

✲.✲ PLANETARY INTENTIONS ✲✶✲	
House	**Associations**
☽ Moon	Travel, messages, the sea and navigation, reconciliation, mothers, female health, obscuration, hiding, protection, Goddesses
☿ Mercury	Speaking, intelligence, wit, divination, writing, science, schools, exams, quickening, communication and technology
♀ Venus	Love, sexuality, partnerships, marriage, arts and creative inspiration, public events, games of pleasure or chance
☉ Sun	Wealth, success in career, success with people in positions of authority, removing hindrances between people, friendship, mental clarity
♂ Mars	War, disagreements, breaking gossip, or scheming, uncovering spies and traitors, to curse, cause ruin, or harm
♃ Jupiter	Honor, acclaim, religious questions, long-distance travel, good health, gifts and donations
♄ Saturn	Mediumship and ghosts, real estate and physical buildings, long-term investments, savings, fathers, estates, wills, things underground, agriculture

WINGED STARS

Angels in Magic and Astrology

⋆˙⋆ The Messengers ⋆˙⋆

Throughout this work, you have seen the names of angels associated with planets and astrological operations. If you begin to study astrological works from previous eras, you will see them even more. We have discussed magical operations and ritual, so we cannot really appreciate or discuss astrological magic without addressing these beings and what they mean within the context of the Art.

For many, angels are solely the product of Abrahamic religions. They belong to the traditions of Judaism, Christianity, and Islam. Many practitioners and seekers can look a bit askance at the inclusion of angelic magic in certain systems because they see it as purely Christian; many who approach esoteric practices are leaving Christianity with a bad taste—and, therefore, are put off by the inclusion of the very Abrahamic language of certain grimoires, astrological texts, and magical treatises. The prayers, exorcisms, and angelic invocations found in the grimoires and in astrological and magical texts from Christendom are, indeed, heavily laced with the language of Abrahamic faiths. This includes the use of biblical prayers, Hebrew names for God, and pieces of the Christian liturgy. It is important, however, to unknit this worry. The angels are part and parcel of the occult and esoteric traditions of the West, and we do not need to forfeit them and their magic just because of Christian connotations.

It is also important to remember that we live in the world and must act within the systems we are exposed to. Power flows through art, religion, history, and daily experience. For many centuries, Christian language dominated many parts of the world, and, because of this, there is power in the rituals and prayers of the system. The grimoires do not necessarily preach Christian dogma so much as they recognize the performative power of Christian liturgy and Hebrew prayer. The constant "muscle memory" of repeated Christian worship has given immense power and weight to certain names, acts, and images. It is a real and present egregore that we all experience, whether we believe in the religion or not. The images of the angels, their names, and attributes resonate with us because we have the experience of Christendom and its years of history and cultural influence. From the pageantry of Catholic and Orthodox prayer to the cultural weight given to Abrahamic houses of worship, holy books, and sacred items, we are all touched in some way by the influence of these systems. Astrology and its magic are no different, and the Art has passed through this cultural and spiritual system as much as it passed through Babylonian religion, Hellenistic philosophy, and pagan Roman rule.

It is also interesting to note that historical magical texts often approached magic as a contractual process with higher intelligences, and not simply a working of energy and will. Modern New Age

Illustration of Cassiel from The Magus, Francis Barrett (1801)

concepts of magic are quite different than what we find in many historical texts on magic. Modern New Age ideas, New Thought, and other concepts are rooted heavily in the vaguely Neoplatonic theologies and "natural magic" of Renaissance occultists such as Marsilio Ficino or the writings of occultists like Agrippa. The concept of "natural magic," which was explored heavily in the Medieval and Renaissance occult worlds is a development, a different worldview, than the more theurgic or spiritual concepts of magic in older texts such as the Greek Magical Papyri. The grimoire traditions itself, although rife with natural magical correspondences, is also based in working with higher (or lower, in the case of demons) beings.

For many of the grimoires, magic is by its very nature a communicative, almost contract-based agreement with higher spiritual beings.[1] The Witchcraft trials, when accusing others of working with "familiar spirits," were attacking this very concept that had been part and parcel of magic for ages. Angels are some of the most explored beings in this conceptual framework, and there are powerful associations, rites, and ideas behind them. They are also the most frequently associated beings with planetary magic in the tradition of astrologically based systems in the Christian West. This is also found in Islamic sources, a religion where belief in angels is a foundational dogma. Jewish Kabbalah, particularly practical Kabbalah, is also full of angels.

It is important to know, however, that angels predate the Abrahamic religions and exist outside of them. According to many, the root of the concept of angels is found in the Persian religion of Zoroastrianism. In the religion of Zoroastrianism, the will of the supreme deity is worked into the world by the action of certain spirits that obey divine command. This concept of the divine will being worked into reality by spirits that serve would heavily influence Hebrew concept of angels, particularly after Hebrew contact with the Persian religions during the Babylonian captivity and beyond. Hebrew scripture after exposure to Babylonian and Persian thought begins to speak of angels in much more esoteric ways.[2] Names, attributes, and complex angelologies come even later, in the Rabbinic period, and are taken even further in Kabbalistic thought.[3] Kabbalah, particularly what was known as "practical Kabbalah" (which was magical and occult in nature), would go on to include vast and complex angelic theology, employing angel names and angelic magic into detailed

---

[1] For an investigation in how Solomonic treatises viewed magic as contractual with higher spirits and not purely causal, see: Stephen Skinner, Techniques of Solomonic Magic (Singapore: Golden Hoard Press, 2017).

[2] The *Book of Daniel* and other Hebrew scriptures speak heavily of this, painting the angels in unique symbolic and esoteric ways.

[3] Kabbalah is a complex system with multiple schools. Practical Kabbalah, which includes a lot of magical practice and was deeply controversial in certain circles, engages extensively with angelologies.

systems of Jewish magic. This development, for me, shows a deeper history of working with higher intelligences and seeking them for spiritual enlightenment and magical workings.

Neoplatonist, Gnostic, and Hermetic texts use the term angel as well, from the Greek *angelos*, meaning messenger. Theurgic and mystical literature that was Hellenistic was comfortable with the concept and vocabulary of the angels, even if they were non-Christian writers using the terminology. Early Christianity mingled with many other Hellenistic and Judaic religious trends, and thus the angels were part of multiple traditions that did not all line up with what was perceived as orthodox Christian or Jewish theology. The angels were worked into complex hierarchies and spiritual cosmologies that may have had communication with Christian thought but could hardly be called orthodox or solely Abrahamic by any stretch of the imagination. Therefore, a writer such as Iamblichus, a pagan, could use the term "angel" as easily as a Christian.

Pythagorean, Neoplatonist, and Hermetic philosophies all used complex hierarchies of spiritual beings to describe the emanation of the divine One into the myriad dynamism of creation. The conceptual framework of "the angels" fits very well into this attempt to understand the divine emanation—an attempt that astrological magic works with as well. As pagan authors used pagan god-names and Hellenistic philosophical terms, Christian authors used angelic names to describe these same frameworks in a way that worked within their own lived experience with magic and astrology.

In Hebrew scripture, the angels are referred to by many names. Predominately, they are called *malakhi*, meaning "messengers." This is where the Greek word *angelos* (also: messenger) comes from in the Christian scriptures. It is a continuation of this Hebrew term. Other Hebrew titles for these beings include "Sons of God"[4] and "The Holy Ones."[5] The biblical references to angels can be surprising, deeply disturbing even, and returning to these texts is important to shake the beautiful Renaissance image of angels as sweet infants, or beautiful noble-faced visitors, out of

---

4   *Bene Elohim*, םיהלאה ינב

5   *Ha Kedoshim*, םישדוקה

our heads. Jewish authors after the Biblical period began to create hierarchies of the angels that would be detailed and enumerated by Jewish
theologians and writers, both in traditional orthodox literature and mystical Kabbalistic literature. The *Zohar*, a central Kabbalistic text, gives a
complex hierarchy of angels. Kabbalistic writers developed the hierarchy
further, often disagreeing on ranks or titles. Maimonides, the *Rambam*,
a more traditional voice in Jewish thought, gives a hierarchy from which
many others seem to be derived[6]:

1. **Chayot Ha Kodesh** *"Living Beings"*

2. **Ophanim** *"Wheels"*

3. **Erelim** *"The Courageous Ones"*

4. **Hashmallim** *"The Brilliant Ones"*

5. **Seraphim** *"The Seraphs"*

6. **Malakim** *"The Messengers"*

7. **Elohim** *"Godly Creatures"*

8. **Bene Elohim** *"Sons of the Godly Beings"*

9. **Cherubim** *"The Cherubs"*

10. **Ishim** *"Manlike Creatures"*

The references to the angels in Jewish scripture are often prophetic
and esoteric. They are described by Ezekiel (the *Ophanim*, at least) as
four-headed, with winged eyes and much fire. Other prophetic books
in Hebrew scripture contain equally terrifying images of angelic beings.
They are, essentially, divine will made manifest. Being the execution of
divine will they are, by nature, terrifying and awe-inspiring to the mortal
onlooker because of the chasm of difference between the highest divine
nature and the human senses. Prophetic literature used extremely powerful

---

6   Maimonides, *Yesodei hTorah*, trans. Eliyahu Touger, Chabad, accessed October
2020, https://www.chabad.org/library/article_cdo/aid/904962/jewish/Yesodei-haTo-
rah-Chapter-Two.htm.

imagery to work through complex theological and social issues and the angels reflect that awe-struck power of true noetic experience. The *Book of Ezekiel* gives an example of angelic descriptions:

> " *"Also out of the midst thereof came the likeness of four living creatures. And this was their appearance; they had the likeness of a man. And every one had four faces, and every one had four wings. And their feet were straight feet; and the sole of their feet was like the sole of a calf's foot: and they sparkled like the colour of burnished brass. And they had the hands of a man under their wings on their four sides; and they four had their faces and their wings. Their wings were joined one to another; they turned not when they went; they went every one straight forward. As for the likeness of their faces, they four had the face of a man, and the face of a lion, on the right side: and they four had the face of an ox on the left side; they four also had the face of an eagle. Thus were their faces: and their wings were stretched upward; two wings of every one were joined one to another, and two covered their bodies."* - Ezekiel 1:5-11 [7]*

In Christianity, angelic hierarchies and angelic attributes vary depending on tradition and writer, but they are vastly different in most works than their Jewish predecessors. The most enduring hierarchy is that of Pseudo-Dionysus the Areopagite. In his work *The Celestial Hierarchy*, he breaks the angels down into nine orders grouped in threes. [8]

---

[7] Bible sources are from the King James Version of the Bible. Although modern translations are sometimes more useful in academic research and clarity, I have chosen to remain with the KJV for no other reason than Elizabethan English is pretty. *We all have our things.*

[8] Dionysus the Areopagite, *The Celestial Hierarchy*, The Tertullian Project, accessed November 2020, http://www.tertullian.org/fathers/areopagite_13_heavenly_hierarchy.htm#c6.

Order of Angels

The Seraphim	The Dominions	The Principalities
The Cherubim	The Virtues	The Archangels
The Thrones	The Powers	The Angels

This hierarchy draws on New Testament verses to support its breakdown. This system of ordering would go on to be used by multiple Medieval sources and in Christian devotional art as well as magical and occult texts that worked with angels. In canonical western scripture, the only named angels are Michael, Gabriel, and Raphael.[9] The names of the other archangels come from apocryphal Christian literature, Gnostic texts, and other early Christian writings that were not accepted into the canon of the Bible in the Roman church. Eastern Orthodox and Oriental Orthodox scriptures contain further angelic names and sources, but these are not found in Roman Catholic biblical literature.[10]

The tradition of there being "seven Archangels" comes from texts in the Abrahamic tradition. In the *Book of Tobit*, the Archangel Raphael states, "For I am the angel Raphael, one of the seven, who stand before the Lord."[11] The *Book of Enoch*, which was almost considered canonical in the West and *is* part of the canonical scriptures of the Ethiopian Church, also contains references to the celestial hierarchy of seven Archangels and goes into great detail about angelic attributes and names, to a degree not found in other scriptures. It is not difficult to see why the number seven was significant to these writers. There are seven visible Heavenly Spheres. There are seven candlesticks in the Temple, etc. The associations with seven are common.

This number of seven would go on to be central to astrological magic and the grimoire tradition. With few exceptions, grimoires would link angelic

---

9 Protestant Bibles do not include the *Book of Tobit*, and, therefore, the only truly named are Michael and Gabriel. There are demonic or fallen names as well, but of the traditional archangels, it really is just these three (or two, for Protestants) in scriptures that are canonical in the West.

10 The Ethiopian Church, for example, contains more esoteric literature in its canon that is not found in other Christian denominations.

11 *Book of Tobit 12:15*. Deuterocanonical Biblical quotes are from the Douay-Rheims version.

magic and astrology together very tightly, including angelic powers, in the discussions of the seven planets of traditional astrology.[12] Even works focused almost entirely on the use of astrology for prediction (horary) or the reading of nativities, such as *Christian Astrology* by Lilly, include the angels for each planet. The enduring legacy of the link between the angels and the planets is everywhere in the historical corpus of texts.

So with all of this history, the seeker can come to an appreciation of the angels that is more grounded in a view of the divine made manifest in the world than it is with any specific religious tradition or set of dogmas. The angels are the divine will made real. They are almost, to use a perhaps bizarre analogy, like computer programs. They are not necessarily separate, isolated intelligences with free will that exist somewhere in the cosmos but instead are executed ideas and will manifesting in the world. The *Janua Magica Reserata*, says of angels that they "... exceed not in desire, desire not, because they want not in beholding their creator ... [they] suffereth neither change nor end, for they are immutable & Divine, & are swift Messengers to execute the commands of the Highest at his divine pleasure & appointment."[13]

We are using names, sigils, numbers, and signs to understand these concepts because it allows our sense-laden and corporeal bodies to interact with these ideas in a real way in our magic and divination. The angelic powers are pathways, programmed to create, execute, rectify, and order. They are the messengers, bearing truths of the Divine that we can work out and experience for ourselves. We are tapping into a network with these named beings, a neural pathway, a celestial pathway, a programmed set of powerful correspondences and teachings that can add to magical working and spiritual progression.

In my own work, I have come to have an appreciation for angelic astro-logical magic as a useful and powerful system. Understanding the worldview at the heart of an esoteric approach to astrology requires a language for how the divine light radiates and moves through the Heavenly Spheres.

---

[12] A major exception is the *Book of Abramelin*, which is probably the least astrological grimoire commonly known or used.

[13] Stephen Skinner and David Rankine, *The Keys to the Gateway of Magic: Summoning the Solomonic Archangels and Demon Princes* (Singapore: Golden Hoard Press, 2005), 64.

Angels really are a useful way to understand this process. Although the planets bear the names of gods, it can be difficult and sometimes awkward to approach them as true singular divinities. By engaging with the angels of each planet, we can see the celestial intelligence of each Heavenly Sphere as a pathway of light, a specific channel of communication and correspondence to our earthly experience. Angelic systems allow us to remember the divine unity behind the system while still appreciating the diversity and unique nature behind each sphere—because the angels do not operate as completely independent beings in most theological understandings, but instead as messengers and conduits. Tapping into these unique beings and working with the magical systems they inspire allows us to retain a holistic relationship with the celestial realms as well as draw on the rich art, literature, and devotional works of traditional religious and esoteric writings as well. Dionysus the Areopagite reminds us that the Angels still participate in the divine Oneness, in the form of Light, that we all carry:

> *"Let this truth be spoken—that it was through goodness that the superessential Godhead, having fixed all the essences of things being, brought them into being. For this is the peculiar characteristic of the Cause of all things, and of goodness surpassing all, to call things being to participation of Itself, as each order of things being was determined from its own analogy. For all things being share in a Providence, which bubbles forth from the superessential Deity, Cause of all things. For they would not be, unless they had participated in the Essence and Origin of things being."* [14]

---

[14] Dionysus the Areopagite, *The Celestial Hierarchy*, The Tertullian Project, accessed November 2020, http://www.tertullian.org/fathers/areopagite_13_heavenly_hierarchy.htm#c6.

⋆⟡⋆Angels and the Art ⋆⟡⋆
The Seven

The tradition of linking angels with the celestial spheres comes from early grimoire works such as *Picatrix* and became a fully fleshed-out system throughout the Renaissance's magical writings. The angels are found in earlier texts as well, in Hermetic and Coptic tradition. As mentioned before, the tradition of naming seven archangels corresponded too neatly with seven Heavenly Spheres not to be used and adapted by occultists and magicians. Agrippa, Ficino, Mirandola, Trithemius, and others all worked angelic hierarchies and planetary angelic magic into their understanding of the occult. The difficulty arises for the seeker when they begin to see the different systems at use in these writings. Spelling conventions and copying errors add to the confusion as European authors tried to render Hebrew and Greek into Latin letters, which sometimes creates multiple spellings and versions of the same angelic name. [15]

The number seven was also important in Christian and Jewish scripture. In Christianity, the Epistles of Paul are written to the seven churches of Asia. The number seven is found throughout sacred items in the Hebrew scriptures, relating to items within the Temple, or to items associated with the Levitical priesthood. Grimoires and astrological treatises imbibed this number, easily linked to the seven wandering stars, and worked it together into a complete system that relies intensely on the number seven for its sacred numerology. The *Sepher Raziel*[16] puts the following words into the mouth of Solomon, linking the planets to sacred scripture: "And Solomon said that the prophets call these brethren the 7 living spirits, and holy and wise men said that they were 7 lamps burning, or 7 candlesticks of light & of life, and all the prophets call them the 7 heavenly bodies which are the 7 planets."[17]

---

[15] This can be confusing for students, so I recommend keeping a list of the various spellings of certain angels. It is easy to mistake certain Hebrew names that have been transliterated and translated by those without a strong knowledge of Hebrew.

[16] This is a 16th century grimoire, not the Kabbalistic text of a similar name.

[17] *Sepher Raziel: Liber Salomonis a Sixteenth Century English Grimoire*, ed. Don Karr & Stephen Skinner (Singapore: Golden Hoard Press, 2017), 154.

Trithemius, taking from Albertus Magnus and other historical sources as well as some of the earliest translations of Kabbalistic literature available to Christian readers, was a powerful early source for planetary angelic magic that would come to heavily influence later occult and esoteric writers and thinkers. [18] As the systems developed and cross-cultural exchanges became common in the literature of Renaissance and post-Renaissance occult circles, a system of seven angelic correspondences became common in magical literature across European circles. This system is the system I use and teach. It is important to remember, though, that the seeker can explore even further angelic systems that link to astrology. Some systems give angelic powers to every single degree or to the decans of the zodiac signs, while others use unique "Olympian Spirits" for the seven Heavenly Spheres. There is also the complex system of angelic magic developed by John Dee, the "Wizard of Mortlake," which is a system completely unique within the history of angelic magic and Western occultism. [19] The twisting paths of angelic magic in the literature of occult and esoteric circles during and after the Renaissance are extremely rich.

Despite these rabbit holes, some of which can be very rewarding, I want to introduce you to the seven archangelic correspondences most common in the occult and astrological writings available to us. These seven beings are worked into the grimoire tradition as well as instructive literature on astrology from the Renaissance and post-Renaissance world. Each angel has developed a unique historical egregore and mythology that is available to the seeker to explore and work with in a ritual setting and in personal magical undertakings. Planetary squares, sigils, secret names, and other correspondences were given over to these seven beings, these planetary angels, so that magicians could tap into and work with the Heavenly Spheres in practical ways.

---

[18] Nicholas Goodrick-Clarke, *The Western Esoteric Traditions: A Historical Introduction* (Oxford: Oxford University Press, 2008), 52.

[19] Enochian magic, as it has come to be called, is extremely complex. Dee's angels often differ dramatically from the traditional angels of Western esotericism. This is due to the fact that Dee worked with a scrying system and encountered his own system of spirits that is worked in with the traditional angelologies. Dee also worked with a new language, which he believed to be the original language of Creation—the language of the angels themselves.

GABRIEL—THE MOON

The Archangel Gabriel is the ruling angel of the Moon, associated with the Western direction and the element of Water. He is one of the most attested angels in traditional religious literature, being the angel of the Annunciation in Christianity and named in canonical scriptures even in orthodox circles. In Islam, it is Gabriel (Arabic *Jibril*) who first tells the Prophet to "Recite!" and thus produce the Quran. Gabriel is attested in Medieval and Renaissance art, often bearing a lily, announcing to the Virgin Mary the coming birth of Jesus of Nazareth, the Christ. His heavy association in Catholic art with the Virgin Mary only strengthens the magician's association of this angel with the Moon, the Divine Mother. Mary herself is often shown standing upon the crescent moon, a reference to the Apocalypse of scripture, and this angel, announcing to the lunar mother the birth of light is a powerful image for lunar magic.

His name in Hebrew means "God is my Strength," and traditional Jewish sources place him as the angelic creature mentioned in the books of Daniel and Ezekiel. In Kabbalah he is the angel of the sephirah *yesod*, the sephirah above that of *malkuth*, the Kingdom, the created and material world we all know. So, Gabriel is that first experience above creation. *Yesod*, in Hermetic writings on the Kabbalah, would come to be the sephirah of the Moon and Gabriel the ruler of that Heavenly Sphere. Other Jewish sources paint the mercy of Gabriel, showing him taking pity on Adam and Even after the expulsion from Eden by instructing them on how to live.[20]

In apocryphal literature, Gabriel is present. He is in the *Book of Enoch*, taking orders from God and given rulership of serpents and of Paradise.[21] He is given rulership over the Cherubim, one of the ranks within the echelons of angelic spirits. In Gnostic literature, he is part of the heavenly

---

[20] "Gabriel," Solomon Schechter, Ludwig Blau, and Emil G. Hirsch, *Jewish Encyclopedia*, accessed September 2020, http://www.jewishencyclopedia.com/articles/6450-gabriel.

[21] The *Book of Enoch the Prophet*, trans. R. H. Charles (San Francisco, CA: Red Wheel/Weiser, 2012), 17.

hierarchy of beings. [22] In more orthodox Christian literature, he is the angel of Annunciation, named as the angel who visits both Elizabeth and Mary. Over time, a tradition developed that he was the angel that blows the trumpet at the end of time. This is a common theme in many Christina hymns, but it is not from any Biblical sources or orthodox religious texts; it is more a custom that developed over time within Christian churches.

In magic, Gabriel rules over all things lunar and watery. He is the angel of *yesod*, and of the West. He is invoked for all magic that falls under the auspices of the Moon. It is interesting that many things that may be associated with lunar magic can be found in Christian images of the archangel, even very orthodox ones. From lilies, to silver lamps, to white or pale-blue garments, all of these seem to unite both the lunar approach to this angel as well as his Christian associations.

RAPHAEL—MERCURY

Another named angel in orthodox scriptures, named in the *Book of Tobit*, Raphael's name means "God heals." Although absent from the canonical Hebrew scriptures of the *Tanakh*, he is present in Talmudic literature. He is also present in apocryphal Jewish literature as an archangel and worked into the hierarchy of angels presented by Jewish theologians. In the *Book of Enoch*, the Archangel Raphael is associated with healing, as his name insinuates, with the Prophet saying of him, "[Raphael] is set over all the diseases and all the wounds of the children of men." [23] The associations with Raphael as healer are found in the *Book of Tobit* as well,

---

22   The Gnostic concept of the hierarchy of spiritual beings is known as the *Pleroma*. This concept was central in Gnostic literature, expanding upon and commenting on the seemingly endless hierarchies and intelligences that exist within the spiritual realm of the Godhead and the world of disincarnate, spiritual beings. Gnosticism was highly dualistic, often viewing the base material world as evil, or fallen, and the higher spiritual realm as the only real or meaningful expression of Truth.

23   The *Book of Enoch the Prophet*, trans. R. H. Charles (San Francisco, CA: Red Wheel/ Weiser, 2012), 33.

a book accepted by Catholic and Orthodox Christians but not by most Protestants.[24]

In Islam he is *Israfil* and blows the horn at the Day of Judgment. He is a beautiful angel, with multiple wings, and he makes music and art all at the behest of God. He prays to God in a thousand different languages, and this links beautifully with the Heavenly Sphere of Mercury, which is the sphere most associated with communication, language, and mutability. It is also interesting to note that in Catholicism, he is made patron of apothecaries, pharmacists, and the like, all which bear the image of the caduceus. This caduceus is none other than the sacred staff shown in images of Hermes and Mercury throughout classical times.

ANAEL—VENUS

Anael is often encountered with the spelling Haniel or Hanael. This name comes from the Hebrew for "Grace of God." Along with classical grimoires and sources of classical planetary magic, Anael appears in the Enochian tables of Dee and Kelley as well. There are fewer direct explanations of this angelic nature than others in traditional sources, with many grimoires and treatises seeming to only tie the angel into those things that have been assigned by magicians to Venus.

In classical grimoires and magical works, Anael does bear all of the attributes of Venus, including associations with grace, beauty, creation, and love. It is important to remember, however, that love can mean different things. We are not understanding this angelic being correctly if we are only thinking of love as a romantic attraction between two people. There is also divine love, and charitable love for others—*agape*. These ideas of love should come into play with the angel Anael, who represents much more than just sexuality. Venus is a benefic planet, with multiple associations beyond just marriage and copulation. The angel of this Heavenly Sphere

---

24 Some Anglo-Catholics (more conservative members of the Church of England and its affiliate bodies) do accept the deuterocanonical books.

is no different, able to be benefic in multiple arenas under the purview of the Morning Star.

MICHAEL—THE SUN

Michael is the archangel of the Sun and one of the most sourced angels in tradition. His name can be translated as, "Who is like God?" Michael is named in canonical Biblical scripture as well as the liturgy of Christian worship. Masses often end with the prayer to the Archangel Michael:

> "*St. Michael the Archangel, defend us in battle, be our protection against the wickedness and snares of the devil. May God rebuke him we humbly pray; and do thou, O Prince of the Heavenly host, by the power of God, cast into hell Satan and all the evil spirits who prowl about the world seeking the ruin of souls. Amen.*"

This warrior-like language is common in attributes to Michael, who is associated with defeating and casting out Satan in the apocalyptic literature of Christianity.[25] This tradition of Michael fighting against the sources of Evil and protecting God's chosen children is found in Jewish tradition as well, where the Book of Daniel names him as a special guardian of the children of Israel.[26] This tradition continues even in the revelations of Islam, where the Quran names Michael and Gabriel specifically as servants of God.

> "*Whoever is an enemy to Allah and His angels and His messengers and Gabriel and Michael - then indeed, Allah is an enemy to the disbelievers.*"[27]

---

25   Revelation 12:7.

26   Daniel 12.

27   Quran, surah 2: *Al Baqara*.

In esoteric traditions, Michael was such a potent name that carried such a weight to it that it was used even in traditions of magic that were heterodox, unique, or completely outside of the Abrahamic religious canon. The power of the supreme commander of the Hosts of Heaven is something that can transcend dogma, affiliation, or petty disagreements. Just like the light of the Sun, his star, Michael shines in all spaces.

SAMAEL–MARS

Samael is the angel of Mars and has a curious, devilish history due to the common linking of this angel with Satan, or the many other incarnations of the "fallen angel." His name is a clear indication of the darker aspects of this being, given that it means "poison" or "venom of God." It is important, though, to realize that the concept of Satan (literally: the accuser, in Hebrew) is different across traditions. Although we have inherited the Medieval, Renaissance, and early Modern concept of Satan as the enemy of God who fell from Heaven, this is not the entire theological history of the concept of Satan.

In Hebrew thought, the Accuser was just that—an accuser. He was a prosecuting attorney for the Divine Godhead, or the one sent to do the difficult and more grim duties of godly service. In Rabbinic literature, we can find Samael as the "Accuser" who argues against mercy vis-à-vis Michael, who argues for it. [28] This tradition often separates the concept of "Satan" from "Samael," the latter being a servant of God still, and not in rebellion against God. If God is everything (and in true monotheism, he must be), then he must also be the more difficult aspects of existence.

---

28 "Samael," *Jewish Virtual Library*, accessed September 2020, https://www.jewishvirtuallibrary.org/samael.

This is why Mars, and the angel Samael, are often equated with the Kabbalistic sephirah of *geburah*, literally: "severity." [29]

Samael fulfills another role in some Hebrew sources, which is that of the angel of death. Whether he is tied to catastrophes and calamities on Earth, or simply exacting the wrath of God, Samael can fulfill that role of the reaper if need be. This does not necessarily make Samael cruel, or wicked, simply a force of nature that must be dealt with and accepted if we want to progress. Death is as much a part of life as birth. The entire cycle is necessary and holistic.

It is important to say, however, that some Hebrew sources very much do paint Samael as a figure of evil. He is paired, in early literature, with Lilith, the demoness. [30] He is assigned rulership over hells in mystical Jewish literature and interpreted as a tempter and a figure of evil tied to the fall of humanity and the introduction of evil and woe into the world. This may be a difficult dichotomy to understand—Samael as both accuser and fallen devil—but it fits quite easily into a traditional understanding of Mars in the astrological Arts. Mars really was a malefic influence, a difficult planet that could bring calamity as easily at it could bring revolution. No better figure could rule over this sphere and connect it to us than the Devil, who can be enemy or liberator given the circumstance.

SACHIEL—JUPITER

The Angel of Jupiter has many variations of his name, many being linked to a Hebrew name meaning "Righteousness of God" or "Grace of God." There is disagreement about whether this angel is the same being as

---

[29] Some sources link other angels to the *sephirot*, in systems that do not always agree. There are even sources linking Gabriel to *geburah* which is in stark contrast to more Hermetic, Christian interpretations. I have tended to give precedence to the later, hermetic Kabbalistic associations due to them being more in my wheelhouse and out of a respect for the more traditional, Jewish systems that are outside of my expertise. Hermetic Kabbalah (often spelled Qabalah to differentiate it) is a system in and of itself that is not necessarily within the same practice as more traditional Jewish sources.

[30] "Samael," *Jewish Virtual Library*, accessed September 2020, https://www.jewishvirtuallibrary.org/samael.

Raziel, an often-encountered being in magical treatises, or if he is the same as Zadkiel, or other angels such as Satquiel, Zaphkiel, etc. I believe there is a continuity between the beings, all being associated with Jupiter in various astrological treatises or magical texts.

Being associated with the Kabbalistic sephirah of chesed, or "mercy," this angel of Jupiter bears all the dignity and benevolence of the greater benefic planet. Working with the angel is invoking the benevolent and kingly nature of the largest planet in our system. He is often invoked along with a host of other spirits associated with Jupiter, with Thursday, and with the signs ruled by Jupiter.

Cassiel—Saturn

Also known under other spellings, this angel's name is usually translated as the "cover of God." He appears in the writings of the Enochian system of Dee and Kelley as well as classical grimoires in the Western magical traditions. He is the angel of Saturn, a powerful creature also associated with the North. In Francis Barret's grimoire *The Magus*, he is shown astride a dragon, bearing a crown and scepter, a full beard, an arrow, and scale-covered arms and legs. [31]

Cassiel rules over all things saturnine and is called in magical works for all those dealings that have the aspects of that final gateway planet to the beyond. He presides over workings for the dead, for kings and fathers, and for time, discipline, and restriction. He is temperate and strong, bearing the same Father Time egregore of Saturn's correspondences. Saturnine energy is tied to black and dark objects in nature, to reminders of finality and temporality. This angel is the perfect spirit when our souls are in need of a timekeeper, a teacher, a disciplinarian with a view toward destiny and fate, an understanding of the natural cycles of life, and how the reaping and ending of something can be as crucial as its birth or insemination.

---

[31] Francis Barret, *The Magus, or Central Intelligencer; Being a Complete System of Occult Philosophy* (New York, NY: Citadel Press, 1967), 103.

*˙*Embracing the Angels? *˙*

I leave it up to each practitioner and student to see if the angelic planetary systems strike a chord or fall flat. I am fully cognizant that even with the arguments I have made, some souls are just not going to connect in any meaningful way to a system so entrenched in Abrahamic scripture and worship. That is understandable. I always hope that students of astrological magic can use these systems with an understanding that they exist beyond the pure confines of their religious roots—but I also know that the wounds inflicted by traditional religious belief can be deeply felt and act as a real impediment to connection.

With that in mind, it is also possible to associate the Heavenly Spheres with beings completely outside of the angelic or Abrahamic worldview. The planets do bear the names of pagan gods, after all, and those names carry a mythology, power, and list of correspondences all their own. Jupiter, or Zeus, is the great King of the gods and can be prayed to and petitioned as easily as any angel in the above system. And there are a plethora of sources linking Zeus to various correspondences, such as oak trees (from his oracle in Dodona), to eagles, a favored animal in depictions of the god. These same correspondences exist for all the gods linked with the seven traditional planets.

Babylonian, Greek, Roman, Egyptian, and other cultures have lent their gods to the naming of the stars. This can be a rich place to look for ways to connect to the spirits behind the Spheres and to find a system that works. Magic must, if it is to be of any use to us at all, work. There is nothing more disappointing and futile than empty ritual that achieves nothing. If experimenting with the traditional, angelic, and heavily grimoire-inspired tradition does not yield spiritual growth or magical results, remember that these other systems exist as well and that you have much more to look into than just translations of *The Key of Solomon*. You can, for example, probe the Greek Magical Papyri, or Babylonian hymns to Ishtar, or the Orphic or Homeric hymns of Greece. All of these link to astrology and planetary magic. The divine is everywhere in the Art. Find the spirits that speak—and listen!

CONTINUING

My hope is that students of astrology begin to see the connection between the Art and their own lives. I always believe that astrology thrives and grows when it seen as a spiritual worldview that organizes our lives and thoughts, beginning from our grounded experience and moving toward the cosmos. This journey is an ever-evolving one, even if the sources and traditions are old or esoteric. Any student of the Art can use it to explore not only the highest concepts of the cosmic order, but also the very real truths of being human in a fascinating, broad, and even terrifying universe.

As much as modernism tries to empty the world of meaning, astrology stands as a defiant 'No' against this, refusing to give up the beauty of magic. The Art categorically denies this dead and empty sky that so many seem to want us to believe in and accept. I refuse to accept it. The Art refuses to accept it. And you do not have to accept it. I have seen the Art work as a transformative, explanatory, and organizing tool for many students, and I know what it has brought to my own practice and spiritual life. Given this, I hope this final chapter gives advice on how to continue exploring. So, I end with the following recommendations, keeping in mind exactly what the Biblical writers meant when they penned that the glories of heaven reveal the glories of God. [1]

*⋆*Make Lots of Charts *⋆⋆*

We learn by doing. The only way to really delve into the Art is to construct charts. Do nativities for friends, yourself, or clients. Do birth charts for figures in history you find fascinating. Look up examples of natal charts from other astrologers using varying systems. Ask questions using horary techniques, and incorporate horary astrology into your arsenal of divina-

---

1   Psalm 19.

tion. If you are plagued by indecision about the timing of an event or the possible outcome … cast a chart. I am not suggesting giving into paranoid obsessions. Far from it. I am only saying that astrology is learned best by doing it. If you are really interested in growing your skills, then you will need to build up experience looking at and interpreting horoscopes.

Keep notes of your charts and references that you can look back on when interpreting. You will notice trends, correspondences, and repeated patterns. These patterns begin to become second nature when we are diligent in our practice and our record-keeping. It can do a lot to make the student more confident in their work. Don't be discouraged if the first tries or attempts are confusing or if you have to use references or ask for help. That is all part of learning. Too often, occult subjects are treated so preciously by pompous teachers that students feel completely shut out of starting down a path or asking for clarity or guidance. This should not be the case. Make mistakes and make them freely. You'll learn from them and continue to improve as you work with the system.

And do not try to work a chart to death in the beginning of your studies. One of the mistakes many students of astrology make is to over-analyze a chart. This is tempting, given all the various aspects of the Art we can investigate when examining a horoscope. It is, however, not a very helpful practice when you are beginning to interpret. For nativities and horary charts, stick to the most crucial aspects when you are starting out, and do not get bogged down in minutiae. You can develop unique and detailed interpretations as you grow and expand your knowledge, but trying to be absolutely perfect and cover every single thing in the beginning is only going to discourage you. It is also very off-putting to friends, family, or clients that come to you for readings if you get so focused on arcane details that you cannot provide clear answers or focus on areas of life that actually matter to people.

*⋅*Research and Read Questions*⋅*⋆

One of the most common ways that traditional astrologers taught astrology was by organizing entire works around lists of specific questions. Traditional treatises are frequently organized this way, which can seem disjointed to modern students who expect a more clearly defined textbook when approaching a new subject. When we crack open an older text on astrology expecting to find a chapter akin to: "How to Interpret the Seventh House" we are often instead greeted by chapters like:

Will the client have a wife from noble blood, or common blood?

What will happen to the business of the client when they are aged?

What is the relationship of the client to his monarch?

Will the client have stomach troubles or a cancerous sore?

Will the war end badly for the nation?

What weather will this Winter bring?

This may seem old-fashioned and hard to apply in modern contexts to the reader, but in fact these are especially useful tools for learning astrology. The questions explored in traditional texts give us a deeper understanding of how the planets work in the Art in their dance across signs and houses and in their relationships to one another. These question-based systems also tend to have large lists of aspects, astrological situations, and planetary conditions. I cannot recommend exploring these enough. Going over how the great teachers of the Art interpreted specific situations can give us the foundation we need to work our own systems into place.

Many of the authors sourced throughout this work contain these lists of astrological situations and specific questions. Explore and taste a bit from everywhere, and begin to build up your knowledge of these questions and the advice given to answer them. Studying this is also, frankly, hilarious at times. Classical works on astrology were frequently death-obsessed, awfully morbid, and outlandish. And the shocking nature of this can legitimately help you as a student. It can break down our New Age concepts of astrology as all-gentle, "scientific" explanations of Sun-signs and how they interact with one another. There is a certain *spirit* or *feel* to a lot of traditional astrological texts, and you begin to pick it up and live within it the more you study. To put it another way, if you want to join the club, you have to learn the lingo.

⋆⋆⋆Look at the Stars⋆⋆⋆

This may seem like it does not need to be said, but to be an astrologer is to be a stargazer. I always tell my students to observe the night sky and begin to build a relationship to the stars as they actually appear in the sky and not just as they are written in horoscopes. Find a good star atlas at your local bookshop, or download an app to help you locate the stars where you live. Spend some time observing the stars at night, looking for the ones that shine brightest and noting the movement of the planets. If you have the means, you can invest in a good telescope and keep notes of your experiences. Rituals involving the stars, or the spirits and intelligences given to them in the Art, are always more powerful if you can actually *see* the stars in question. The light is right there, just as it was to the ancients and the pre-Modern writers that penned the works we reference in astrology. Be a stargazer. Put your head in the clouds, for once, despite popular opinion against it.

⋆⋆⋆Good Ritual is Learned⋆⋆⋆

Remember: Good Ritual is a Learned Skill. If you are drawn into the planetary magic and ritual of astrological workings, remember that ritual is not something you are born with. It is a learned set of skills that includes repetition, trial and error, and a built-up system of experiences from which to draw inspiration and guidance. You are not going to knock it out of the park with every single ritual, and some rituals are going to feel empty, or tedious, or even downright bizarre or embarrassing. But that is the entire point. You must experience them to get to know them and to find out what works for you. The spiritual paths available in magic are as varied as the paths of traditional religions. Allow yourself the freedom to explore and try. The worst possible approach is to keep putting off a working because you are worried it won't *feel* right or maybe you *don't know enough* yet. You have to start somewhere.

And once you experience what *good* ritual feels like, you'll be able to create it for yourself more and more. You will learn, easily, what forms and systems work for you and which ones are dead on arrival. For some students, the ceremonial magic of the grimoires provides a beautiful, ordered system in which to engage with astrological magic. For others, it will be more folk-inspired practices. Try different approaches and wait to see what really speaks to you. Don't force yourself into one singular practice if it is not producing results. I always advocate discipline and repeated practice, but only if it is truly moving you toward growth and results. If you've been calling angels for months, and you feel hokey and tired after your rituals, then maybe, just maybe—the angels aren't showing up for you. That doesn't mean you aren't able to connect to anything greater than yourself. It only means that you need to speak to something different, or speak in a different way. Ritual is the language we use to communicate to the divine, and you might need to learn a few languages before you can speak to the manager.

⋆⋆⋆Remember to Stay Grounded ⋆⋆⋆

I have written about the spirituality of the astrological worldview, but it is important to remember: This is not a religion. Astrology is a path, and an Art, and many other things—it is not the Church. Astrology can be one aspect, a very rewarding one, of your path. It does not have to be the central part of your path, and you do not have to agree with every nuanced teaching of the system that has been passed down by teachers. That goes for this book as well. There are systems within astrology itself that are contradictory and require you to choose sides. Many astrologers are very passionately devoted to particular schools of thought in the Art. This is good! It breeds healthy debate. Keep this healthy debate open in your own work and always be willing to examine new sources.

There is a tendency in modern times, with such a secular world, to turn absolutely every undertaking into *the thing*. I've seen modern occultists treat the four elements as an entire religious system almost. I've seen them do the same thing with astrology. Remember that the path is a holistic one, and this is but one part of a very varied and impressive historical collection of practices known as magic. Explore them all. Astrology is practiced by Christians, Jews, Muslims, Witches, contemporary Pagans, and more. This isn't exclusive, because it isn't a dogma.

*⸰*Dance With Fate *⸰*

I wrote in the beginning of this work that astrology exists in a unique position between Fate and magic. In the modern world, I often find that we are constantly flitting between two contradictory positions that can be debilitating to our sense of purpose and our spiritual well-being. The first position is fatalism. Everyone has felt nihilistic at times, convinced that the machinations of the world are so far beyond our control that we are truly helpless. We are victims of time, and circumstance, and illness, and past mistakes. We feel hopeless and drained. Other times we are pushed, often by a consumerist society, to constantly "better" ourselves. We are put down and degraded constantly so that snake-oil peddlers and glittering gurus can sell us something to make ourselves better. If their systems and contraptions don't actually work to make us better, then we are told it is our fault. We must have done something wrong. We didn't try hard enough. We didn't believe in ourselves. We didn't manifest our Will with enough strength, or commitment.

Both of these approaches are dangerous. And the Art exists to help us dance the razor-thin line between them. On one hand, astrology is a touch fatalistic. But it is fatalistic in the best possible way. It is not afraid of Fate. The stars are so beyond us, so large and patient, that they have much to teach us about acceptance and peace. The movements of the stars let us know that there may be a time to plant seeds, but there is also a time to let the fields lie fallow. Often, hyper-individualistic mantras of *Go forth! Change yourself! Reinvent yourself!* are nothing more than the poisoned chalices of a hustle culture that does much damage to our psyches. The Art reminds us to think of everything from a larger perspective. Understand that there are cycles to our time here on Earth. We have to remember that some things are bigger than us. Modern astrology may be Copernican and traditional astrology may be geocentric, but they both agree on one thing—*you are not the center of the Universe.*[2]

But fatalism needs to be balanced with the belief in change. The magic of astrology brings us to a place where we can really believe that we can step in and change our situation. When the time is ripe, perhaps the cycles are calling for us to do something. The stars can whisper to us of a higher place, a hope that kindles inside of us and pushes us to strike out against circumstance. We can raise our voices from their terrestrial woes to a celestial place where they will echo more forcefully, more meaningfully. This understanding, balanced with an understanding that sometimes the stars simply are what they are, allows us to escape from the dichotomy of fatalism vs. incessant change. The machinations of the heavens reflect the machinations of the soul.

So, enjoy the dance. Investigate and probe to the fullest the Art and what it can spark inside the interior castle of your soul. I have full faith that the library of the stars proves a rewarding exercise, and there is much to learn from it. I agree with the writers of the Rosicrucian works, be those works real or satire, when they say:

> 66 *"Thus the Book of Nature is opened wide before the eyes of all, though few can either read or understand it."*[3]

Read away, be it written in ink on a page or in fire in the heavens—and you *will* understand.

---

[2] This seems to be a particularly difficult truth for some people who are absolutely convinced that everything always revolves around them.

[3] *Rosicrucian Trilogy*, trans. Joscelyn Godwin, Christopher McIntosh, & Donate Pahnke McIntosh (Newsburyport, MA: Weiser Books, 2016), 47.

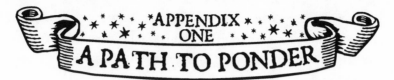

Emanation: The Journey

In the beginning, middle, and end of all things is the One. It is not a static being but a dynamism. It is being and non-being interlocked in perpetual rising and falling. It is the *heiros gamos*, the sacred marriage of two impossibly different things that do not understand their own distinctions. It is the light of the fixed stars, burning to create, exploding in nuclear fusion in the cosmos as the perpetual billion beating hearts of the heavenly furnaces, the crucibles of the elements. It is the All, the Nothing, literally no-thing, but instead *is-ness*, the *ipsum esse*, the *fons et origo*. All is here, all potentiality and possibility crashing together eternally.

SATURN

Awareness happens. What *can be*, becomes. What *might be* then *is*. This brings distinction. It brings boundary and time. If something can exist, then not existing immediately follows. To create is to admit the possibility of destruction. Self-awareness creates its own shadows, mirrors itself in the Other. Realization creates distinction. Unity is fractured, unstable now as it explodes in self-realization. Acknowledging the light brings the darkness into focus. Why is there anything? Why this? Why something? Why not … nothing? Here I am death and time. Here I am clarity of endings and beginnings.

JUPITER

And so creation expands. It explodes outward, constantly creating and un-creating itself. The known searches to fill the void of the unknown. A horror of empty space fills existence, expanding outward, endlessly eating up the nothing. Creation desires to be throned, to crown itself, to claim its own existence. It rages against the nothing and refuses to admit the dichotomies it creates. The king is hungry, thirsty, ravenous to eat away at the prison of time. Creation must expand. It must continue. It must ponder and build up philosophies, religions, and systems. Here I am an administrator, a thinker, a noble, and a royal birthright made manifest. Here I am creating.

Mars

And thus: Rage. Fire burns. The expansion brings death and destruction. Chaos rises against order, and the two fall and mingle together, constantly locked in battle. The darkness is sharp, contrasting against the brilliant shard of light that aches to burst forward, to keep moving and creating. Nothing can be built as bloodless as we would desire. Mistakes are made, and calamities occur. Fate deals blows and time eats at what we make. Fires burn up and lay the ground for the new. Here I am anger, rage, and war. Here I am ready to strip down illusion. Here I am lost in my acts of creation. Here I am uneasy.

Sun

The light knows. It knows what has happened, and hope is kindled. Sacrifice is understood now. Something must be given up to go back, to return, to experience. The eternal dance has purpose now, a guiding light, a memory of the One, a reflection, however dim, of the original light of Creation. Light bears weight on biological life, able to be energy itself in flora, and thus to fauna, to sentient beings. Here I am alive. Here I am bright, and ready to kindle the fire. Here I tend the living world.

Venus

Desire is born. The differentiated parts long to know each other. Biological life flourishes in moisture, heat, and generation. The explosion of creation that was born in the awareness of the One is fractured and longs to be reunited. Each fracturing has removed a piece of something, made something un-whole, disintegrated, full of longing. These disparate parts now ache to reattach, to know again, to be whole. Unity is hinted at for the first time since the emanation began. The possibility of once again experiencing bliss makes itself known. Here I am in love. Here I want to find my other half and reintegrate myself. Here I am hopeful and see beauty and connection in what I make.

MERCURY

And so the mind begins to order things. Logic steps in, now able to label and name all things. Communication spreads the truths that have been learned. Here we take our desires and codify them, naming and delineating the world. Here I speak what I desire into existence. I move beyond sheer thought and emotion into ordered action and conversation. Here I discuss with the angels. Here I speak to God and to my fellow creatures. Here we synthesize and I understand.

MOON

And the birth pangs find their finality. A child comes. The mother's wails fill the empty space. Shifting memories are knit into the astral mind of sentient beings, bearing infinite sparks of a divinity that is beyond comprehension but is hinted at in the pale light of the night. The memory of what once was shifts and moves, in phases, waxing and waning in the sentient soul. Here I feel my purpose intently, having ordered it correctly. Here I taste magic and change.

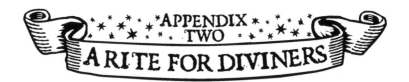

APPENDIX TWO
A RITE FOR DIVINERS

This rite is intended to be used before any astrological undertaking. I recommend it for the practitioner who is about to create a nativity, or before a serious horary reading. This is meant to prepare our minds for the divine knowledge that may be given to us through the use of the Art. I do not believe you must complete a rite like this before any reading, but I do believe a ritual such as this one can help to shift our consciousness. It can prepare us to engage in divination in a receptive way and to better understand the messages that come down to us from the Heavenly Spheres.

Cleanse and purify yourself and the space with a mixture of water, rosemary, salt, and hyssop. As you sprinkle and purify, invoke:

> "I make clean and ready the Temple. I am purified and made right and holy before the Watchers of the Heavens. Beneath the Vault, I am seen and heard. Open my eyes and make ready my heart. Breathe into me the wisdom of the Mysteries that I may work them into the Earth."

Prepare a censer with charcoal and place frankincense into it, allowing the smoke to drift through the space where you will be working.

> "Airy Spirits, open the gates between knowledge and wisdom. Make clear the path to the doors of Heaven."

Light a single candle, of beeswax or any other natural wax, near your work space.

> "Light of Mind, precious vision, illuminate the tabernacle of my soul that therein may dwell the good, and gracious spirits of the Art."

Center your breathing, taking in the scent of the frankincense, and focus on the work at hand. When you are ready, invoke.

"One. Mother.

Come again and be the Wheel of Glories. Cast forth the darkness of clouded mind.

Two. Speech.

Speak again and make clear the truth."

Three. Love.

Conjoin Heaven and Earth so that in me is the Great Work accomplished.

Four. Light.

Heal the troubled spirit and make ripe the fruit of wisdom.

Five. Strength.

Cast down all enemies and disperse all hindrances.

Six. Mercy.

Be gracious in the giving of your knowledge.

Seven. Fate.

Let a perfect Will be made manifest in me."

All divination or work may now be undertaken. When finished, extinguish the candle, with the following:

"I stand within the Seven, both servant and beloved. Unto the stars I send my blessing and from the Heavens I draw my peace. Let it be done."

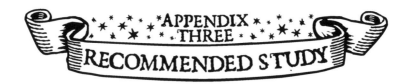

I am including the following list for recommended study. I have tried to
focus on foundational writers for the systems used in traditional astrology
and magic. This is by no means an exhaustive list, but I believe it provides
a good foundation and starting point for anyone who wishes to examine
the Art further. These authors have been translated, collected, and com-
mented on by various scholars and multiple translations are available. I
have also only included original sources.

CLASSICAL SOURCES

Claudius Ptolemy
Tetrabiblos

Almagest

Dorotheus of Sidon
Carmen Astrologicum

Julius Firmicus Maternus
The Mathesis

Marcus Manilius
Astronomica

Olympiodorus the Younger
Commentary on Paulus Alexandrinus' Introduction

Paulus Alexandrinus
Introduction (Eisagogika)

Vettius Valens
Anthologies

Unkown Authors
The Corpus Hermeticum

The Greek Magical Papyri

ARABIC AND JEWISH SOURCES

Abraham ibn Ezra
(Multiple Works)

Abu Ma'shar
(Multiple Works)

Al-Biruni
Book of Instruction in the Elements of the Art of Astrology

Al-Qabisi
Introduction to the Art of Judgments of the Stars

Masha'allah ibn Athari
(Multiple Works)

Sahl ibn Bishr [1]
(Multiple Works)

LATER EUROPEAN ASTROLOGY SOURCES

Guido Bonatti
Liber Astronomiae

William Lilly
Christian Astrology

GRIMOIRES

Francis Barret
The Magus

Unkown Authors
The Key of Solomon

---

[1] Masha'allah, Abu Ma'shar, and Sahl (as well as many other Arabic and Persian astrologers) have been translated by Benjamin Dykes and are all available for the English reader.

Picatrix

The Sworn Book of Honorius

MAGIC, OCCULT PHILOSOPHY, ESOTERICISM

Agrippa
Three Books of Occult Philosophy

Albertus Magnus
(Multiple Works)

Eliphas Levi
(Multiple Works)

Giovanni Pico della Mirandola
(Multiple Works)

Johannes Trithemius
Steganographia

Marsilio Ficino
Platonic Theology

Paracelsus
(Multiple Works)

Robert Fludd
(Multiple Works)

MODERN ASTROLOGERS USING AND TEACHING TRADITIONAL TECHNIQUES

Benjamin Dykes

Chris Brennan

Christopher Warnock

Deborah Houlding

Demetra George

John Frawley

Joseph Crane

✦✧✦ BIBLIOGRAPHY ✦✧✦

Agrippa, Henricus Cornelius. *Three Books of Occult Philosophy*. Edited by Donald Tyson. St. Paul, MN: Llewellyn, 1993.

Al-Biruni. *The Book of Instructions in the Elements of the Art of Astrology*. Translated by R. Ramsay Wright. Bel Air, MD: Astrology Classics, 2006.

"Albertus Magnus on Talismans." *Renaissance Astrology*. https://www.renaissanceastrology.com/albertusmagnustalisman.html.

Ashcroft-Nowiki, Dolores. *The Shining Paths: An Experiential Journey Through the Tree of Life*. Loughborough: Thoth Publications, 1997.

Bardon, Franz. *Initiation into Hermetics*. Translated by Gerhard Hanswille and Franca Gallo. Edited by Ken Johnson. Merkur Publishing, 1999.

Barret, Francis. *The Magus, or Central Intelligencer; Being a Complete System of Occult Philosophy*. New York, NY: Citadel Press, 1967.

Battistini, Matilde. *Astrology, Magic, and Alchemy in Art*. Translated by Rosanna M Giammanco Frongia. Los Angeles, CA: Getty Publications, 2007.

Bellizia, Luzia. *Of the Judgments on the Lunar Nodes*. Translated by Margherita Fiorello. https://www.apotelesma.it/wp-content/uploads/2016/02/Of_the_judgements_on_the_lunar_nodes.pdf.

Bentley Hart, David. *The Experience of God: Being, Consciousness, Bliss*. New Haven, CT: Yale University Press, 2014.

Bobrick, Benson. *The Fated Sky: Astrology in History*. New York, NY: Simon & Schuster, 2007.

Bonatti, Guido. *Liber Astronomiae*. Translated by William Lilly & Henry Coley. Renaissance Astrology. https://www.renaissanceastrology.com/bonatti146considerations.html.

The Book of Enoch. Translated by R. H. Charles. San Francisco, CA: Red Wheel/Weiser, 2012.

Boxer, Alexander. *A Scheme of Heaven: The History of Astrology and the Search for our Destiny in Data*. New York, NY: W.W. Norton & Company, Inc., 2020.

Campion, Nicolas. *Astrology and Cosmology in the World's Religions*. New York, NY: NYU Press, 2012.

The Chaldean Oracles: Text, Translation, and Commentary. Translated by Ruth Dorothy Majercik. Dilton Marsh, Westbury, Wiltshire, UK: The Prometheus Trust, 2013.

Conjuring Spirits: Texts and Traditions of Medieval Ritual Magic. Edited by Claire Fanger. University Park, PA: The Pennsylvania State University Press, 1998.

Cornelius, Geoffrey. "Interpreting Interpretations: The Aphorism in the Practice of the Renaissance Astrologers by Geoffrey Cornelius." In *From Masha'Allah to Kepler: Theory and Practice in Medieval and Renaissance Astrology*, edited by Charles Burnett and Dorian Gieseler Greenbaum. Sophia Centre Press, 2015.

Dionysus the Areopagite. The Celestial Hierarchy. The Tertullian Project. http://www.tertullian.org/fathers/areopagite_13_heavenly_hierarchy.htm#c6.

Dorotheus of Sidon. Carmen Astrologicum. Translated by Benjamin N. Dykes. Minneapolis, MN: The Cazimi Press, 2019.

Dykes, Benjamin N. *Bonatti on Basic Astrology: Treatises 1-3 of Guido Bonatti's Book of Astronomy, Theory, Signs, Houses, Planets, Configurations.* Minneapolis, MN: The Cazimi Press, 2010.

Faivre, Antoine and Joscelyn Godwin. *The Eternal Hermes: From Greek God to Alchemical Magus.* Grand Rapids, MI: Phanes Press, 1995.

Goodrick-Clarke, Nicholas. *The Western Esoteric Traditions: A Historical Introduction.* Oxford: Oxford University Press, 2008.

The Greek Magical Papyri in Translation. Edited by Hans Dieter Betz. Chicago, IL: University of Chicago Press, 1996.

Hauck, Dennis William. *The Emerald Tablet: Alchemy for Personal Transformation.* New York: Penguin Compass, 1999.

Hermetica: The Greek Corpus Hermeticum and the Latin Asclepius in a New English Translation with Notes and Introduction. Translated by Brian P. Copenhaver. Cambridge, UK: Cambridge University Press, 1992.

Homeric Hymns. Translated by H.G. Evelyn-White. Theoi. https://www.theoi.com/Text/HomericHymns3.html#8.

Hymns of Orpheus. Translated by Thomas Taylor. 2015. Kindle.

Iamblichus: On the Mysteries. Translated by Emma C. Clarke, John M. Dillon, and Jackson P. Hershbell. Atlanta, GA: Society of Biblical Literature, 2003.

The Illustrated Picatrix: The Occult Classic of Astrological Magic Complete in One Volume. Translated by John Michael Greer and Christopher Warnock. Renaissance Astrology, 2015.

Julian. *Hymn to King Helios.* Translated by Emily Wilmer Crave Wright.

Jung, C.G. *Jung on Astrology.* Edited by Safron Rossi and Keiron Le Grice. New York, NY: Routledge, 2018.

Kerényi, Carl. *Dionysos: Archetypal Image of Indestructible Life.* Translated by Ralph Manheim. Princeton, NJ: Princeton University Press, 1976.

Kieckhefer, Richard. *Magic in the Middle Ages*, 2nd ed. Cambridge: Cambridge University Press, 1989.

Klaassen, Frank. *The Transformations of Magic: Illicit Learned Magic in the Later Middle Ages and Renaissance.* University Park, PA: The Pennsylvania State University Press, 2013.

Lehman, J. Lee. "The Conjunction of Electional Astrology and Magic." In *The Celestial Art:*

Essays on Astrological Magic, edited by Austin Coppock and Daniel A. Schulke. Three Hands Press, 2018.

"Liber Jurata Honorii." Esoteric Archives. http://www.esotericarchives. com/juratus/juratus.htm.

Lilly, William. *Christian Astrology: Books 1 & 2.* Edited by David R. Roell. Bel Air, MD: Astrology Classics, 2004.

Lilly, William. *Christian Astrology: Book 3.* Edited by David R. Roell. Bel Air, MD: Astrology Classics, 2004.

Luck, Georg. *Arcana Mundi Magic and the Occult in the Greek and Roman Worlds: A Collection of Ancient Texts.* Baltimore, MD: Johns Hopkins University Press, 2008.

Maimonides. *Yesodei hTorah.* Translated by Eliyahu Touger. Chabad. https://www.chabad.org/library/article_cdo/aid/904962/jewish/ Yesodei-haTorah-Chapter-Two.htm.

Manilius, Marcus. *Astronomica.* Tanslated by G. P. Goold. Cambridge, MA: Harvard U.P., 1977.

Paracelsus: Essential Readings. Translated by Nicholas Goodrick-Clarke. Berkeley, CA: North Atlantic Books, 1999.

Ptolemy, Claudius. *Tetrabiblos.* Translated by F.E. Robbins. Cambridge, MA: Harvard University Press, 1956.

Rosicrucian Trilogy. Translated by Joscelyn Godwin, Christopher McIntosh, and Donate Pahnke McIntosh. Newsburyport, MA: Weiser Books, 2016.

Rüpke, Jörg. *Pantheon: A New History of Roman Religion.* Translated by David M. B. Richardson. Princeton, NJ: Princeton University Press, 2018.

Sepher Raziel: Liber Salomonis a Sixteenth Century English Grimoire. Edited by Don Karr and

Shaw, Gregory. *Theurgy and the Soul: The Neoplatonism of Iamblichus, Second Ed.* Kettering, OH: Angelico Press/Sophia Perennis, 2014.

Skinner, Stephen. *Techniques of Graeco-Egyptian Magic.* Singapore: Golden Hoard Press, 2017.

Skinner, Stephen. *Techniques of Solomonic Magic.* Singapore: Golden Hoard Press, 2017.

Skinner, Stephen and David Rankine. *The Keys to the Gateway of Magic: Summoning the Solomonic Archangels and Demon Princes.* Singapore: Golden Hoard Press, 2005.

Skinner, Stephen and David Rankine. *The Veritable Key of Solomon: Three Different Texts from*

Those Translated by S.L. MacGregor Mathers. Singapore: Golden Hoard Press, 2017.

Uzdavinys, Algis. *The Heart of Plotinus: The Essential Enneads Including Porphyry's On the Cave of the Nymphs.* Bloomington: World Wisdom, Inc., 2009.

Valens, Vettius. *Anthologies.* Translated by Mark Riley. https://www.csus.edu/indiv/r/rileymt/vettius%20valens%20entire.pdf.

Works of Sahl & Masha'allah. Translated by Benjamin N. Dykes. Minneapolis, MN: The Cazimi Press, 2010.

Zoller, Robert. *Arabic Parts in Astrology: A Lost Key to Prediction.* Rochester. VT: Inner Traditions International, 1989.

*.*INDEX *.*

Abrahamic Religions: 237, 255

Accuser: 252-253

Agrippa, Cornelius: 21, 55, 68, 78, 93, 108-109, 145-146, 149

al-Biruni: 14, 91, 133, 155, 164, 176, 269, 271

Alchemy: 10, 12, 40, 67, 272

al-Qabisi: 14, 169, 269

Angels: 81, 109, 215, 237, 239-255, 260

    Anael (Venus): 250

    Cassiel (Saturn): 109, 111-112, 254

    Cherubim: 241

    Gabriel (The Moon): 109, 243, 248-249, 251, 253

    Michael (The Sun): 243, 251-252

    Raphael (Mercury): 109, 243, 249

    Sachiel (Jupiter): 94-95, 253

    Samael (Mars): 81, 252-253

Aphrodite: 50-52, 54

Apollo: 64, 67

Aquarius: (SEE: Zodiac)

Archangels: (SEE: Angels)

Areopagite, Dionysus the: 242, 245, 272

Aries: (SEE: Zodiac)

Ascendant: 158, 178, 186-187, 190-191, 195, 205

Aspects: 41, 55, 80, 127, 131-132, 160, 179, 185-186, 188, 193, 198, 252, 257

    Combustion: 66, 133

    Conjunctions: 54, 132-133, 193

    Opposition: 134, 193, 196, 208

    Sextiles: 137, 193

    Squares: 55, 110, 131-132, 138, 193, 196

    Trine: 135-137

Asteroids: 161-162

Astral Temple: 224-227

Astronomy: 161-162

Babylon: 6-7, 117, 238-239, 255

Behenian Stars: 146, 148-149, 151

Benefics: 53-56, 78, 89-94, 121, 135, 154-155, 180-181, 191, 250-251, 254

Bonatti, Guido: 24, 104, 157-160, 187, 269, 271-272

Calendars: 229

Cancer: (SEE: Zodiac)

Capricorn: (SEE: Zodiac)

Catholic: 93, 238, 243, 248, 250

celestial spheres: 7-9

Chaldeans: 6

Charts and Diagrams

    Calculating the Days and Hours of the Planets With the Seven-Pointed Star: 235

    Example Chart for "Pat": 190

    Mars and Venus in Opposition: 135

    Mercury Squared Jupiter: 139

    Quadruplicities on the Zodiac: 175

    Saturn and Jupiter in Conjunction in Sagittarius: 134

    The Moon and Jupiter in Mutual Reception by Exaltation: 130

    The North and South Lunar Nodes: 154

    The Sects of the Heavens: 167

    The Sun Trine Mercury: 136

    The Twelve Houses of Heaven: 180

    Triplicities on the Zodiac: 172

    Venus in Sextile with the Moon: 137

Copernicus, Nicolaus: 63, 153, 262

Correspondences: 9, 13-14, 31, 46, 59, 72, 85, 98, 113, 147, 149, 176, 178, 201, 247, 255

Days of the Week

    Monday: 232-233, 235

    Saturday: 232-233

    Sunday: 66, 218, 232-233

    Thursday: 232, 254

    Tuesday: 232, 235

    Wednesday: 235

Debility: 114, 125-127, 129, 138, 188, 205

Decans: 124-125

Dignity: 93-94, 109, 114, 122-123, 126-127, 138, 188, 190, 192, 194-195, 208-209

Diurnal: 106

Divination: 3, 150, 164, 185, 198, 200-204

Domicile: 116, 129, 208

Dorotheus of Sidon: 118-119, 122, 176, 268, 272

Dykes, Benjamin: 80, 104, 106, 119, 187, 211, 269-270, 272, 274

Egyptians: 123-124, 144, 230

Electional Astrology: 80, 163-164, 273

Elohim: 240-241

Emerald Tablet, The: 10

Empyrean Realm: 8, 103, 141, 170

Ephemeris: 165, 200, 219, 233

Equinoxes: 119, 146, 169, 171

Exaltation: 117-119, 129, 188, 193-195

Face: (SEE: Decans)

Falcifer: 103, 108, 111

Feminine: 22, 38, 155, 207

Ficino, Marsilio: 9, 55, 145, 238, 246, 270

Firmicus: 125, 268

Fixed Stars: 141-146, 150, 164, 169-170, 185, 189

Four Elements, The: 142, 171-172, 175, 187
        (SEE: ALSO: Triplicity)

Frawley, John: 211, 270

Fumigations: (SEE: Incense)

Gemini: (SEE: Zodiac)

Gnosticism: 249

Greek Magical Papyri: 25, 54, 108, 215, 238, 255, 269, 272

Grimoire: 246

Grimoires
        Honorius, Sworn Book of: 79, 270
        Key of Solomon: 23, 39, 55, 66, 68, 81, 108
        Picatrix: 14, 22, 40, 53, 55, 68, 76, 93-94, 145, 246, 270, 273
        The Grimoire of Abramelin: 212-213, 216, 244

Hanael: (SEE: Anael)

Hebrew: 239-240, 246, 252-253

Hekate: 20, 28-29

Helios: 64-65, 67, 273

Hermes Trismegistus: 10, 35, 37

Hermeticism: 10, 37, 146, 240, 253, 272

Hinduism: 156

Horary

    Querent: 164, 187, 205-210

    Quesited: 205-206

Horary Readings: 164, 200-201, 203-205, 207, 209-210, 256

Horoscopes: 2, 163, 165, 185

Houlding, Deborah: 125, 211, 270

Houses: 114, 160, 165, 178-180, 182-183, 187, 190-191, 201, 207

    Angular: 180, 187, 191

    Cadent: 179-180, 187, 191, 207

    Succedent: 180, 187

Husbands: 90, 208-209

Iamblichus: 3-4

Incense

    Incense of Jupiter: 96

    Incense of Mercury: 43

    Incense of the Moon: 27

    Incense of the Sun: 69

    Incense of Venus: 57

In Detriment: 120, 188, 192

In Fall: 120-121, 188

Islam: 149

Judaism: 149, 217, 240-241, 248-249, 253

Jupiter: (SEE: Planets)

Kabbalah: 239, 248

    Sephirah: 81, 248, 253

Kepler, Johannes: 3, 270, 272

Leo: (SEE: Zodiac)

Libra: (SEE: Zodiac)

Lilly: 64, 80, 92, 105, 127, 131, 134, 150, 154, 273

Lilly, William
    Christian Astrology: 64, 80, 92, 105, 127, 131, 133-134, 138, 150,
154, 164, 244, 269, 273
Lots: 96, 153, 156-160
    Part of Fortune: 157-158, 190-191
    Part of Spirit: 158
Lucifer: 51
Macrocosm, The: 5, 132, 182
Magic: 1-3, 5-7, 9-10, 12-15, 19-20, 23-25, 36, 38-40, 54-56, 63, 67-68,
76, 81, 93-94, 107-109, 144-147, 149-150, 163, 173, 185, 204, 212-
223, 226-227, 232-234, 237-240, 243-244, 246-250, 254-255, 259-261,
272-274, 277
Maimonides: 241, 273
Malefics: 56, 68, 76, 79-80, 82, 103, 106, 108, 119, 132, 138,
181, 197, 253
Manilius: 1, 169, 268, 273
    Astronomica: 1, 268, 273
Mars: (SEE: Planets)
Masculine: 38, 66, 155, 207
Mercury: (SEE: Planets)
Microcosm, the: 5, 13, 132, 182-183
Midheaven: 179, 191
Mode: (SEE: Quadruplicity)
Modern Astrology: 130, 183
Monad: 67, 90
Moon, The: (SEE: Planets)
Mutual Reception: 128-129, 192
Natal Chart: (SEE: Nativity)
Nativity: 185-187, 194-195, 198
Natural Magic: 9, 145, 149, 238
Necromancy: 107
Neoplatonism: 4
Occultism: 24, 55, 68, 145-146, 238, 246-247, 270-271, 273
Oil of Venus: 57
Orphic Hymns: 52
Paracelsus: 5, 9, 13, 270, 273

Peregrine: 126, 192, 194-195, 208

Persian: 80, 239

Philosophy: 3, 156, 270-271

Pisces: (SEE: Zodiac)

Planets: 1-2, 4-9, 13-14, 21, 23-24, 35, 38, 40, 54, 63, 66, 82, 90, 92-94, 103-104, 106-108, 110, 114, 116-129, 131-138, 140-146, 149-150, 155, 160-162, 164, 167, 174-175, 179-180, 182, 185-188, 191-192, 194, 197, 205-208, 212, 233, 244-246, 254-255

    Jupiter: 89-94, 98, 129, 191-193, 196, 232, 253-254

    Mars: 56, 76-82, 85, 106, 128, 142, 191-193, 196, 208, 232, 235, 252-253

    Mercury: 25, 35-36, 38-41, 43-44, 46, 110, 121, 127-128, 130, 133, 190-191, 193-195, 209, 235, 250

    Neptune: 161-162

    Saturn: 56, 103-110, 113, 116, 119, 121, 146, 191-195, 254

    The Moon: 6, 16, 19, 21-25, 27-28, 31, 56, 116, 119, 129, 153, 155, 158, 191-196, 205, 208, 219, 229-230, 232-233, 235, 248

    The Sun: 6, 11, 22-23, 62-70, 72, 116, 119, 127-128, 133, 155, 158, 168, 179, 191, 193-194, 199, 208-209, 231, 233, 251

    Uranus: 161-162

    Venus: 5, 50-57, 59, 121, 133, 175, 191-196, 208, 250

Plotinus: 3-4, 274

Porphyry: 4, 178, 274

Prayers, Praying: 237

Priesthood: 66

Psychic Shielding: 224

Psychopomp: 35, 40

Ptolemy, Claudius: 22, 65, 123

    Tetrabiblos: 22, 65

Pythagoras: 7, 156-157, 240

Qabalah: (SEE: Kabbalah)

Quadruplicity: 173-175, 187

    Cardinal Signs: 173-175, 191

    Fixed Signs: 141-146, 150, 164, 169-170, 173-175, 185, 187, 189, 191

    Mutable Signs: 18, 35, 173-175, 191

Reception: 128-129, 192

Religion: 3, 7, 92, 144, 154, 202, 215, 230, 237-239, 255

Retrograde: 130-131

Rising Sign: (SEE: Ascendant)

Rituals: 9, 14-15, 25-26, 30, 41, 43, 56-57, 68-69, 79, 82, 94-95, 110, 150-151, 212-213, 217-218, 220-222, 237, 259-260, 266

    A Rite for Diviners: 266

    A Rite for Jupiter: 94

    A Rite for Mars: 82

    A Rite for Mercury: 40

    A Rite for Saturn: 109

    A Rite for The Moon: 25

    A Rite for The Sun: 68

    A Rite for Venus: 56

    A Ritual for the Old Stars: 150

Rulerships: 162

Sagittarius: (SEE: Zodiac)

Saturn: (SEE: Planets)

Scorpio: (SEE: Zodiac)

Sect: 115-116, 122, 167, 188, 192

Seraphim: 241

Seven-Pointed Star: 235

Sidereal: 141, 168-169

Sirius: 144, 230

Solomonic: 23, 39, 55, 66, 68, 81, 108, 239, 246, 274

Sun-sign Astrology: 126, 177, 200, 259

Sun, The: (SEE: Planets)

Tables

    Astrological Symbols: 140

    Egyptian Terms: 124

    Planetary Hours: 234

    Planetary Intentions: 236

    Planetary Joys: 181

    Planetary Lots: 159

    Planets in Detriment: 120

    Planets in Fall: 121

    Precise Exaltations: 118

Quadruplicities: 174
The Behenian Stars: 148
The Houses: 182
The Zodiac: 177
Triplicities: 171
Triplicity Rulers: 122
Tables of Planetary Correspondences
Jupiter: 98
Mars: 85
Mercury: 46
Saturn: 113
The Moon: 31
The Sun: 72
Venus: 59
Taurus: (SEE: Zodiac)
Terms: 3, 6, 123-126, 141, 173, 176, 192, 196, 240
Theurgy: 13
Touchstone Texts
Jupiter: 91
Mars: 78
Mercury: 36
Saturn: 105
The Moon: 21
The Sun: 65
Venus: 52
Trigons: (SEE: Triplicity)
Triplicity: 121-122, 171, 187-188
Air Signs: 171-172
Earth Signs: 171-172
Fire Signs: 171-172
Water Signs: 171-172
Valens, Vettius: 22, 25, 37, 51, 66, 79-80, 91, 105, 122, 133, 164, 176, 195, 268, 274
Vedic Astrology: 66, 90, 165, 169
Venus: (SEE: Planets)
Virgo: (SEE: Zodiac)

Witchcraft: 20, 24

Zodiac: 116, 141, 145, 168-170, 172, 176-178

    Aries: 117, 124, 171, 179, 196, 208

    Cancer: 129, 168, 171, 176, 192, 195-196

    Leo: 128, 179

    Libra: 192, 208

    Pisces: 38

    Primum Mobile: 116, 141, 170

    Taurus: 129, 177, 192, 195-196, 199

    Virgo: 38, 177

Zoller, Robert: 156, 158-160, 274

ABOUT THE AUTHOR

Levi Rowland is a professional astrologer working and living in New Orleans. With over 15 years of experience, he offers astrological consultations, workshops, and classes through online platforms and in-person at events such as WitchCon and Hexfest. Levi is a High Priest of the Alexandrian Tradition and teaches and works with:

- Traditional Astrology
- Hermetic Qabalah
- Cartomancy
- Ceremonial Magic

Levi's work in traditional Astrology is informed by his years of occult training and his work as a teacher, both in magical systems and in the mundane world where he teaches languages, interprets, and translates. His translation work has allowed him to open up classical texts to new audiences and help preserve traditional magical techniques for contemporary practitioners.